British Studies Series

General Editor JEREMY BLACK

Published

John Charmley **A History of Conservative Politics, 1900–1996**

David Childs **Britain since 1939**

David Eastwood **Government and Community in the English
Provinces, 1700–1870**

Brian Hill **The Early Parties and Politics in Britain, 1688–1832**

Kevin Jefferys **Retreat from New Jerusalem: British Politics,
1951–1964**

T. A. Jenkins **The Liberal Ascendancy, 1830–1886**

David Loades **Power in Tudor England**

Alexander Murdoch **British History, 1660–1832: National Identity
and Local Culture**

Anthony Musson and W. M. Ormrod **The Evolution of English
Justice: Law, Politics and Society in the Fourteenth Century**

Murray G. H. Pittock **Inventing and Resisting Britain: Cultural
Identities in Britain and Ireland, 1685–1789**

Andrew Thorpe *A History of the British Labour Party*

Forthcoming

D. G. Boyce **Britain and Decolonisation**

Glenn Burgess **British Political Thought from Reformation
to Revolution**

J. B. Christoph **The Twentieth-Century British State**

Gary De Krey **Restoration and Revolution in Britain**

W. H. Fraser **The Rise and Fall of British Trade Unionism**

Jeremy Gregory **The Long Reformation: Religion and Society in
England c. 1530–1870**

Katrina Honeyman **Women and Industrialization**

Jon Lawrence **Britain and the First World War**

(List continued overleaf)

F. J. Levy **Politics and Culture in Tudor England**
Allan Macinnes **The British Revolution**
G. I. T. Machin **The Rise of British Democracy**
Thomas Mayer **Britain, 1450–1603**
Michael Mendle **The English Civil War and Political Thought**
W. Rubinstein **History of Britain in the Twentieth Century**
Howard Temperley **Britain and America**

British Studies Series
Series Standing Order
ISBN 0–333–71691–4 hardcover
ISBN 0–333–69332–9 paperback
(*outside North America only*)

You can receive future titles in this series as they are published by placing a standing order. Please contact your bookseller or, in case of difficulty, write to us at the address below with your name and address, the title of the series and the ISBN quoted above.

Customer Services Department, Macmillan Distribution Ltd
Houndmills, Basingstoke, Hampshire RG21 6XS, England

British History 1660–1832

National Identity and Local Culture

Alexander Murdoch
Senior Lecturer in Scottish History
University of Edinburgh

First published in Great Britain 1998 by
MACMILLAN PRESS LTD
Houndmills, Basingstoke, Hampshire RG21 6XS and London
Companies and representatives throughout the world

A catalogue record for this book is available from the British Library.

ISBN 0–333–60031–2 hardcover
ISBN 0–333–60032–0 paperback

First published in the United States of America 1998 by
ST. MARTIN'S PRESS, INC.,
Scholarly and Reference Division,
175 Fifth Avenue, New York, N.Y. 10010

ISBN 0–312–21634–3

Library of Congress Cataloging-in-Publication Data
Murdoch, Alexander.
British history 1660–1832 : national identity and local culture /
Alexander Murdoch.
p.   cm. — (British studies series)
Includes bibliographical references and index.
ISBN 0–312–21634–3
1. Great Britain—Historiography.   2. National characteristics,
British—Historiography.   3. Great Britain—History, Local–
–Historiography.   4. Nationalism—Great Britain—Historiography.
5. Historiography—Great Britain—History.   I. Title.   II. Series.
DA1.M87   1998
941'.007'2—dc21   98–6883
                                                                        CIP

This book is printed on paper suitable for recycling and made from fully managed and
sustained forest sources.

10   9   8   7   6   5   4   3   2   1
07   06   05   04   03   02   01   00   99   98

Printed in Hong Kong

For my parents

CONTENTS

Contents

Preface and Acknowledgements

This book is intended as a short and accessible introduction to a complex subject. The idea of attempting it first came to me as long ago as 1974, when I read Professor John Pocock's now famous essay, 'British History: A Plea for a New Subject', in the Periodicals Room of the University of Edinburgh Library. It helped me place my efforts as an American student with a Scottish name, who found it difficult to understand why Scottish history was not considered relevant to the British history taught at American universities, and indeed at universities in Scotland or England. My ferociously sectarian paternal grandparents, emigrants to America from the West of Scotland, had passed down to their family a view of Britishness much at variance with this. The idea occurred to me again in 1979 while reading Professor J. C. Beckett's *The Making of Modern Ireland 1603–1923* on the train from Dublin to Galway to be interviewed for a lectureship in 'eighteenth-century history' at University College Galway, where it was clear that American and Irish history were taught in an emphatically Atlantic rather than a British context, in the assumption that each was mutually exclusive. Thus, in 1992, having moved from Edinburgh to the East Midlands of England, the invitation from (then) Dr Jeremy Black to write on the theme of 'centres and localities' in Britain and Ireland during the eighteenth century was most welcome.

I would like to acknowledge Professor Black's help and support in this project, particularly in what proved to be a successful application for a British Academy Research Leave Award held while I was an employee in Northampton of Nene College of Higher Education Corporation. I am grateful to those at Nene College who endeavoured to ensure that I benefited from this award, particularly its Director, Dr S. Martin Gaskell. Peter King, Professor of Social History at Nene College, always encouraged and supported me in this project, and shared with me unreservedly his love for the work and vision of Edward Thompson as an historian of eighteenth-century England. Richard Moss, former Head of History at Nene College, set an example of quiet academic integrity in changing times which I will remember for the rest of my career.

I must also record a particular debt to Professor Linda Colley, who has corresponded with me on aspects of this subject, not uncritically, and has been generous in her encouragement. I must also acknowledge my debt to two former employers. The late Ian R. Grant trained me as an antiquarian bookseller and employed me as his assistant and cataloguer from 1978 to 1986. Few people realise his role as a publisher in producing the four-volume *Edinburgh History of Scotland* with Professor Gordon Donaldson from 1965 to 1975, and as co-editor with Donald Withrington of the new edition of the *Old Statistical Account of Scotland*, in twenty volumes, from 1973 to 1983. Dr Robert J. Cain employed me from 1986 to 1990 as researcher for the Scottish Records Program of the North Carolina Colonial Records Project, administered by the Historical Publications Section of the North Carolina Division of Archives and History, and always treated me as a friend and a colleague rather than an agent. He made it possible for me to take up academic employment when the opportunity arose late in 1990.

Since the autumn of 1995 I have been privileged to be a member of the Department of Scottish History at the University of Edinburgh, and the completion of this book owes everything to the support I have received from Professor Michael Lynch as Head of Department. My colleagues Dr John Bannerman and Dr Ewen Cameron have taught me much about the Scottish Highland perspective on the idea of Britain, and the Honorary Fellows of the department (Professor Geoffrey Barrow, Dr Pat Dennison, Dr William

Ferguson and John M. Simpson) have always been willing to discuss aspects of this subject with me. It has been a pleasure to return to the university and encounter as colleagues my former supervisors in the Department of History, Professor H. T. Dickinson and Dr N. T. Phillipson. I owe a particular debt to Dr Phillipson for his support and encouragement over many years. Ronald Black and Dr Robert Mullally of the Department of Celtic Studies at Edinburgh have helped by gently reminding me that the perspective of a monoglot anglophone is not the only one relevant to the study of the idea of Britain.

There are many other scholars I would wish to thank, but there are limits to how long a list once can include in a short book! I would be remiss, however, in not mentioning how much I have gained in the past from collaborating with Dr John Dwyer, Dr Roger Mason of the University of St Andrews and Professor Richard Sher of the New Jersey Institute of Technology, Newark, New Jersey. Other scholars I would like to mention include Dr John D. Brims, Dr David J. Brown, Professor J. Stewart Brown, Dr Alan Day, Dr Hugh Dunthorne, Owen Dudley Edwards, Dr Martin Fitzpatrick, Professor Tim Harris, Dr Colin Kidd, Dr Murdo Macdonald, Professor Rosalind Mitchison, Professor Aubrey Newman, Professor Frank O'Gorman, Dr John Robertson, Dr Stuart Wallace and Professor T. C. Smout. Any errors or omissions in this little book, however, are my responsibility alone.

I am grateful to the Research Centre in Scottish History at the University of Strathclyde for inviting me to discuss aspects of this subject with them and to acknowledge how much I learned from three important conferences relating to this subject: that on 'The Formation of the United Kingdom' held at the Institute of Historical Research, University of London, in July 1994; that on 'National Identities in Eighteenth-Century Britain' held at Manchester Metropolitan University by the North-West [England] Branch of the British Association for Eighteenth-Century Studies in September 1994 and that on 'Conflict and Change in English Communities and Regions' held at the University of Liverpool in March 1995. All of these conferences were attended with the help of financial support from the School of Social Sciences, Nene College, Northampton.

While receipt of a British Academy award added to the excitement of pursuing this project, the arrival of my daughter Lydia during the period of that award, and the opportunity to move to Edinburgh which arose just before her birth, made the period during which this project has been completed almost, I can truthfully state, unbearably exciting. I owe much to the love and support of my partner Catherine Rylance, our daughter Anna and our son Jos for negotiating the many changes we have had to face together. I owe a particular debt to Catherine, who was determined to drag me from the library and seminar room to encounter her native England in places like 'the Bush' near Upper Lydbrook in the Forest of Dean, or the public bar of the Jolly Potters at Hartshill in the Potteries, or the village fêtes of Northamptonshire or the footpaths of the North Norfolk coast. In return I have tried to persuade her, in consideration of her mother from Renfrewshire and her paternal grandmother from County Cork, that no matter how English the rose, a little bit of the idea of Britain can be found to have affected us all.

Edinburgh
August 1997

1

INTRODUCTION: REGION AND LOCALITY

British history has at last begun to attract substantial interest from historians who teach 'British History' at universities in Britain itself and elsewhere. This may seem to be a curious statement, but as David Cannadine has pointed out recently, 'during the heyday of the *British* state, nation and Empire, it was the *English* version of Whig history which was the prevailing mode'.[1] A curious dichotomy crept into British historiography during the twentieth century, reflecting the domestic political tensions of imperial decline, in which the multi-volume *Oxford History of England*, most obviously, reflected a particular perspective on national history, including Alan Taylor's denial that such a thing as Britain ever existed, while in contrast, schools of Welsh and Scottish history began to develop within the ethnic fastness of the University of Wales and several of the Scottish universities. In one sense Alan Taylor, in denying there ever was a British History, was stating a common belief, leaving aside the particular conundrum of Ireland as a place beyond Britain itself where people were killed over the issue of whether or not a person could be both British and Irish.[2] For those who were interested in British history but were not British themselves, particularly if they were anglophone, the easy-going use of

1

the term England to encompass everything from the country itself to the entire British Empire was difficult to understand.[3] To the imperial historian T. O. Lloyd, Britain as a term was itself too indistinct because it 'smelled too much of woad', and the resistance to the term by historians of the constituent countries of what has sometimes been called 'the British Isles' reflects the imperial origins of the term in contrast to social and historical identities of greater currency amongst most 'British' people.[4]

John Pocock, a New Zealander by birth, led the way in trying to think critically about the implications of this phenomenon. It was no accident that it first became particularly apparent to him at the time that negotiations to allow Britain and Ireland to join the European Union were reaching the point of commitment and success.[5] Nor was it an accident that this point was marked by, on the one hand, a revival of the national historiographies of Ireland, Wales and Scotland, and on the other hand, the almost evangelical fervour of the practitioners of the new English social history established by Edward Thompson, a school of history which gloried in its Englishness as a celebration of a national, cultural and class identity that was not linked to any of the things that the idea of Britain represented; empire, cultural superiority and militarism.[6] Beyond Britain, it affected the English-speaking populations of Canada, Australia and New Zealand, many of whom still thought of 'England' or 'Britain' as 'home'. Subsequently, British history has slowly attracted more interest, to the point that in the time since this book was first proposed and its appearance, the subject can justly be said to have become fashionable, although still very much the subject of debate.[7]

This is partly because, in periodisation, the historians who have found the idea most useful have been those working in particular sub-periods of medieval and early modern history, such as the reigns of Edward I and his immediate successors; or Britain at the time of the English Civil War. Geoffrey Barrow wrote *Medieval Britain* as a successful textbook more than forty years ago, before he went on to write his biography of Edward's great Scottish foe, *Robert the Bruce and the Community of the Realm of Scotland*.[8] J. C. Beckett, more than thirty years ago, was the begetter of the term 'War of the Three Kingdoms' as a result of his own efforts to write a history of modern Ireland.[9] Neither was writing from the standpoint of English history, but each historian had concluded that they could not adequately write their own nation's history without an understanding of its 'British' context. More recently, historians writing from an English perspective have come to share this view, and a series of influential books have resulted that have substantially altered the state of scholarship for each period of historiography.[10]

For the eighteenth century, the situation in historiographic terms has been slightly different, partly because there has been an increase in historiography which followed Barrow's lead in an eighteenth-century context, and sought to write Scottish history in a British context.[11] William Ferguson sought to balance this by deliberately adopting a historical perspective of more depth and a greater range in time to avoid presenting political union with England as inevitable or (perhaps more contentiously) immutable. In his *Scotland's Relations with England*, as he explained in the preface, he presented the public with a book that dealt with British history until 1707 as a result of embarking on a project to write about it *after* 1707, because he became convinced that modern history 'would be all but meaningless if robbed of the earlier perspectives'.[12] Other historians, particularly Nicholas Phillipson, have tried to follow up John Pocock's call for a British History by placing Scottish political and intellectual history more precisely in a British context: as a means of understanding more exactly how an incorporating union which sacrificed political independence should have been followed by a period of unprecedented cultural activity and economic growth in Scotland after 1745.[13] There are still debates over whether eighteenth-century Scottish history can be understood in relation to the union with England, or whether the Union has been used as a political explanation for far more complex transformations which had more to do with industrialisation and urbanisation than the politics of the Scottish landed class.[14]

More recently, Linda Colley has published a major study of the development of British patriotism during the eighteenth and early nineteenth centuries which has sought to move beyond John Pocock's definition of British history as the history of four nations within the British Isles, and has, as a result, attracted considerable attention and stimulated a measure of debate amongst a wider community of scholars. Although she was careful to endeavour to incorporate what might be called a nationalist perspective in her book, she also considered gender, sectarianism and, more controversially, class, by arguing that there was a popular sense of British patriotism which went beyond the culture of the landed and commercial elite.[15] She also pointed out that there was no contradiction during the eighteenth century in individuals holding concurrent identities relating to their locality, religion or country (in the sense of England, or Scotland, or the Vale of Trent or Eskdale), while at the same time accommodating themselves to a larger British identity, which partly represented a common identity against the 'other', most obviously a France which was initially Catholic and absolutist, but which, after 1793, became atheistic (or deistic) and Republican. The nature of France as the 'other' in opposition to Britain may have changed, but the effect was the same. Most English, Welsh and Scots people, and an appreciable number of Irish as well, could identify themselves as 'British', in opposition to whatever was represented by France during the long wars between the two 'states'.[16] It is as well to remember that what France represented continued to change even as it continued to represent an enemy, or even if in peacetime it represented what could be conceived of as a contrast to Britain. Under Napoleon, France ceased to be a republic, but remained a threat, as a military dictatorship bent on European domination, and briefly world domination as well, as Napoleon's expedition to Egypt demonstrated.[17] Even after peace in 1815 the nature of the restored Bourbon monarchy was not recognisable in terms of British ideas of limited monarchy. The abject failure of the French Constitution of 1792 appeared to demonstrate that constitutional monarchy could not be adopted beyond Britain, while, in contrast, the American Republic appeared prone to all the degeneracy of the Italian and Dutch republics which had preceded it.[18]

The legacy of the American and French revolutions thus appeared to be that only the British were capable of preserving a limited monarchy which incorporated both stability and personal liberty, and, in this sense, the term actually appeared to mean the English, and those in Scotland, Wales and Ireland who adopted or were willing to accept as a positive good the model of English polity. Indeed, Henry Dundas persuaded Pitt to move for an incorporating union with Ireland as a means of extending British government in a way that had proved impossible in America, but which the geographical proximity of Ireland and the precedent of success in the case of Wales, as well as the example of Scotland, appeared to indicate was feasible within the British Isles.[19] What is more, the precedent of Oliver Cromwell and William of Orange indicated that Ireland could be subdued militarily, whereas the American War had proved beyond a reasonable doubt that the American colonies most emphatically could not.

In this awareness of 'otherness', Colley took up an important concern of Pocock's earlier articles on British history that is often overlooked. Pocock contrasted what appeared to him to have been the successful maintenance of concurrent identities in Scotland after 1707 as Scots, and as North Britons, with the failure of anything similar to emerge in Ireland.[20] The contrast in historical experience was such that by the twentieth century one had to choose between being Irish or being British if one lived in Ireland, and the choice was an absolute one, involving the complete rejection of its alternative, and sometimes a choice between life and death. Anyone resident in Britain will still read about these issues every day.[21] Indeed, much of the reluctance and uncertainty over the use of the idea of Britain in modern England arises from a reluctance to incorporate the idea of Protestant settler Ireland in its framework, because to do so implies acceptance of the tragedy of modern Northern Ireland as a central rather than a peripheral issue to the English. Britishness is of use in opposing European integration, but it is an embarrassment in its Irish context to most people in England, and probably Scotland and Wales as well.[22]

It is often forgotten that in Welsh and Scottish history as well as Irish history there is a frontier area of engagement with, and in opposition withdrawal from, an expanding England. Were Celtic peoples essentially aboriginal and in retreat before the civilisation represented by the English language and the culture that went with it? Or were they peoples with a unique and rich cultural inheritance of their own which has been obscured by the imperial process of Anglicisation? Another forgotten dimension is that within England, or indeed Britain, as W. G. Hoskins pointed out years ago when he established 'English Local History' as a separate academic discipline, it is possible to write about upland and lowland areas with very different economies and societies that are not necessarily amenable to a framework of analysis which is political or constitutional.[23] A 'British' context is not necessarily the best one to comprehend the textile workers of the Vale of Stroud, the lead miners of the Derbyshire Peak District, or the Fenland people of East Anglia expropriated by a landlord programme of drainage and enclosure.[24]

British history, as yet, does not easily intersect with regional or local history, partly because of divisions which have long existed in British historiography between a 'History' which is primarily political and constitutional and an 'Economic and Social History' which is just that, and thus concerned with communities and identities which cannot necessarily be satisfactorily incorporated within a structure of political administrative units or kingdoms created by the use of military power.[25] This is most obvious in relation to the study of the industrial revolution in Britain, at one time in danger of being reduced to the history of the adoption of changing technology and productive process, but now associated much more with a regional and social context of economic change that occurred in some areas but not in others, and nowhere followed exactly the same pattern. J. D. Chambers, for example, published his *Nottinghamshire in the Eighteenth Century: Life and Labour Under the Squirearchy* in 1932, but when he published an updated edition of his work, he gave up the county structure for that of a geographical region in adopting the title, *The Vale of Trent 1670–1800*, which discussed Nottingham's industrial hinterland as it extended into Derbyshire and Leicestershire as well as part of, but not all of, Nottinghamshire.

But what of social history? David Rollison's recent work on the Vale of Stroud incorporated a pronounced 'social' perspective, but also found the use of a region within which manufacturing activity of a new kind occurred more useful as a framework than that of the county identity of Gloucestershire, although this is used in the title of the study to provide a context, and the importance of Gloucester as a crossroads for the exchange of goods and ideas is central to the book. Yet while the Vale of Stroud was a cradle of early textile manufacture and thus the scene of social changes which would transform much of English society, so it was also marked by empire and cultural exchange thousands of miles away. The Iroquois Indians of upper New York during the eighteenth century demanded Stroud-made Gloucestershire cloth from those who wished to trade for the furs they obtained from the animals they hunted. The cloth was of good quality and used for the clothes of the British agents and soldiers who dealt with the Iroquois, so they desired it too. The social context of its production provides a different perspective on empire and who, within Britain, was part of the construct and who was not. James Wolfe, the victor of the battle for Quebec in 1759, was leader of a company of soldiers sent to Stroud in 1756 to protect local clothiers from striking workers. Within four years, as part of the same war, Wolfe's opponents included striking textile workers in the West Country, as well as the French in Canada and their Indian allies. The red cloth of Stroud was a manufacture in England, but a badge of empire and commerce abroad.[26] Empire and the British state were remote from a locality yet impacted on it, and this hidden history of the local influence of state formation and empire, and its relationship to economic change and social development within Britain, has yet to be fully explored.[27]

Thus while the early modern British or indeed European world was one in which only a self-regarding political elite transgressed traditional boundaries, these boundaries were being crossed more often by more people as internal migration increased, most obviously to London, and markets began to intersect in a way that was not national, and of course was not British either, if we confine ourselves to what is understood by the geographical expression.[28] During the eighteenth century, regions and localities were subject to as much redefinition as the concept of Britain itself. In addition to county market towns at the centre of a region, or towns like Beverley or Chesterfield, which were not county towns but served the function of urban market centre for a rural hinterland, there were towns which operated on a 'cusp' between different regions. Towns like Northallerton, Daventry and Newcastle-under-Lyme, Crieff, Pitlochry and Berwick-upon-Tweed, or Kenmare, Enniskillen and Clonakilty, all provided a forum for cross-cultural contact and trade across established market boundaries rather than within them.[29] At this level, however, we have few studies to tell us whether these frontiers related to British history or operated independently of it, but it is clear that there were those who looked to 'the people above' and found some significance in what they could learn of their world, and there were those who did not engage with authority and the state if they could escape it.[30] It is impossible to measure how many people in how many centres and localities fell into either group, but a significant element in eighteenth-century history was that the numbers of those aware of the existence of both 'spaces' in Britain were increasing, and their agency would prove to be a dynamic in its history. Ignorance of the 'other' might have been bliss, but it was less of an option as commerce and the culture of print drew more people together.

An example of the intersection of economy, locality and the impact of state formation and empire was Easter Ross in northern Scotland, which existed on a boundary which did not always coincide with the geographical division of highland and lowland, and which had nothing to do with national identity. When economic and social change were introduced by the landowners in this area, it was 'not primarily, to make money', but to compete on equal terms with an expanded British elite.[31] In this the gentry in Easter Ross and their agents did not act in conjunction with their tenantry, nor in opposition to them, but independently of them. They acted as a class and they had no doubts about the efficacy or propriety of the economic changes they brought to their region. Their behaviour might be termed 'revolutionary', in reference to 'a small, highly motivated group of people' who carried out substantial economic change because they wanted to increase their own standard of living and because they had come to believe, such was the impact of Enlightenment ideology, that in the modern world of the eighteenth century all things were posssible.[32] The power of the new science, as the late Paul Edwards once paraphrased Adam Smith, was that one 'could be both good, and rich'.[33]

This was not a regional development, although perhaps it developed particularly rapidly and with particular ferocity in the Scottish Highlands. War speeds social change, and many of the 'revolutions' which social and economic historians discuss in relation to the end of the eighteenth century – industrial revolution, agricultural revolution, transportation revolution – really did take place in a period of revolutionary political conflict in which those who saw themselves as agents of economic and social revolution presented their activities as 'improvement', while in political terms their class systematised empire as part of an extended financial system that embraced monarchy, aristocracy and landowning as talismans of continuity. In contrast, those whose politics were presented by the elite as radical or revolutionary were actually seeking to defend customary tradition, and to gain access to the mechanism of constitutional activity in order to further that defence of their way of life, and by implication their autonomy as members of the society in which they lived.

The work which follows is an attempt to examine this theme in the light of the many substantial and important contributions which have appeared in the 1990s that bear upon it directly or indirectly. Many scholars have seen the need to look for new approaches to traditional English and British history, although there remain important differences in emphasis which are not necessarily exclusive, but might still be perceived in that light. Imperial, constitutional and political British history can be viewed as complementary to, rather than in opposition to, 'four-nations' history, which denies that there is any meaningful British history at all. It also complements social, economic or popular political history, which assumes that to direct historical attention to the politics and culture of 'the people above' is to valorise their imperialism, rather than part of an attempt to understand why the British Empire established itself so successfully, and to measure the cost of that development to groups within British society who did not benefit from it.

The three chapters which follow discuss the dynastic origins of British history and the relationship between the extension of the dynastic power of the Stuarts and the emergence of a state which, by 1707, acted as a dynamic receptacle of a sovereignty which was both political and economic. John Pocock wrote recently that the great lesson 'the English' learned from their civil war was that 'sovereignty' was 'precarious and contestable'.[34] Where did ultimate political authority exist in English society? The very question reveals the essential relationship of English history to British history and the reason why a Scottish historian like Barrow or an Irish historian like Beckett found it essential to comprehend a British perspective whereas, until so recently, very few English historians experienced the same intellectual process.

The Wars of the Three Kingdoms had been horrible civil wars in all three kingdoms. There were no unified national groups, although it is true that Wales was almost uniformly Royalist. The lesson of war was that no one part of Britain could solve the problem of establishing sovereignty in its society without extending it throughout Britain. This it was that brought Oliver Cromwell to Scotland and Ireland and brought about a reluctant unity of experience which was his legacy to Britain. The development of a new constitutional idea of a sovereignty of shared authority involving monarchy with aristocracy and gentry under the law would occur in England, and the extension of this constitution would provide the dynamic of British history up to the outbreak of war with revolutionary France in 1793.

Chapters 5–7 consider important aspects of the underlying themes of the entire book. If the idea of Britain originated in an idea of Protestant empire which, by 1660, had been completely subsumed within the dynastic identity of the Stuarts, by 1707, or 1713 with the Treaty of Utrecht, or certainly by the time of the Treaty of Aix-la-Chapelle in 1748; Britain had become an imperial idea based on the security of the state as the custodian of political sovereignty. In British geographical terms, this involved securing the government and the new monarchy against the challenge of Jacobite revolt by extending the authority of the state, not just to Ireland and Scotland, but to provincial England and Wales, and also over London. In extra-British terms this involved the legitimisation of the financial and commercial markets which were evolving in London. Their origins lay with the financial needs of the Tudors and London's ever-increasing growth as an urban centre, but the arrival of William of Orange in 1688–89 as a Dutch king in a Protestant cause also marked a marriage of financial interests between new English monarchy and the Dutch Republic, which enticed more English commercial capital further and further afield into the Atlantic economy and beyond. In one sense this is a familiar history, but it has been restated recently in important and interesting ways by several innovative scholars, including John Brewer, Patrick O'Brien and Christopher Bayly.[35]

Chapter 6, 'Peripheral Nations?', directly concerns the keystone of the book, which is the tension between the metropolitan character of traditional British history and the critical reaction on the part of many scholars to the essential imperialism which it implied. It concerns the effect of this on those

11

who were not within the magic circle, not just in terms of class, but in terms of the 'other' nations that were incorporated with England in constructing Britain as a state, and the English provinces which, as a result, found themselves as colonised from the centre as the frontier nations that were incorporated in the new polity. In some cases, the result was that certain English regions found themselves subordinated to non-English urban centres or regions by the end of the eighteenth century, the most obvious example being that of the North of England to Edinburgh.[36]

The last of the more broadly thematic chapters considers the problem of relating the history of an expanding financial, commercial and manufacturing empire to the history of the culture which harboured it, and as a result considered itself as 'enlightened', rational, progressive and above all else, superior, to 'other' cultures on a national, provincial, local and class basis. Britons were enlightened and free, 'others' were not, even if they were English. The use of terms like independence, liberty and slavery permeated the expanding culture of print which came into contact with more and more areas of traditional culture during the eighteenth century, and created areas of friction and interdependence between two cultures which in one sense had existed previously independent of one another. Court culture involved a very narrow though powerful world, detached and insulated from the larger society around it; yet in another sense by being detached, it did not involve an element of opposition, of choice, and fundamental conflict which began to become apparent in Britain by 1820 and was evident for all to see by 1830.

The last section of the book considers the last quarter of the eighteenth century and looks forward to the Britain which had come into existence by the time victory over the European empire of Napoleon finally had been achieved in 1815. Linda Colley has termed this 'one of the most formative periods in the making of the modern world and – not accidentally – in the forging of British identity'.[37] It involved the secession of the American colonies of what was, until

12

1763, British North America from the British Empire, while the Canada so triumphantly conquered by Wolfe and his Scottish successor, General James Murray, was retained, and became a new 'British North America'. A sense of acute domestic as well as imperial crisis within Britain ensued during the 1780s, which was resolved by more rapid change brought about by war rather than the rational and progressive period of reform anticipated by so many of the educated, commercial and professional classes. Reform would not come until half a century later. In the meantime, Britain created a new empire centred on the Eastern rather than the Western hemisphere, it became a more overtly militaristic state, and it no longer justified possession of empire on the grounds of the civilising power of commerce as much as upon institutional superiority in law, government and administration – an alteration that contained the seeds of the racism which later took over the 'undefended minds' of those who secured their crust and livelihood from that empire during the nineteenth century.[38]

At the same time the nature of social relations within Britain was changing as well and becoming in one sense more inclusive, in that commercial culture as well as participation in the war effort involved ever larger numbers of people, but more exclusive as well, in that the prosecution of British political reformers during the 1790s and the 'Church and King' riots in defence of the established order against those perceived as challenging it led to an atmosphere of internal division which may have varied in intensity from region to region in Britain, but certainly existed alongside popular patriotism.[39] Here we find a hidden English nationalism which has continued to the present day, often in uneasy juxtaposition with British patriotism and in some ways accommodating it. The very success of the British state, in addition to mobilising its financial power, at mobilising the energies of as much of its population as possible to counter the unprecedented mobilisation efforts of its French enemy, led to an increased expectation of participation in the polity of the state and the wealth it generated. This would form the

13

basis for the renewed strength of the postwar reform movement. More people wanted to be Britons, and no one within
the traditional ruling elite was really prepared to conceive of
what that would mean, and in the end the financial achievement in paying for the war could not be matched by an
ability to construct a reasonable transition to a peacetime
economy.[40] Revolutionary British economic change could be
perceived as subjugation of traditional English culture, but
really the 'tradition' which was perceived was the domestic
aspect of a booming wartime economy, while subjugation
consisted of the failure of the political and financial classes
to turn their wartime economic invention to more peaceful
pursuits. At the time that he wrote *The Making of the English
Working Class*, Edward Thompson felt that no unified British
working class had emerged until the 1820s.[41] Jonathan Clark
has written that Catholic Emancipation of 1829 undermined
the old order in Britain and brought about political reform in
1832–33.[42] Given that these events coincided with Revolution
in France and unrest in many other parts of Europe, as well
as the origins of the British Chartist movement, perhaps the
latter date helps relate the social and economic change which
was undermining more and more of traditional society to the
political and constitutional experimentation that reflected
recognition, even among the enfranchised elite, that in
order to preserve the old order, it would have to change.[43]
When it did change, it did so in a British context that incorporated Ireland. Both the limitations of political reform for
most British working people as revealed by the mass movement for a People's Charter and the failure of the British
state to prevent demographic collapse in Ireland during the
1840s provided stark evidence of the social and political
limitations of the idea of Britain at its apogee.

2

THE STUART MONARCHY AND THE IDEA OF BRITAIN

The idea of modern Britain could be said to have originated in the ambitions of James VI of Scotland to be recognised as king of England and Ireland in succession of Queen Elizabeth. His achievement of that ambition made him a monarch who accomplished what Edward I or the Tudor monarchs had never achieved, which was the unity of all of the island of Britain under one monarch. His coinage when he first went to England bore the Latin inscription 'Henry [VII united] the Roses, James the kingdoms'.[1] Thus would the poor king of an equally poor kingdom, peripheral not just in European but also in British terms, become the founder of a Protestant dynasty which would exceed the glory of the Tudors as monarchs of an imperial state of European and world consequence, through its influence over Protestantism as a religious cause and its wealth as a trading nation.[2] James succeeded in uniting Britain under one monarch, after a fashion, but he failed in his efforts to bring about a union between his native kingdom of Scotland and his new kingdom of England and Wales.[3] Ireland, of course, although having James as its king, remained a separate case. By failing to achieve a union between Scotland and England as monarchies, James could be seen very early to fail to follow the

15

success of the Tudors, as it was Henry VIII's union of Wales with England which provided the most telling precedent for James's ambitions to unite Scotland with the Tudor kingdom.[4] Ireland was another matter, because failure to achieve union with Scotland precluded any idea of further consolidation, but even before the accession of James there were those who saw the incorporation of Wales with England as the future for the English interest in Ireland.[5]

James's accession did change the course of Irish history, however, for Ulster became redundant as a frontier border próvince to insulate the Pale against the Scots. Under James's direction, drawn from his experiences of attempting to colonise and control his own Gaels in the Scottish Highlands and Islands, Ulster became a new area of plantation for Scots as a parallel Irish world to the plantation of south-east Ireland by men of West-Country England. Ireland as colonised kingdom thus became, courtesy of the first British Stuart king, both separate from Britain and subordinate to it, but also another place where Scots and English met and sometimes clashed in conflict, on neutral territory, and sometimes made common cause against the threat of the alien Gael. In that sense, from 1603, Ireland really did become the forerunner and progenitor of British, as opposed to English, empire.[6]

This became evident during the years of the so-called English Civil War, which the Irish historian J. C. Beckett aptly referred to as 'the war of the three kingdoms'.[7] Charles I, in his desperate efforts to retain and reinforce his authority as monarch, became ever more deeply embroiled in schemes to use his Scottish and Irish kingdoms as the means of subjugating those who opposed his authority in England. This would initiate a pattern of Jacobite activity which would persist into the eighteenth century, and really only end when the French finally abandoned the House of Stuart in their peace with Britain in 1748. There was a pronounced irony in the actions of Charles, given that the English Civil War was rooted in his attempt to recall the English Parliament, whose services he had successfully dispensed with over the previous decade, to enable him to raise an English army to impose his royal will on Scotland. Thus it could be argued that if Charles had been able to ignore Scotland completely rather than merely neglect it, his reign might have taken a very different course. As Conrad Russell commented so aptly, one might say of Charles that to lose one kingdom might be seen as a misfortune, but to lose all three really could only be interpreted as being careless.[8] It was Charles I, in his spider-like manoeuvres at the centre of a British web, who brought his three kingdoms together to the point that they became intertwined. For more than a century afterwards, it was the machinations of the Stuarts which ensured that Britain remained a multinational state rather than an English empire.[9] The continuation of the romantic myth of Jacobitism in popular historiography is possibly a legacy of this dynastic element to the origins of British history, as the fortunes of the Stuarts as a royal family and the beginnings of the idea of Britain are inextricably bound up with one another.

If James VI claimed to have united the kingdoms, it was Oliver Cromwell who actually did it in 1651–52, in a whirlwind, and in a way which genuinely did suggest that God was on his side. The defeats he inflicted on the Scots at Dunbar in 1650 and Worcester in 1651 effectively destroyed the tradition of Scotland's martial independence which went back to the fourteenth-century Wars of Independence. Or if catastrophic defeat, not unknown to the Scots at the hands of the English before 1650, was not new, the ruthlessly effective occupation of the country which succeeded it was.[10] The Scots never recovered from the subsequent defeat, not just during the war which followed, but historically, from the utter subjugation which Cromwell imposed on them. Cromwell's conquest, not just of Scotland and Ireland, but of thoroughly Royalist Wales and the Royalist regions of England, really marks the beginning of modern British history as something other than an episode in the continuing misfortunes of the House of Stuart.[11] Why? Because the success of the Cromwellian army demonstrated that Britain possessed an elementary unity.[12] It demonstrated that there could be no final settlement in any one part of it unless that settlement could be accepted for the entire archipelago, including Scotland and Ireland, which previously could be conceived of in entirely different terms. The Kingdom of the Scots had, arguably, never submitted to foreign rule. It had certainly maintained political independence from the time of Edward I and Robert Bruce at the beginning of the fourteenth century.[13] If Ireland as a kingdom had not quite the same claim to feudal independence, it was equally the site of a Celtic/ Gaelic other world which was never completely subdued in a military sense until the arrival of the English New Model Army in 1652. Henceforth the Irish and the Scots shared the memory of total military defeat at the hands of an English army. There were no wars of independence, only military occupation and expropriation, although the Scottish and Irish experiences differed in that in Scotland heavy fines and taxes maintained an army of occupation, whereas in Ireland many landowners who were Catholic and Gaelic were expropriated and replaced.[14]

Thus the Restoration world of Charles II came about in the wake of Britain's first experience of unitary rule, under a Protectorate which demonstrated the military and economic supremacy of the prosperous South of England and its metropolis, the largest city in Europe, the City of London. Charles II restored the multiple kingdoms because his father had ruled them as separate kingdoms and the English New Model Army had not. His reign was all about restoration of a sense of continuity in the aftermath of fundamental change. The Restoration regime was as gaudy and superficial as the monarch himself, but embodied also his detached assessment of his kingdoms and what was necessary to keep them at peace. He was King of England first, but like his father saw his additional realms as resources to be drawn upon to maintain his authority and give him a degree of independence from his over-mighty English subjects. In that sense his attitude towards them was colonial. He never visited Ireland or Scotland after 1660 and he certainly never wanted to. Years later he sent his bastard son to Scotland with the pronouncement that it was no better than a place to go and 'wink and shit', such were the people there.[15] Ireland he had no experience of and saw only as a source of tax revenue and soldiers, for which he would not have to account to his English Parliament.[16]

This was of course why Charles II wanted to be king of three kingdoms and not just of one, whether of England or of greater Britain. If, like his father, he was unable to dispense with his English Parliament, by keeping Scotland and Ireland separate kingdoms he retained part of his realm beyond the scrutiny of parliamentary committees, although his biographer Professor Hutton makes a good case to see him as essentially returning to his father's agenda by the end of his reign, in despair of ever reconciling royal policy with the prejudices of Parliament.[17] The Parliaments of Scotland and Ireland were very different from that of England and much easier to control. Thus they could be delegated to trusted servants, or workhorses upon whom a watch could be set, and provide an extra-English dimension to the reign without diverting attention and resources from its focus at court in London, in what was coming to be perceived as the 'heart' or 'home' of England. The war of three kingdoms was succeeded by the reign of a king of three kingdoms, with the centre of the web every bit as English as before. Nevertheless, the King participated in three parallel political histories which were never completely separate, sharing him as they did amongst the dramatis personae, subject to a king who saw the survival of his majesty and his dignity in the separation of his kingdoms.[18]

The manner in which this was carried out again differed significantly between Scotland and England. Charles had been crowned King of Scotland at Scone, the ancient place of that rite and in circumstances not all that distant from those prevailing at the coronation of Robert Bruce three and a half centuries previously. He knew many of the great Scots peers and some of the ministers of the Kirk, and at his restoration he had both scores to settle and a clear idea of how Scotland as a kingdom would relate to his primary

responsibilities in England. The Marquis of Argyll was executed in 1661, and soon the heads of others joined his on
public display in Edinburgh.[19] The Earl of Lauderdale
shared his king's memories of the raising of his standard in
Scotland and for many years acted as his alter ego there. If
never quite a viceroy on behalf of Charles, for many years
Lauderdale came as close to that role as any Scot in history.
The debate over the idea of having a national secretary for
Scotland within a united kingdom becomes particularly clear
from the time of Lauderdale onwards. Lauderdale was his
master's servant. Charles gave him his power and supported
it for many a year, but in the end it was clear that although
Lauderdale had great power in Scotland, it counted for
nothing without royal approval.[20] On the other hand, the
semi-royal nature of that authority was evident in the fact
that although Charles began to consult others towards the
end of the Lauderdale era, he never replaced his informal
viceroy directly. Instead, the future James VII and II,
enmeshed in the depths of the Exclusion Crisis in England,
journeyed to Scotland as his brother's representative to hold
a Stuart court once again in the ancient palace of Holyroodhouse in 1679, rebuilt on the express orders of Charles II
after the Restoration and lined with the portraits of the
Stuarts, real and imaginary, back to the very origins of Scotland itself in the seventh century, painted in a job lot at so
many shillings per head by a Dutchman named De Witt.[21]
Lauderdale experienced opposition from aristocratic rivals
and members of the Scottish landed class who opposed his
arbitrary power, as well as Presbyterians who opposed the
religious policy of the Crown, but for many years Charles and
his English advisers were happy to leave Scotland to its
dominant politician as an alien Presbyterian place.[22]

The case of Ireland, as Ronald Hutton has remarked, was
very different during the Restoration years. 'English politicians were happy to let [Scotland] look after itself,' he has
written, 'but [Ireland] represented, from the post of Lord-
Lieutenant down, a gigantic spoils system in which all wished
a stake.' 'All' refers to all at court rather than all in Ireland,

and reflects the more overtly colonial relationship between England and Ireland. The Duke of Ormonde and the Earl of Essex were conscientious Lords-Lieutenant of Ireland, and in Ormonde Charles employed a deputy who had a unique range of experience of recent Irish history and knowledge of the complex interaction between Old Irish, Old English and 'New English' interests there, as well as the divisions within the so-called 'New English' Protestants between the Scottish Dissenters in Ulster and the Episcopalian landowners and their clients in Leinster and Munster to the south. But even more than Scotland, Ireland 'was governed from Westminster as well as from Dublin', and a Lord Lieutenant, no matter how sympathetic to Ireland and the interests of that country, would forever be undermined by those who could question his authority at court, and that court was in London, not Dublin.[23] There was also, of course, the well-known curse of 'Poynings' Law', obtained by the English deputy Sir Edward Poynings from the Irish Parliament which met at Drogheda in 1495, which in effect precluded the Irish Parliament from originating legislation, leaving it only with the right to accept or reject measures presented to it by the King's ministers. Such was the ignorance and neglect of Irish affairs in London, however, that often legislation was obtained by proposals from Ireland being sent to England for confirmation and approval before being set before the Irish Parliament. So it was that both executive and legislature in Ireland were subject to the monarchy in England, although in practice this was not very much different from the actual situation in Scotland from 1603 to 1638 and again from 1660 to 1707, when the Scottish Parliament could consider only legislation presented to it by a committee of its members, 'The Lords of the Articles', appointed by the monarch.[24]

Charles II was King of three kingdoms, but like his father, he was never master of any of them, and this was because the religious settlement in all three kingdoms was problematic. This was not unique in Europe, riven by a century and a half of religious warfare, with France still divided between

Catholic and Huguenot and the Holy Roman Emperor elected by both Protestant and Catholic electors, but the idea of Britain was essentially a sectarian construction, rooted in the complex culture of the Reformation and the powerful idea of a Protestant emperor to oppose the Hapsburg servant of the Pope as Antichrist.[25] The Stuarts had adapted the idea to the fortunes of their dynasty, in the case of Charles I and Charles II in all probable ignorance of its origins, but both the second and third 'British' Stuart king valued hierarchy, order and, in particular, their own majesty, over the needs of the Roman Catholic Church. James VI and I had famously stated, 'No bishop, no king', and if these words were not always in the mind of his son and his grandson, their policies often reflected its message.[26] What was different about Charles II as Restoration monarch was that he had the rather dramatic evidence of his father's execution and his own exile to reflect the limits of royal authority, particularly in the matter of religion and the right to dictate the manner in which it was observed.

Under the rule of Charles II the Episcopalian churches of England, Scotland and Ireland were restored, but nowhere were they restored absolutely.[27] The British monarchy presided ever after over a pluralist religious regime, albeit one in which there were favoured churches supported by the monarchy and the state. Much of real Restoration policy concerned the elaboration of a religious settlement which would become as subtle and subject to almost imperceptible alterations in emphasis as Charles II himself. His brother James's inability to grasp the complexity of what was evolving would prove his undoing and demonstrate that, while the authority of the monarchy had been restored in 1660, the dynamic of religious change could only be tempered rather than controlled. The restored monarchy was attracted to Catholicism but tied to the Tudor idea of a national Catholic church. In all three kingdoms by 1660 there were substantial numbers of people from all walks of life who were opposed to either of these alternatives and were willing to suffer much for their beliefs. In the narrative history of a reign which was often intolerant, it is sometimes possible to fail to note just how much of the regime's domestic policy was predicated on the acceptance of religious toleration. The Stuart restoration regime was not based on religious toleration for Protestants alone. That was what would distinguish it from its successors, and that was what would subject the regime to periodic crises, but the dramatically different religious demography of the three kingdoms would necessitate separate policies in each, which were in conflict with the collective British memory of shared crisis as well as the instability implicit in religious pluralism. Charles II wanted a pluralistic monarchy and probably (it is impossible by its nature to document the argument) wanted a pluralistic religious settlement, but his great enemy the Marquis of Argyll had put the alternative, and very Protestant, view to a committee of the Scottish Parliament in 1646:

> let us hold fast that union which is happily established between us [Scottish and English Parliaments, but properly speaking in alliance rather than union]; and let nothing make us again two, who are in so many ways one; all of one language, in one island, all under one King, one in Religion, yea, one in Covenant, so that in effect we differ in nothing but in name – as brethren do – which I wish were also removed that we might be altogether one, if the two kingdoms shall think fit.[28]

If the Britain of England, Scotland and Wales was largely Protestant by 1660, Ireland as ever before and ever after, was not. The fact that Argyll's speech was made in response to the crisis caused by the defeat of the Scottish Covenanting army in Ireland at Benburb in 1646 underlines the difficulty and the continued connection, as did Cromwell's subsequent conquests and the restoration of Charles II to all three kingdoms rather than to two . . . or one. Charles cared little for Ireland and never went there. The Duke of Ormonde was the House of Stuart in Ireland, although his royal masters did not always appreciate this.[29] It has sometimes been argued that the Stuarts used Ireland and Scotland as testing-grounds for absolutist policies which they hoped to introduce to England

and Wales later, but there is little evidence for this, and much to suggest that it entered the literature as part of the Whig teleology of an ever more independent English Parliament successfully resisting the plots and policies of arbitrary monarchs.[30] Genuine religious pluralism was probably not the aim of the Restoration regime, but there is little evidence that it ever found favour with the champions of English parliamentary independence, driven by a fear of popery as well as of higher taxes, and thus opposing toleration for Roman Catholics as well as arbitrary government.

Charles wished to permit toleration of Roman Catholicism in Ireland without causing dissension amongst its predominantly Protestant political elite. How well established that Protestant elite was has caused some debate recently, with emphasis on the one hand of the pedigree of Protestant plantation by 1660, while on the other hand, no one can deny that the majority of the population of Ireland was Roman Catholic, and that the massacres of Protestants by the Catholic Irish rebels of 1641 persists in the demonology of Protestant Ireland to the present day. How secure was Protestant ascendancy in 1660? Did Charles II wish to undermine it? Perhaps the Roman Catholic remonstrance of 1661 provides one measure of this, when over a hundred prominent laymen, priests and even a bishop declared that, as Irish Roman Catholics, they conceded absolute authority to the Crown in the temporal sphere, viewing their allegiance to the Church and its head in Rome as spiritual only. Ormonde was always in favour of tolerating the religious beliefs and worship of what he recognised as the faith of the majority of the Irish population, provided that their political loyalty to the Crown was always clearly expressed. This was wise counsel for Ireland, but even a hint of toleration for Roman Catholicism provoked suspicion of the Stuart regime in England, Wales and Scotland, aware of the Roman Catholicism of the king's mother, sister, wife, and from 1672, of his brother as well. In 1666 Ormonde allowed a congregation of Roman Catholic Irish clergy to meet in Dublin to discuss the remonstrance of 1661, although when it failed to agree, priests known to oppose the measure were imprisoned.[31] Not all Irish politicians shared his perspective, and were quick to advise the King and his ministers that the Protestant interest in Ireland could only be undermined at their peril.

The tensions in Irish society during the Restoration were most noticeable, not surprisingly, in the land settlement administered by the new regime. Many Protestants had not been Royalists and had received lands taken from those who were. Many Royalists were Catholic and could claim restitution of their lands on the basis of political loyalty rather than religious uniformity. Which way would the new regime go? The eventual settlement has been termed 'a classic political fudge', which certainly reflects the innate caution of the monarch. Catholic landownership recovered to about a quarter of the total. This, of course, still condemned the majority of the population in terms of confessional allegiance to a minimum of political influence, in a traditional polity where power reflected ownership of land. That ownership was not strictly sectarian, however, in that the Irish royal government was almost as concerned about the threat posed by Protestant Dissenters in Ulster, or even Dublin, as it was by the prospect of Catholic revolt, although the Duke of Ormonde regarded the one threat as in some degree cancelling out the other.[32] Whenever there was a prospect of Covenanting disturbance in Scotland during the 1670s the Dublin government sent troops into Ulster to preclude Presbyterian assistance to the Scots.[33] Although from 1672 there was a tangible sign of an acceptance by the regime of the Presbyterians in Ulster in the granting of a *regium donum*, as a contribution to the maintenance of Presbyterian ministers, payable out of the customs revenue of the port of Belfast.[34]

Restoration government of Ireland must be accounted a success. There were no rebellions. Three very different religious groups, themselves divided in the case of Catholics ('Old' England and 'New' English) and Dissenters (Ulster Presbyterians and Cromwellian English Dissenters), largely went about their business in peace. The Irish government kept the peace and generated a surplus of revenue in some years, as well as raising regiments for the war effort when needed, both of which were sent to England. Indeed, from an Irish perspective uncluttered by the pretensions of a courtier, that was the problem. Ireland was administered to English needs, not just in its favouritism towards the Protestant community (which naturally did not share that perspective), nor its provision of sinecures and income for English politicians, but also in the subjugation of Irish economic interests, although this appears to have been the province of an English Parliament which undoubtedly saw its economic role in national rather than British terms.[35] Much depends on whether one wants to emphasise assertive policies (there were none formulated with the express intention of benefiting Ireland) or protective ones, as in the Duke of Ormonde's protection of Ireland from the excesses of the Protestant reaction in England to the discovery of the 'Popish Plot'. The execution of Irish primate Oliver Plunket in what was essentially a judicial murder, while an atrocity which can comfortably be laid on the tombs of English bigots, indicates to a discomfiting extent the subjection of Irish interests to English priorities during the Restoration regime.[36]

In England and Wales, after a period of initial uncertainty over the extent of popular feeling, the 'Cavalier' Parliament, intensely Royalist, restored the Church of England, and enacted in its support the so-called 'Clarendon Code' named after Charles's first great minister and mentor in government.[37] The initial intention to comprehend English Presbyterians within the national Church ran into trouble in the face of enthusiastic Episcopalian responses to Restoration. By October 1661 Charles had entrusted the task of revising the prayer book of the Church of England to a Convocation meeting at York and Canterbury.[38] Although this established Episcopalianism, it did not mean that Charles marked the Presbyterians down for persecution – indeed he always differentiated between them and Protestant dissent in a broader sense – but it did mean an uncompromising re-establishment of Episcopalianism as the system of government for the state Church. Here we see not royal repression as portrayed in older books such as Thomas Richards's *Wales Under the Penal Code 1662–87* (1927), but the operation of a government which served a monarch whose commitment to religious belief was minimal, and whose need for state security was maximum. Grateful, rather than rebellious, Dissenters were less likely to rebel, and an obedient rather than an assertive national church would serve the purposes of the state much more conveniently.

Tim Harris has made the useful observation that it was not religious persecution which created friction between Dissenters and Anglicans; it was disagreement between those who were sympathetic to Dissent and those who were not.[39] In some boroughs, such as Coventry, where there was a strong Dissenting community, Dissenters continued to hold office in local government. In London Dissenters were also influential, and a noticeable element in the financial markets which were already beginning to evolve there. Between 1660 and 1688 more than a third of those who held directorships of the great trading companies of London, such as the East India Company, were Dissenters.[40] Such economic importance amongst the Dissenting community meant many moderate Anglicans were against discrimination towards Dissenters. There were many who had conformed to the Anglican Church at the time of the Reformation who may have accepted the idea of bishops and a state church, but were much less interested in enforcing religious uniformity. It was to this constituency that the King gravitated, most likely out of pragmatism. What is certain is that the Cavalier Parliament was more Anglican than the King, and that the so-called 'Clarendon Code' was imposed on Charles and Clarendon rather than initiated by them.[41] The King and the monarchy became associated with a policy of toleration for much of his reign, but the problem, of course, was the evident desire of the King to extend toleration to Roman Catholics rather than limit it to Protestants. Roman Catholics in England were a minority, of influence only in a few localities such as parts of Lancashire and, most visibly, at Court, but as we have discussed, the Stuart kingdom of Ireland held up a very different example before English Protestants, Dissenter and Anglican alike, and the King's links with absolutist France were but too evident, even before suspicion of secret negotiations by the Court with France became apparent. Toleration of Roman Catholicism as a religion was viewed with deep suspicion in England, Wales and Scotland.

All this crystallised, of course, in the Exclusion Crisis, and the possibility of the openly Roman Catholic Duke of York emerging as the first Roman Catholic monarch of England since Queen Mary, an unhappy precedent that formed part of the basis of the anti-Catholic hysteria of the Popish Plot, which drew upon the imagery of Ireland in 1641 in Titus Oates's tale of a plot to massacre thousands of English Protestants. The British nature of this English crisis was also evident in the names which Englishmen now used to discredit their opponents; Tory defenders of the Anglican Church and religious uniformity were likened to the Catholic Gaelic-speaking Irishmen who murdered Protestants in Ireland during the 1640s, while Whig proponents of Protestant dissent, trade and the limitation of the royal prerogative were likened to the Whigs – Scottish Presbyterian zealots who opposed both Cromwellian protectorate and restored Royalism, determined to impose their Presbyterianism on all of Britain.[42] Remote and neglected as the other Stuart kingdoms were, they nevertheless acted as parallel poles in the demonology of English religious and political conflict. Perhaps it was suitable, then, that both those members of the royal family most affected by Exclusion were sent to Scotland when Presbyterian opposition to the regime broke out into open rebellion – James, Duke of York as King's Commissioner, the King's bastard son Monmouth as commander of the King's forces there against the covenanting rebels he would defeat at Bothwell Brig. It was the Scots, not the Irish, who appeared to threaten the Restoration peace by 1679, given the outbreak of open rebellion in south-west Scotland.

It was not always thus. Charles used viceroys in Scotland very effectively, as we have seen, and in Lauderdale he found the ultimate Restoration political animal; cold, calculating, quick to take pleasure, driven by ambition, utterly convinced that only stable state authority could prevent a recrudescence of the disasters which had overtaken his country (not to mention himself) between 1638 and 1660. But the history of Lauderdale's rule in Scotland is the history of a series of royal 'indulgences' which attempted to contain the force of Lowland Presbyterian religious feeling.[43] Presbyterianism and the heritage of the covenant held sway south of the Tay and Clyde only at a time when the population of Scotland, meagre as it was, was much more evenly distributed across the entire area of the country than it is now. Lauderdale and the King's Scottish Privy Council, drawn from the Scottish aristocracy on a national rather than a regional basis, may have been sympathetic to the rights of an ancient kingdom, but represented a political class whose disenchantment with the national Kirk was well-nigh comprehensive. Nevertheless, they were on the whole also conversant with the strength of Presbyterian feeling in Lowland Scotland and the strength of the influence of the clergy over much of the population, including clergy who had lost their livings for refusing to accept the reintroduction of episcopacy at the time of the Restoration.

The Scottish clergy were divided, as they had been for years, between the 'protesters' or 'remonstrants'. They saw the Scottish National Covenant of 1638, as well as the Solemn League and Covenant adopted in conjunction with the English Parliament in 1643, as binding perpetually on the Scottish Kirk and the Scottish people. The 'resolutioners', in contrast, the larger party of Presbyterian ministers in Scotland, were convinced Royalists who harboured hopes, not without some justification, that Charles might accept a moderate form of Presbyterianism for his national church in all three kingdoms. In this they were betrayed, not so much by the King, as by events, and perhaps by Lord Chancellor Clarendon's memory that when the Royalist ship of state had previously floundered, it had shipped water first in Scotland.[44] Thus, episcopacy was extended to Scotland because it was established as the preferred basis for a restored national church in Ireland and then, through the insistence of the

Cavalier Parliament rather than Clarendon, as the form of church organisation adopted in England. Lauderdale had his doubts, but he was initially eclipsed by the Earl of Middleton in Scotland, and by the time he had demonstrated his superiority as a political lieutenant to Charles, the decision to restore episcopacy in Scotland had been taken.

Lauderdale did his best. Repression alternated with indulgence. The first indulgence of June 1669 resulted in the restoration of forty-two Presbyterian ministers to their parishes, and in 1672 a second indulgence restored another ninety. Ministers were not required to denounce Presbyterian church government to resume their places, but both 'indulgences' were accompanied by additional measures against those who chose not to come to terms with the state, such as an act of 1669 fining landowners on whose lands open-air conventicles were held, one of 1670 imposing fines on any unlicensed preacher, and a 1672 law making baptism by the state Church compulsory. By 1677 landowners in theory, or to be more accurate by direction of the Scottish Privy Council, were required to sign commitments guaranteeing the loyal behaviour of all those residing on their lands. In 1679 outright rebellion broke out in Scotland, but was put down by royal troops led by the Duke of Monmouth, who thus demonstrated his loyalty to monarchy and the state in precedence to toleration and dissent, hitherto a potential source of support for his ambitions towards the throne. This was followed in Scotland by a third set of measures intended as royal indulgence towards Presbyterianism, pardoning most of the recent rebels and legalising private worship according to conscience. The intention, as with all the measures of indulgence, was to separate those who could be reconciled to the regime from the determined minority who would continue to oppose it.[45]

Monmouth, having demonstrated his loyalty to his father by putting down the covenanting rebellion of 1679 in Scotland, was then sent into exile at his father's behest to help the dynasty during the Exclusion Crisis. James, focus of opposition attention during the crisis, although he initially accompanied Monmouth into exile to the Netherlands, was soon recalled and sent to Scotland, where to the surprise of many, the royal Roman Catholic scored several notable successes with the political nation of the country, as opposed to the Lowland Presbyterian population, alienated from him by his religion.[46] James acquired a new base of support in the Highlands of Scotland by undermining the government backing for the Earl of Argyll and the expansionist policies of Clan Campbell, and also by providing Scotland with a royal court again.[47] The Scots Parliament of 1680, with James as King's Commissioner using his Scottish title as Duke of Albany, confirmed James as heir to the Scottish throne. The Scottish bishops, used as they were to Presbyterian opposition, were not averse to royal recognition of their place in church and state, even if it was at the hands of a Roman Catholic, and hereafter Scottish Episcopalians would be distinguished by their strong loyalty to what became a Roman Catholic dynasty.[48] James's advent in Scottish affairs would have far-reaching consequences in the origins of a Scottish Jacobite movement which would unsettle Scottish politics for more than three subsequent generations.

In Restoration Britain it was the religious issue which was at the root of the inextricable entanglement of the political fortunes of all three kingdoms, but in Scotland the nature of the regime also led to proposals for an economic union between Scotland and England in 1668, ostensibly at the instance of the King, but probably originating in recognition by Lauderdale and the Scottish Privy Council that the economic protectionism of the English Parliament was going to have adverse effects on the Scottish economy, both by making trade with the Continent, Ireland and the English plantations in America more difficult, and by the effect of English wars with trade rivals, as in the Second Dutch War of 1664–67, in which the Scots found themselves embroiled in hostilities which were neither in their interest or about which they were consulted.[49] Lauderdale and Charles II, however, like James VI and I, foundered on the rock of English parliamentary intransigence. In 1669 a royal letter recommending political union with England was presented to the Scots Parliament, to be met with a complete lack of enthusiasm by the Scottish nobility who dominated that institution. Commissioners were, however, appointed to treat with English representatives, although Lauderdale wrecked the negotiations by raising his demands, perhaps because Charles was using negotiations for union to divert the attention of the English Parliament from other aspects of his foreign policy.[50]

One part of Lauderdale's proposals would have long-term effects even greater than the subsequent intervention of James, Duke of Albany in Scottish affairs. It was proposed to effect a parliamentary and economic union without fully following the Welsh precedent, allowing the Scots law courts and the Scots Church to continue to function on a separate basis. This in fact would prove to be the basis of the Union finally achieved in 1707, which brought about a British state for the first time, certainly if the Cromwellian regime is classified as an English military dictatorship. Why this alteration? Scottish lawyers during the Restoration, partly in response to the legal integration of the Cromwellian years when English judges had been introduced into the Scottish courts, began to codify Scots Law, drawing heavily on Dutch Civil Law. Both Dalrymple of Stair and Mackenzie of Rose-haugh, although their politics differed in emphasis, produced published *Institutions* of Scots Law during the 1680s which established a firm basis for asserting the independent status of Scots Law.[51] The consequences were dramatic in effect. Law and learning became a basis for asserting Scottish independence, rather than Scottish military and political independence or Presbyterian imperialism, which could be shown during all the period of the Wars of the Covenant and the conflict during the Restoration to be fatally divided in that it was the creed of southern Lowland Scotland rather than the country at large. Eventually, this development would contribute to the evolution of a British state which was legally and politically as well as religiously, pluralistic, and provide a unique basis for British political authority when it was extended to an empire.

3

JAMES LOSES THE KINGDOMS: THE REVOLUTIONS OF 1688 IN THEIR BRITISH CONTEXT

If Charles II as a Restoration king had begun his reign as a king of three separate kingdoms, by the end of his life he clearly had become an admirer of the absolutism espoused by France and the centralisation represented by that tradition.[1] James II and VII continued the policy of centralisation in power, and in locating that power in the Stuart dynasty rather than in institutions of polity, or law, or even state religion. It would be his failure to appreciate the importance of state religion which would lead to his exile. Unlike his brother, however, James also had strong support on the peripheries of the Restoration state both in Catholic Ireland and in the Scottish Highlands.[2] These were areas which would provide support to the monarch when he attempted to assert his influence in England and alter the basis of the state passed on to him by his brother, and they were the areas of Britain which would again be beyond the pale when James hurled himself and his followers into political oblivion. Perhaps the way he did it tells its own tale, as arguably his greatest miscalculation, or from another perspective his most pronounced gesture of rejecting part of his kingdoms,

was to throw the Great Seal of England into the Thames as he
began his first flight from London in December 1688.[3]

His support in Scotland originated in his activity there as
his brother's commissioner from 1679 to 1682, when his
opposition to the over-mighty Argyll dynasty in the West
Highlands won him many friends amongst the Scottish
clans who had suffered from Campbell Argyll expansionism
for centuries. James also was the first Stuart to visit Scotland
since his brother's coronation in 1651, and the first to dwell
in the reconstructed Palace of Holyroodhouse which Charles
had ordered to be rebuilt after his restoration. This counted
for much with Scottish Royalists.[4] It is not often realised that
the strength of Scottish Jacobitism over so many subsequent
years was based on a deep sense of the Scottish origins of the
Stuart dynasty and the symbiotic relationship between the
survival of the dynasty and the survival of Scotland as an
independent entity. This was much of the reason why James
was able to attract and retain the loyalty of successful professionals such as Sir Robert Sibbald and George Mackenzie
of Rosehaugh, as well as more overtly political creatures such
as the Drummond brothers of Perthshire, later Duke of Perth
and Earl of Melfort.[5] The Roman Catholic chapel at
Holyroodhouse came to symbolise the identification of royal
authority with Catholicism and its determination to secure
toleration for those whose religion it was. Scotland was so
secure under James's power, despite the strength of the
Presbyterian movement, that its entire army was posted
south in 1688 to help defend James's position in England
without any danger to his Scottish regime.[6]

In Ireland, of course, Tyrconnell retained absolute control
over a kingdom almost, but not quite, absolutely committed
to James as a monarch and the policy of religious toleration
he had espoused. James was the first Catholic king of a
Catholic nation at a time when old ethnic divisions between
the Gaelic Irish and the Catholic 'Old' English families were
beginning to pass away, with both groups perceiving themselves as Irish and Catholic and thus sharing in a common
identity. Tyrconnell was their leader and 1685 to 1691 was to

be their brief moment in British history.[7] The defeat of their aspirations condemned the majority of the population to the status of a colonised and conquered society, dominated by an essentially alien elite until the twentieth century. James's policy of toleration extended to all of his kingdoms, but in Ireland there was the added twist that toleration and encouragement were being proposed for the great majority of the population after more than a century of acute sectarian conflict, interrrupted only by periods of uneasy peace such as that represented by the reign of Charles II. James's own instincts were for caution in Ireland to avoid alarming English opinion and so jeopardising his rule and his programme in his richest and most populous kingdom. That is why the Protestant Earl of Clarendon was James's initial choice to be Lord Lieutenant of Ireland. It was only after Tyrconnell acquired the Lord Lieutenancy himself in February 1687 that the Jacobite regime achieved an unbridled supremacy, although there were rumbles of what was coming. Before Clarendon lost office, his secretary reported in July 1676 that 'the Irish talk of nothing now but recovering their lands and bringing the English under their subjection, which they who have been the masters for above 400 years know not how well to bear'.[8]

The key issue was not religious toleration, but ownership of land. The clergy of the Roman Catholic Church began to agitate for possession of the lands and buildings of the Church of Ireland, but this James was very reluctant to grant. Even when James was in Ireland and summoned a parliament to help him regain his other kingdoms, it was the Church of Ireland bishops who were summoned to join it, not those of the Catholic Church. Yet by August 1687 Tyrconnell was planning to revise the Restoration land settlement. His plan was that beneficiaries of Cromwellian and Restoration grants would be required to restore one-half of their estates to former owners. One of Tyrconnell's advisers argued that 'nothing can support Catholic religion in that kingdom [Ireland] but to make Catholics there considerable in their fortunes, as they are considerable in their number.

For this must be the only inducement that can prevail upon a Protestant successor to allow them a toleration as to their religion, and a protection as to their estates.'[9] The hope of the Protestants before 1689 was that James would not dare countenance Tyrconnell's plans because of the harm it would do to his prospects of support in England.

Tyrconnell's instrument was the Irish army, which James gave to him to reform and which, under his control, became a formidable, and Catholic, military force. It was control of this army that caused Tyrconnell to think of accomplishing more for Catholics in Ireland, and it was fear of how James might use this force outside Ireland which helped precipitate opposition to him in England. The Irish army was already large in 1685, but deficient in almost every other military virtue. James favoured the military in general in all of his kingdoms, but in Ireland he had a lieutenant in Tyrconnell with a clear, independent policy he intended to follow, which was not so much sectarian as an attempt at restoration of the Old English Roman Catholic landed class to the privileges which were theirs before the Reformation. Although some regiments retained Protestant officers and men, by 1688 more than 7000 Protestant soldiers had been dismissed from the service and replaced by officers and men whose religious loyalty was Roman Catholic. The largely Protestant militia was disbanded in 1685 on the grounds of security in the aftermath of Monmouth's and Argyll's rebellions, as a potential source of opposition to the regime. Under both Cromwell and Charles II the Irish army had reflected the dominance of the Protestant minority over the Catholic majority of the island's population.[10] By 1688 that had changed. There is evidence that Tyrconnell had obtained James's permission to use it as a basis for making Ireland a semi-independent state, which is just what it was before the multi-national army of William III reconquered it during 1690–91.[11] Some Irish troops were sent to England in 1688 to help repel the Dutch invasion, but this does not seem to have been part of any long-term plan by James and Tyrconnell to use the Irish army to support James's policies and aspirations in

England. This was not the way the process was viewed in England and Scotland, however. Gilbert Burnet wrote in his *History* that 'the king resolved also to model Ireland so as to make that kingdom a nursery for his army in England and to be sure at least of an army there while his designs were to go on more slowly in the isle of Britain',[12] and this probably reflects much contemporary opinion. There was a long tradition of perceiving British kingship as uniting both isles, and what is more, uniting both isles in the Protestant interest. Indeed, that perception lay at the very origins of the Stuart accession to the English throne. James, by adopting the religion of his paternal grandmother Mary, Queen of Scots, had likewise created a British problem which it is difficult to see could exclude Ireland, any more than Ireland could escape the effects of the English Civil War.

Nevertheless, there was one very non-British aspect to James's loss of his kingdoms in 1688, or more particularly his loss of his richest kingdom. This was the Dutch support which enabled William III to claim what he might plausibly have regarded as his inheritance, but one which certainly would have been inaccessible to him if he had not been able to draw on the resources of the Dutch Republic. It has recently been pointed out just how substantial these were, amounting to a fleet four times the size of the Spanish Armada, and an army to match, in the form of the best regiments of the Dutch army, although the English and Scottish regiments of the Dutch army also accompanied the invasion force to provide it with a more 'British' identity.[13] Why did the Dutch do this? Not so much because of the Protestant religion, although sectarian wars had linked the English and Dutch together from the time of Elizabeth, but more a realisation that Holland could only successfully oppose French expansionism if it could obtain resources from England in particular, and that the possibility of this occurring while James II was King of England was slight. William, of course, was part Stuart himself. He was not only James II's son-in-law, but his nephew as well. His was a Protestant dynastic marriage to his uncle's eldest daughter at a time when it was politic for the

House of Stuart to make such an arrangement. Charles II had viewed his marriage with some detachment, however, encouraging his nephew on his wedding night with the ironic benediction, 'Now, nephew, to your work! Hey! St George for England.'[14] William and Mary had thus always formed the focus of a powerful English reversionary interest, a kind of middle way between the Duke of Monmouth and James himself. The birth of a Catholic English prince jeopardised all this, and pushed William into action, not so much for England and for Protestantism as for the Dutch Republic and the cause of preventing French domination of Europe, and no doubt, of course, for William himself.

If, on one level, the arrival of William in England in 1688 was part of a dynastic dispute in which he and his wife wished to safeguard their interests, and if, on another level, his motivation had more to do with European diplomacy and the security of the Dutch Republic than the idea of Britain, his accession to the thrones not just of England, but Scotland and Ireland as well, became known as a revolution by those who helped bring it about. Whose revolution was it, and what did it stand for? The change in regime marked not just a revolution in the English Constitution and in the fortunes of Catholics and Protestants all over Britain, but a revolution in the culture of the English political elite which had British repercussions of enormous consequence. Peter Dickson's use of the term 'financial revolution' has stood the test of time for almost thirty years, and is referred to time and time again by historians of the period. It also marked a revolution in the way the idea of Britain altered from an essentially dynastic construct which, at certain times, had become important in a sectarian sense, to an imperial idea which was not dynastic or religious, but constitutional and political, as well as financial. What was to become Britain really began in 1688, mutated in 1776, and survived into the twentieth century by combining the stability of monarchy with the flexibility of a commercial republic. Part of this process involved making Lowland Scots and Protestant Irish part of what it was to be British, while deferring the assimilation of the Gaelic-speaking people of north-west Scotland and the West of Ireland for a hundred years, and another desperate series of wars, which were yet again directed externally against France.[15]

The English Revolution of 1688 was a political event and, in the eyes of many, an elitist one. An episode in patrician politics, in which a king who would not share power with a landed elite and support a national church that embodied their interest, was replaced by a king who would happily concede this in return for the money and the troops to help him pursue his vendetta against Louis XIV and the French monarchy. Whereas traditional emphasis had been placed on the use of Parliament to limit the arbitrary power of the monarchy, and guarantee the individual rights of the subject, more recent work has emphasised that the change in the regime led to 'an increase and not a decrease in the power of the state'.[16] Nevertheless, it is worth restating that, in two respects, the Revolution of 1688 in England did make a revolutionary impact on British, and indeed European, culture, in that important aspects of European radical and Enlightenment ideology are rooted in the events in England of 1688 and 1689.

In Enlightenment terms, the Williamite regime and its successor, as it came to embody and act as the core of opposition to absolutist France, also came to succeed the Dutch Republic as the embodiment of a society in which individual liberty led to increased commerce, increased wealth and to cultural efflorescence in an Augustan age which attracted European-wide admiration. England did not need an Enlightenment because the European Enlightenment consisted of an attempt to introduce the conditions of Augustan England into other societies, notably Bourbon France, during the long and variegated reign of Louis XIV. It also involved increased English influence on Germany after the accession of the Hanoverian Elector as George I of Great Britain and Ireland in 1714, and on other European regimes through the medium of increased trade and the ever-expanding medium of print.[17]

There were also radical aspects to what happened in England, Scotland and Ireland between 1688 and 1691 which would resonate further and, indeed, mark the parameters of political ideology in Europe for more than a century. A monarch ruling by Divine Right was replaced by one whose authority was essentially based on the approval of those he governed. It was true that the English settlement involved careful semantic niceties to retain the loyalties of those who yearned for a hereditary monarchy of one king with one national church, something which James Stuart either stupidly or courageously had refused to give them. Yet when all was said and done a hereditary King and his rightful heir, whose ancestors had ruled in Britain (although not, significantly, England) for time out of mind, were rejected and replaced by a relative with an inferior claim to the throne, backed by military force and the fact that a majority of the political nation of England, and probably the population at large, would not support the King God had given them in his personal commitment to Catholicism.[18]

There were, of course, efforts to enlist God in the Williamite cause. 'Well, doctor,' William of Orange said to Gilbert Burnet as they stood on English soil on Guy Fawkes' night in 1688, watching his troops land after a voyage which had been beyond the might of the Spanish Armada a hundred years before in 1588, 'what do you think of predestination now?'[19] The risks William ran and the odds he overcame in all three kingdoms provided him with a retrospective authority as success continued to crown his efforts. But there were many who were willing to look to human agency and the power of free individuals to mould their own destinies, not just as kings, but as subjects. In fact, the Scottish convention called by William in 1689 declared that it had the right to dispose of the Crown and to reshape the Constitution before proceeding to do what it was called to do and offer the Scottish throne to William.[20] In England, although the Declaration of Rights and the Subsequent Bill of Rights were tempered by the majority in Parliament, there were still limitations to the power of monarchy introduced under the guise of defence of traditional rights, particularly with regard to parliamentary consent to the maintenance of a standing army.[21]

Even more, as H. T. Dickinson has pointed out, the *circulation* of radical ideas, such as an end to the king's power to call and dissolve Parliament at will, full toleration for all Protestants, and the abolition of the royal veto, all had a lasting effect on English, and eventually British, politics.[22] John Locke's importance as a theorist for the radical English Whigs was his argument for constitutional reform, based on a mutually binding contract between ruler and ruled and an assertion of the natural rights of man, which marked a fundamental departure in English politics, not in its goal of limiting royal authority, but in its secular foundation and confidence in human agency. Locke led the radical Whigs in making an abstract appeal to 'the people', as opposed to God, as the foundation of political authority. Just who 'the people' were became, of course, a matter for considerable debate over subsequent centuries, but even if Locke and his colleagues conceived of the centre of political legitimacy and authority in narrow terms of a propertied elite, it was the open nature of the language they employed which would allow increasing numbers of men, and eventually women, in more and more countries and colonies, to claim inclusion in the political nation and access to the natural rights inherited at birth by every human being.[23] This was a powerful message, and it would echo through subsequent history up to the present day. All this started in 1688, although it would not have occurred to William III as he mused on predestination with Bishop Burnet on 5 November 1688.

In the immediate terms of English politics following the Revolution of 1688, one legacy was a consistent 'country' opposition which drew on the legacy of Locke and the radical Whigs to oppose not only the power of the monarchy, but the influence of political 'management', which grew in proportion to the expansion of state military and financial activity over the course of the eighteenth century. There were times when it could descend to the depths of sectarianism or worse, as occurred during the Jew riots in London in 1752 and, in particular, the Gordon riots against Catholic relief in 1780.[24] Although Sir Robert Walpole was a Whig, his use of management evoked an opposition which drew increasingly on the heritage of 1688 in formulating an opposition to his regime. If Tories could be tarred with the Jacobite brush, it became more difficult with country Whigs in alliance with them as part of a 'broad-bottom' coalition (which eventually brought an end to Walpole's power in 1742, despite jibes from Walpole's followers at a 'fat ass' opposition which featured the corpulent Tory Sir John Hynde Cotton).[25] But this opposition was not just to a regime which relied on grubby bribes and sordid manipulation. It was opposition to a regime based on money and commerce, on financial manipulation, and lacking in respect for traditional values and social organisation. Thus a Jacobite or Tory mob might appeal to the Stuart political cause to legitimise their actions, but not in the sense of defence of the Divine Right of kings; rather the defence of tradition and a moral economy. When rioters wore the blue ribbon, it was not for Jacobitism, nor was it for radical Whig ideas of natural rights in an abstract and universalist sense. It was to declare for the defence of tradition and the good old cause of the way things were in the face of accelerating economic and political change. 'What do you call that blue ribbon, Frank?', one observer of a political demonstration against the ruling oligarchy in the Scottish burgh of Dumfries in 1760 recalled, when he testified during a subsequent legal case. 'I call it liberty and property and be damned to you', came the reply.[26] A similar exchange was recorded during a dispute of journeymen's rights in the Birmingham gun trade during the 1770s, when the contractor Thomas Galton attempted to reduce the payment offered to gun finishers, and was met with a demonstration outside his house by twenty workmen wearing blue cockades, and singing a song denouncing his practices especially composed for the occasion by a ballad singer named Mary Probins![27]

In Scotland Whig radicalism was present but not as developed (Dumfries was in the Scottish border country with England). Much more important was a strong commitment

to Presbyterianism on the part of the majority of the population in Lowland Scotland, who, through twenty-eight years of
Stuart rule after the Restoration, were less attached to the
idea of 'comprehension' than their equivalents in England.
The 'rabbling' of Episcopalian ministers from their parishes
in south-west Scotland and elsewhere in the Lowlands indicated a degree of hostility towards the established Church in
some parts of Scotland in 1688, which was not matched anywhere in England and was quite different from the situation
in Ireland.[28] Nevertheless, although there were Scots about
William, such as his chaplain William Carstares, who emphasised the shared Calvinism of Scottish Presbyterians and
Dutch Reformed Protestants, William was no Calvinist zealot.
He had to accept a Presbyterian Church of Scotland in 1689
because the leaders of the established Episcopalian Church
could not persuade themselves to express their loyalty to the
new sovereigns. The Presbyterians supported William and
Mary because they almost all saw a change of regime as safeguarding their church, even though they had benefited from
James's recent act of toleration in Scotland. Too few Episcopalians were willing to become Williamites, although a comprehensive settlement incorporating Presbyterians and loyal
Episcopalians remained part of William's policy until his
death.[29]

Thus the revolution in Scotland was a religious one rather
than a political one, although the imprint of Presbyterian
Whiggery remained from the initial reaction to events in
England in the Convention which met in Edinburgh to consider the Scottish political situation. William's fear of a quasi-
republican Presbyterian faction – and he had experience of
Protestant republicanism in Holland as a youth – led him to
temper initial approaches from political leaders of the Presbyterian interest. Indeed, it is striking how leaders of both
Presbyterians and Episcopalians managed to offend William
when they appeared at his court in London, with the Presbyterians suspected of fanaticism and the Episcopalians of
treason.[30] William instead turned to courtiers to serve him
in Scotland, like the Duke of Hamilton and the Duke of

Queensberry, or the Earl of Melville and the smooth careerist John Dalrymple, Master of Stair. To oppose the anti-monarchical bent of the Presbyterians' political programme, William eventually adopted it, but entrusted its implementation to a class of politicians whose lack of interest in anything other than their own careers reduced the modern historian Dr Patrick Riley to the very bleakest of views of the Scottish polity at this time.[31] Such a view characterises the entire political nation in Scotland in 1688 and after by close attention to the political careers of a few smiling men with bad reputations, immortalised in the portraits they had painted to glorify their successful achievement of wealth and office, but really not representative of anything other than themselves.

The end result of 1688 in Scotland would be, as Dr David Hayton has noted, 'a long-run gain for the centre at the expense of the periphery, and an extension of English influence over the Gaelic peoples of Ireland and the Scottish Highlands'. In contrast to the traditional Whig view of the Revolution, Hayton has pointed out that 'it can be regarded as a critical moment in the expansion of English control over the other parts of the British Isles; a step towards empire, rather than towards constitutional democracy'.[32] In addition to a swing in the political scales towards the Lowlands at the expense of the Highlands and the north-eastern Lowlands of Scotland, however, the Revolution also led to the reinvention of Scottish Presbyterianism as the church of Whiggish dissent under the Stuarts. This was effected through the medium of 'pope' William Carstares, the Calvinist chaplain William had moved to Edinburgh College (as it then was) as Principal. His brother-in-law William Dunlop became Principal of Glasgow College. Both remodelled their colleges with the Dutch universities in mind, incorporating medicine and science as well as a more liberal divinity curriculum for the future ministry of the new Presbyterian church they sought to create, and whose historian, Robert Wodrow, would receive a pension from George I on the publication of his *History of the Sufferings of the Church of Scotland* in 1722.[33] It is no accident that the man who led the Church into alliance with the Scottish landed and professional classes, Principal William Robertson of Edinburgh University, should end his career reflecting on the importance of the Revolution of 1688 in British history.[34] It can be argued that the later French Enlightenment originated in the more open and commercial society which emerged in England after 1688, and which, after all, would make a key contribution to the defeat of absolutist France in 1713. Much could be said regarding the origins of the Scottish Enlightenment and the ultimate effect of the settlement of 1689 on Scottish society. The immediate impact of 1689 on the Scottish Highlands was harsh, as the massacre of Glencoe demonstrated, but like much else that happened after 1689 and 1707, it reflected deep divisions within Scottish society rather than English oppression. As Paul Hopkins has commented on the infamous massacre of Glencoe, given that it was inflicted by one group of Scottish Highlanders on another group of Highlanders, on orders given by a Scottish politician and approved by a Dutch king, it was 'something for which, naturally, no true Scot will ever forgive the English'.[35]

In Ireland, as we have observed, the Revolution was about land. When the Jacobite Irish House of Commons in 1689 produced an Act 'declaring that over 2,000 named Protestants had forfeited life and property by their rebellion', the response of their very Catholic Stuart king was, 'What, gentlemen, are you for another "'41'"?'[i.e. The Irish Rebellion of 1641].[36] Even as late as 1689 James resisted attempts to overturn the Irish Restoration land settlement, but finally accepted a Repeal and Attainder Act which 'provided the basis for little short of a complete Catholic resettlement of Ireland'. After the Treaty of Limerick, as J. G. Simms has shown, a long and harshly fought struggle occurred between the Irish Protestant landowners and William over first, the generosity of the Treaty of Limerick towards the defeated Catholic gentry who chose to remain in Ireland and second, the spoils of ownership of the land which did change hands.[37] In the end the English Parliament would become involved and Irish land would provide a point of contention between English Parliament and English King. In that sense, however, nothing had really changed. James II may have been a Catholic, but he remained an Englishman all his life. When the Protestant Earl of Clarendon was appointed Lord Lieutenant of Ireland in 1685, James told him 'that though he would wish the Irish see, that they had a king of their own religion,... yet he would have them see too, that he looked upon them as a conquered people; and that he would support the settlements inviolably'.[38] When James arrived in Ireland to try to retake his kingdoms from William, the French envoy who accompanied him remarked that 'he has a heart too English to take any step that could vex the English'.[39] For James knew that the more he placed himself at the head of a resurgent Catholic Ireland, the less chance he ever had of becoming King of England again. Once the outcome of the Battle of the Boyne had put that object beyond his reach, he made his preparations to go. What he left behind was a Catholic warrior nobility and gentry who, after the Treaty of Limerick, were fragmented between the 'wild geese' who sailed for further fighting in France, leaving their women and children wailing behind them in Limerick harbour, and those who remained, who, under the unrelenting pressure of 'the penal laws' passed by the now adamantly Episcopalian Protestant Parliament, began to trickle over to the Church of Ireland to preserve what little was left to them as gentry. The vast mass of the Catholic peasantry were untouched by the penal laws because they had not land or property of their own. Left leaderless, they became an invisible majority in an almost classic colonial situation, dominated by a landowning elite who took their labour for granted and viewed their culture as aboriginal. It is this absolute confidence of the post-1691 Irish Protestant world that S. J. Connolly captured so well in his work on 'the making of Protestant Ireland'. It was not a society held down by force: 'instead, government depended on the continued willingness of the many, most of the time, to accept the domination of the few – even if this was only, as [Samuel] Johnson suggested, because they lacked the ability to establish, or possibly even to imagine, an alternative'.[40]

In 1688 only 22 per cent of land in Ireland was owned by Catholics, whereas by 1703 it had decreased to 14 per cent.[41] The Catholic nobility and gentry had lost in 1691, but the real defeat had come earlier at the hands of Cromwell, and in 1660 at the hands of selfish Restoration courtiers and the stolid Protestantism of the Duke of Ormonde. The real loss in 1691 was of Catholic leadership in the landed class. Sean Connolly has described 1688 in Ireland as a failed counter-revolution by Catholic Ireland, but it reaffirmed the priv-ileged position of Protestantism, and in the narrowness of its victory and the extent of it when it came, it gave Irish Protestants confidence in their place in Ireland and a sense of purpose and mission in their presence there.[42] Although William and his general Ginkel and their regiments repre-sented external intervention, Londonderry and Enniskillin represented successful resistance to Catholic absolutism and the achievement of something like religious uniformity within the landed class, at a point in European history when this class everywhere wielded most power and influ-ence in society. This in turn provided the basis for what J. G. Simms chose to call colonial nationalism. As David Hayton has remarked, ironically, 'the defeat of one form of separat-ism was a step in the evolution of another'.[43] Military inter-vention in Ireland by William in 1689 left a long legacy, and allowed a confident minority to develop a society increasingly independent of the British government during the eight-eenth century, insulated from the majority of the population of its country not just by wealth, but by religion and ideology.

4

THE UNION OF ENGLAND AND SCOTLAND AND THE DEVELOPMENT OF THE HANOVERIAN STATE

William III was not a Briton: if anything, he was Dutch, head of the Dutch Republic as Stadholder. In 1688 he underwent a transfiguration which meant that he became, for a significant number of people, a key symbol of British unity, as we are still well aware today in Belfast, and sometimes in Dublin, Liverpool and Glasgow. From one perspective this involved drawing on a powerful tradition of British monarchy as God's instrument in the defence of Protestantism. Indeed, it would be William's reign in which the crowns of all three kingdoms were forbidden to anyone of the Roman Catholic religion. Yet William's interest in Britain was not sectarian, even if it was sectarianism which led this very Dutch man to become such a very British king. The reasons for this were political and diplomatic and involved opposition to Bourbon France, and it was William's determination to direct the wealth and military might of England against France, without the distraction of entanglement elsewhere in Britain, which led him to create the previously unthinkable religious settlement which would eventually enable the accomplishment of what had eluded the Stuart kings, a parliamentary union of Scotland and England in 1707.[1] By accepting the establishment of a Presbyterian church in Scotland while retaining an Episcopalian settlement for the Church of Ireland and Church of England, with the 1689 Toleration Act in England for the Dissenters, all the major Protestant churches in Britain, with the solitary exception of the Jacobite Scottish Episcopalians, had some interest in the survival of the regime and in preventing a restoration of the Roman Catholic Stuart dynasty.[2] Thus William, in a rough- and-ready, soldierly way, brought about some kind of comprehension of the Episcopalian and Presbyterian interests in Britain as a whole, even including Dissenters additional to the Presbyterians. There was no British national church, but by avoiding the question of denominational religious uniformity (which became, as a result, the defining aspect of Protestant Christianity in British America as well), William opened the way for relating political unity to commercial and economic unity. That opening would have American and imperial repercussions as well as British ones.

William started and finished with Scotland. It was a largely Protestant kingdom, it shared a land border with England, and James had not landed there, as he had in Ireland in 1689. It also had a separate parliament which, after the concessions made to secure the throne for William in 1689, had a considerable degree of room for independent action, in some ways foreshadowing a similar position achieved by the Irish Parliament in 1782, during another period of British political instability. The Scottish Parliament was dominated by the Scottish nobility, most of whom were preoccupied with gaining the favour of the King and the offices of state which went with it. Detailed study of the politics of the Scottish Parliament during William II's reign (for such he was in Scotland), which sat in its unicameral house with lords and commoners together, has led some to conclude that its independence had unleashed a maelstrom of selfish political manoeuvring, with no redeeming features whatsoever, made worse by the fact that it occurred during decades of acute economic hardship for much of the population, in what was even at the best of times a poor country.[3]

There were Scottish contemporaries who agreed. In 1703 the Scottish patriot Andrew Fletcher of Saltoun denounced the Scottish Court Party as creatures of English masters who had no interest in the welfare of their own nation: ''Tis nothing but an English interest in this House [the parliament of Scotland], that those who wish well to our country, have to struggle with at this time.' He argued that 'so long as Scotsmen go to the English Court to obtain offices of trust or profit to this kingdom, those offices will always be managed with regard to the Court and interest of England, though to the betraying of the interest of this nation, whenever it comes in competition with that of England'.[4] Fletcher's patriotism still evokes a compelling vision of Scottish civic independence, within or out of union with England, rooted in his opposition to the Stuart Restoration regime, his exile in Holland, and his participation in the settlement of 1689 in Scotland. Yet during the making of the Treaty of Union with England he was reduced to the status of an impotent outsider, in the end leaving the last Scottish Parliament in disgust at his failure to influence his fellow members. It is easy to idealise his political views and attempt to adopt them to modern perspectives, yet this was a man profoundly set in the culture of the Scottish landed elite. His response to the famine in Scotland of the 1690s was to propose the introduction of slavery for the common people of Scotland on the model of slavery in the republics of the ancient world. This has led to his dismissal by one leading social historian as a panic-stricken landowner reacting to the increase in the number of homeless people with 'class prejudice enlarged by total innumeracy', given his exaggeration of the number of vagrants as a justification for perceiving them as a threat and enslaving them.[5] It certainly reflects the wide gap which had opened up in the early modern period, between the minority who owned the land and those who served them in opposition to the mass of society who still lived on the land and had to try to wrest a living from it.

What follows from this rather bleak equation is a choice between dismissing contemporary politics as the meaningless machinations of a selfish elite, or an acceptance of the fact that a small elite played a disproportionate role in the politics and culture of society due to its hold upon the land, wealth and leisure available to that society. This can be seen in the wider context of the patriotism of Andrew Fletcher of Saltoun. It can also be seen in the contemporary context of the ideas expressed by John Locke, and in the writings of the Irish Protestant patriot William Molyneux. His pamphlet 'The case of Ireland's being bound by acts of parliament in England, stated' (1698) included an extraordinary claim made in asserting Ireland's constitutional rights that most of 'the present people of Ireland' were of English or 'British' descent and that 'there remains but a mere handful of the ancient Irish at this day'.[6] It has been suggested that this might reflect that by 'people' Molyneux meant 'the political nation', or those with political rights. Another possibility was that his statement reflected a belief that the 'Old English' (whose representative Tyrconnell had been) had in fact assimilated the Celtic Irish, so that if Ireland had become divided since the Reformation into Catholic and Protestant populations, almost all of both these populations were of some kind of English or British origin, with a declining aboriginal Irish population remaining only in certain remote areas of the country.[7] The open nature of Molyneux's language in contrast to the narrowness of his political culture is not really unique to the settler population of Ireland, however, as the writings of his friend John Locke demonstrate. Part of the power of 'The case of Ireland's' is Molyneux's use of Locke's language of natural law, although Locke himself rejected its extension to Irishmen, or Ireland as a kingdom. Andrew Fletcher spoke stirringly of the interest of his ancient country, yet coolly proposed enslaving thousands of his countrymen to prevent them from becoming vagrants. Thomas Jefferson, intellectual heir to this tradition and a slave-owner, would write that 'all men are created equal', and James Madison, in the preamble of the US Constitution of 1789, would begin a document approved by an almost self-selected convention of fifty-seven wealthy men with the phrase, 'we the people'.[8]

If the events which led to the parliamentary union of England and Scotland can be perceived as the machinations of a narrow elite, they still must be considered against the background of contemporary public opinion amongst the 'political nation' in both kingdoms. Politicians in the eighteenth century might appear from one perspective to be operating in a vacuum, but they all had constituencies to which they were accountable. In the early eighteenth century in Britain, and even later, these constituencies themselves could be and often were very narrow in comparison to the population as a whole, and this has led some to assert that this narrow electorate was open to manipulation by the politicians rather than the politicians being open to pressure from their electorate. There is, however, a formidable amount of recent work which would appear to refute this.[9] The point which emerges from this research is that there was an early modern political constitutency beyond the political nation: that in many parts of Britain there was not an absolute divide between the landed and commercial class, and the politicians who represented them, on the one hand, and the mass of the population on the other. Indeed, it is the conviction that this could not be so which sparkles so elegantly on the pages written by E. P. Thompson.[10] Yet we know very little about this unenfranchised world of popular political opinion, which has left irregular and elusive evidence of its existence.

It is in this context, however, that the larger political framework of the Union of 1707 must be considered, independent of the 'political chicanery at the highest levels'.[11] There can be no doubt that popular opinion was against it both in England and in Scotland, as the long subsequent history of mutual antipathy and execration illustrates. English motivation for the Union originated in court politics and reasons of state. The Scots were repellent to English popular opinion on account of both the Jacobitism of one part of the country and the dissenting Presbyterianism of the other. They were in addition, like the Irish, seen as susceptible to the arbitrary power of the Crown, and any proposal for parliamentary union provoked English fears of strengthening the power of the Crown by an accession of subordinate Scots MPs.[12] From the view of William III, however, having had to divert his attention and a considerable number of Dutch, German and Danish regiments to the problem of sorting out the possibility of being taken in the rear by an invasion of Britain from Ireland, the prospect of repeating the exercise in Scotland had little appeal. After his death in 1702 Queen Anne continued his policy. 'Nothing ought to be done in the Scotch business but what will do good in England', the Duke of Marlborough advised Lord Treasurer Godolphin.[13] What would 'do good in England' was a parliamentary union which would remove the possibility of having to fight a Scottish equivalent of the Battle of the Boyne. In the long term it did not work, as the 1715 and 1745 rebellions illustrated so tellingly, but it bought (literally) enough time for Marlborough to concentrate on the Low Countries, and as such it secured the Protestant succession to the Hanoverians, or at the very least, considerably strengthened the possibility of such a succession being effected.

Yet English involvement with Scottish politics in an attempt to secure an incorporating union ironically involved English politicians and their parties in Scottish politics. What is often misunderstood about the Union of Scotland and England is that although bribery and corruption secured the votes needed to get it through the Scottish Parliament, this was possible because the Scottish political nation and the Scottish populace as a whole were deeply divided on religious grounds. The union was an act of *realpolitik* secured by English ministers and Scottish court politicians, in an atmosphere of acute sectarian division, which paralysed political debate and reduced a radical political thinker like Andrew Fletcher to the role of a bystander. Almost all of Scotland was opposed to political union with England, and almost all of Scottish opinion, from the politicians to the peasantry, knew that the restored Union of the Crowns had been a failure in Scotland, no matter who the monarch. But the important point is that this negative unity was paralleled by absolute dissension over what was to be done to alter the state of an ancient kingdom.[14]

The Jacobites of the north-east Lowlands and of the Highlands of Scotland were largely Episcopalian, but saw loyalty to the ancient Scottish house of Stewart (which was the ancient Scottish spelling of the surname, as opposed to the francophone 'Stuart') as part of the Erastian nature of their Episcopalianism. They could also, many of them, be described as proto-national in their identification of Stewart kingship, as part of Scottish political identity which was the culmination and continuation of centuries of independent history. The Duke of Hamilton, with a claim of his own to the Scottish throne, was their leader, and if he forfeited his following for court favour in London (and eventual death in a duel there), that does not negate the cause he came to represent.[15] That is what was represented by Lord Belhaven's famous speech to the Scottish Parliament in its last session, with its appeal to 'our ancient mother Caledonia' and the conviction, shared by more Scots than many modern historians realise, that 'the nation of the Scots long antedated parliaments, which in fact came into existence to safeguard the nation's rights and liberties and could not abate them'.[16] Belhaven's speech was printed and read to great applause all over Scotland, and is in a sense part of the tradition of Blind Hary's *Wallace* and Barbour's *Brus*, representing a deeply embedded folk tradition of Scottish identity.[17] Jacobites adhered to that tradition, but all Scots who adhered to that tradition were not Jacobites. When the last session of King William's Scottish Parliament, meeting after his death, refused to vote in 1702 to rule out accepting the rights of James VIII to the throne of Scotland, many of those who voted against did so to assert the independence of the Scottish Parliament rather than the rights of the Jacobite claimant to the Scottish throne.[18]

The other half of the Scottish polity was a Presbyterian party which detested English Anglicanism, but given the strength of the opposition to its re-establishment after 1690 north of the Clyde and Tay rivers, these were Lowland Scots who could look nowhere other than England for support, where the Whig Party was willing to accept the Presbyterians as defenders of the results of the Glorious Revolution of 1688.[19] The strength of Presbyterianism in Scotland at this time was emphatically regional rather than national, but it included a significant proportion of the urban population in the larger burghs of the central areas. Possibly a majority of the political nation were Presbyterian, but the legacy of the Covenanting wars and Restoration repression of Presbyterians was such, along with the fact that the Presbyterian kirk had so recently been re-established at considerable effort, that a guarantee of the privileges of the state Church became part of the Court settlement for union. Why? It divided an opposition which was otherwise overwhelmingly opposed to union and would win over Presbyterian support, or at least the support of the Presbyterian clergy, to a union settlement which, after all, would reduce the immediate power of the great Scottish nobility to directly interfere with the Church. This was the view of William Carstares and his allies, who dominated the General Assembly of the Kirk. They accepted an Act of the Scottish Parliament for the Security of the Church of Scotland in 1706 and, in return, kept Presbyterian anti-unionist feeling from expressing itself through the central agencies of the Church. Carstares had been William's chaplain and was influential in persuading him to re-establish Presbyterianism in Scotland, but he knew that insecure as union with England would be for the Kirk, there was no guarantee that it could maintain its position in Scotland without English support.[20]

The argument for parliamentary union which carried it through the Scottish Parliament itself was economic. The Court Party was not given enough money to buy all MPs, although the promised 'Equivalent' to compensate Scotland for increased taxation was a kind of national bribe, as Burns later presented it in his writing of being 'bought and sold for English gold', which tellingly uses the pronoun 'we'. It was promised that the creditors of the failed Company of Scotland Trading to the Indies, the 'Darien Company', in popular parlance, would be compensated out of this money, and if there were few majorities amongst the Scottish political nation at this time, there was an undoubted majority of those who had lost capital in the Darien adventure to establish a Scottish colony in the Western hemisphere. The famous quotation from a letter of the Earl of Roxburghe about Scottish acceptance of union started with 'trade with most' as its explanation of acceptance.[21] The Court Party was able to get the result its English masters wanted and pocket their bribes and salaries, because most Scottish voters and MPs, however reluctantly, had to accept that there would be economic benefits for the Scottish economy in access to English markets and trade with the English colonies.[22] An illustration of this recognition can be seen in the instructions sent from the burgh of Montrose to its representative in the Scottish Parliament in 1706, instructing him to vote for the treaty, as if Scotland (or at least Montrose) lost access to English markets, 'we shall be deprived of the only valuable branch of our trade, the only trade by which the ballance is on our side and then one needs not the gift of Prophecy to fortell what shall be the fate of this poor miserable blinded nation in a few years'.[23] In fact, the Scottish negotiators of the Treaty of Union succeeded in securing a remarkably good bargain for the Scots, always provided that the terms of the Treaty could be secured in hard reality after it had been signed. Its terms were marked by what has always characterised the operation of the Union of the Scots with the English. Scots access to English residence markets and empire was maximised, while the possibility of English access to Scottish markets, culture and residence, limited and impoverished as they were, was denied or restricted. It was the Scots political class who wanted or consented to be British, but they endeavoured to ensure that, as much as possible, this was a one-way process.[24] After the Union, Scots became divided between those who were and were not British, in a way which did not occur in England, although another way to look at this process would be to see those English who saw their future in commerce and finance accepting that part of this evolution towards a new economy was the expansion of this new English culture to areas beyond the borders of England itself.[25] Part of Scottish society and the Scottish political nation was co-opted to the service of the new English state and economy. Why not let others call it British if it made their acceptance of it easier?

It is not always realised that there was an Irish aspect to the Anglo-Scottish union, although when debate over a union of Great Britain and Ireland came, Daniel Defoe's *History of the Union* was republished to prepare the England and Scottish public for the event.[26] The Protestant Ascendancy in Ireland was re-establishing its authority and consolidating its power to an unprecedented degree through the agency of its own Parliament, at a time when its Scottish equivalent was virtually bankrupting itself in trying to gain access to the wealth that was possible in overseas trade with America and Asia. In Scotland it was the Highland chiefs who, by and large, were excluded from the politics and privilege of the landowning elite as thoroughly as the remaining Catholic Irish landowners were excluded from Irish Civil Society by the penal laws, but in both kingdoms the national elite became acutely aware of their subsidiary status in relation to England in the years after William came to Britain.

In Ireland this feeling was expressed most forcefully in Molyneux's famous pamphlet, mentioned above, published in 1698 in the aftermath of determined English parliamentary interference in the Irish wool trade. At the time it was asserted in England that Ireland and everyone who lived in Ireland were subordinate to the English Parliament both economically and politically. Molyneux's pamphlet would be periodically reprinted throughout the eighteenth century whenever Irish grievances against English colonialism became acute. Although Molyneux received little support from his fellow Irish Protestants, or indeed at the time from his friend John Locke, his pamphlet set out to demonstrate the historical antiquity and independence of the Irish

Parliament and the fact that natural law demanded that no parliament could legislate for those who were not represented in it.[27] Amongst those who responded to Molyneux in England, and there were a substantial number, was William Atwood, the Englishman whose pamphlets demonstrating the precedence of the English Parliament over that of Scotland were ordered by the last Parliament of Scotland to be burned by the hangman in Edinburgh. Atwood was equally dismissive of the claims of the Irish Parliament, tactlessly instancing the Jacobite Parliament of 1689, which had confirmed the rule of James II when the English Parliament had given the throne of England and Ireland to William III in 1689.[28]

When the Irish Parliament and its Protestant politicians did establish their independence of the English Parliament and of the Crown in Ireland in 1782 Molyneux's pamphlet was again reprinted, as it had been at the time of the Union of Scotland and England, at the time of the agitation over Wood's halfpence during the 1720s, and on other occasions in 1749, 1770, 1773 and 1776; but in 1782 one of the passages of the original pamphlet was omitted. This was where Molyneux wrote that if the English Parliament was going to insist on legislating for Ireland, representation in the English Parliament should be granted to Irish Protestants, 'and this, I believe, we should be willing enough to embrace; but this is an happiness we can hardly hope for'.[29] The leaders of Protestant opinion in Ireland when Molyneux published his pamphlet preferred the idea of an incorporating union to parliamentary independence as a means of avoiding restrictions on Irish trade. At the beginning of Queen Anne's reign the Irish House of Commons voted an address to her to that effect, but the Irish Protestants were the victims not so much of their own success as of the fact that an English (and Dutch) financed army had already had to go to Ireland to secure a political settlement favourable to England. Having done that, the English Parliament would not agree to grant concessions to Irish trade as well, and no ministry in England thought it worth the trouble to ask them to do so.[30] In Scotland the local political elite were bought off not just with bribes but with concessions intended to stimulate the economy, in the expectation that they would keep Jacobite dissent under control without the need of external assistance. The uncertain progress of the Anglo-Scottish Union for its first fifty years owed much to the shaky ability of the Scottish Court Party to keep its part of the bargain.

As the Whig state established itself behind the Hanoverian dynasty, its hallmark became 'stability', characterised by increasing secularisation associated with commerce, as well as a dominant alliance between church and state. As has been pointed out recently by Jeremy Black, developments in Britain were not completely exceptional in a European context, where equally state power was on the increase, challenges to the centralising regime were limited, and expanding states entered into less than completely incorporating relationships with subordinate kingdoms, as the history of Iberia in particular demonstrates, amongst other European examples.[31] In political terms Scotland was reduced to the status of a province, but what happened in eighteenth-century Scotland was that loss of political independence was eventually succeeded by continued cultural independence, based on increased wealth and leisure in the urbanised Lowlands. It is interesting to note that the benefits reaped from union with England in Scotland were disproportionately gathered by the urbanised mercantile and professional classes, and that the union only really became accepted by most of even Lowland Scottish people once urbanisation began to gather pace in the central Lowlands. It was thus a cultural independence enjoyed by part of the Scottish population only.[32] Lowland Scotland, like Ulster and Leinster in Ireland, secured its own prosperity and independence by acting as the agent of English state building in a colonial manner that resulted in the virtual destruction of traditional Gaelic culture in both countries.[33]

Throughout much of the eighteenth century it was Scotland and the problems Scotland was experiencing adjusting to union which caused the British state most problems.

Ireland was an area of stability until the time of the American War of Independence, when the balance of political ideology was transformed from a sectarian basis to more secular ideas of political rights and a struggle to embody the rights of man.[34] Up until that time the Hanoverian state, although it was subject to a substantial Scottish Jacobite revolt in the North of Scotland beyond the Clyde and Tay, was able to take advantage of the longest period of peace between Britain and France during the eighteenth century (from 1713 to 1741), and did so to construct a polity which balanced the interests of the traditional landed elite with those of a financial and mercantile class whose wealth was centred in London, but who had links with all the expanding urban areas in Britain. Sir Robert Walpole forged a political coalition between the landed and trading interests which involved persuading one group to accept the operation of commerce and the other to adopt the patina of the squirearchy which had produced Walpole himself. Thus the landed class was reassured by Walpole's efforts to keep the land tax low and to reaffirm the supremacy of the Church of England, while the commercial class was able to make money by an expansion of government activity in finance and encouragement of overseas trade.[35] Walpole did not concern himself over much with those parts of Britain peripheral to his agenda. Ireland was consigned to a series of 'undertakers' who administered Irish affairs in conjunction with the Lord Lieutenant in the interest of the Protestant Ascendancy. Scotland was consigned to the Duke of Argyll and his brother, the Earl of Ilay.[36] Wales was a rural country in which the larger gentry flourished while the smaller gentry suffered poverty in obscurity.[37] The interests of the ministry were on the commercial world of London and its development. Scotland, Wales and Ireland were part of a country interest to be placated by a low land tax and an Erastian ecclesiastical policy, as well as liberal distribution of patronage.[38] What altered the cosy framework of this settlement was the development of overseas trade beyond the primitive mercantilist strategy of Walpole's generation. Commercial trading economies in Dublin and Belfast, Glasgow and Edinburgh, and later in Wales in Cardiff and Swansea would co-opt part of the 'country' to a new commercial economy, every bit as much as the political elites of Ireland, Wales and Scotland had been co-opted to serve the cause of the Williamite settlement after 1688.[39]

5

THE IDEA OF BRITAIN AND THE CREATION OF THE FIRST BRITISH EMPIRE

The essence of what happened to the idea of Britain in the eighteenth century is that it mutated from an essentially sectarian idea into one founded on ideas of empire and racial superiority.[1] Part of this process was the secession of the inhabitants of the pre-1763 anglophone colonies on the mainland of North America during the last quarter of the eighteenth century and their replacement, at the centre of imperial activity outwith Britain by the Scots and to a certain extent by the Irish, so that the Britain of 1829 (Catholic Emancipation) or 1832 (Parliamentary Reform) or 1837 (the Accession of Queen Victoria) was well and truly a very different construct from that of 1707 or even 1763.[2] Although it is obvious that change must have occurred, the profound nature of that change is not always appreciated. The idea of 'gentlemanly', pre-industrial capitalism helps explain the economic changes which underpinned the use of Britishness as a unifying concept for a society negotiating the passage from the early modern world of the Renaissance and Reformation to the thoroughly modern yet still pre-industrial war economy forged by the British to achieve world domination between 1793 and 1815.[3] Britishness has always been about state building, but during the eighteenth century the focus shifted from dynastic power to financial power through the control of trade, and in the process the political state turned away from a model of power centred on an executive monarchy, to a limited monarchy which represented and safeguarded an alliance of landed and commercial wealth.[4] Finance, trade and agricultural improvement became part of the same process. While the political history of Hanoverian Britain appears detached from the economic and social dynamic which would eventually subsume it; the politics of the period represent political conflict amongst the landed and commercial classes in which divisions over the superiority of interest between land and commerce was, until mid-century, obscured by the conflicting dynastic loyalties represented by Hanoverians and Jacobites; after unification of loyalty to one dynasty represented by George III was accomplished, divisions of a different nature emerged over constitutional reform, ironically made into a clear issue of principle by the completion of the transformation of dynastic identity.[5]

The landed conservative elite who consolidated their hold on power against a potentially absolutist monarchy by supporting the change of regime in 1688, and maintained their privileged position at the end of the eighteenth century by maintaining their unity, were open to ideas of civic responsibility which looked back to the classical world and to ideas of encouraging commercial and financial wealth, which gave them a modern outlook that really did make them different from landed elites elsewhere in Europe. 'If the English went to Italy to see Antiquity,' Roy Porter has commented, 'foreigners came to England to see Modernity.'[6] That modernity was largely urban, but it was an urban world peopled by men and women who owned land in the country. Later in the process more and more people who did not own land began to behave like people who did, and they could do so if they could get access to money through finance, through trade, through the professions, and even through shopkeeping![7] If some of the ways to wealth were still unacceptable to gain access to this society initially, wealth usually found a way in the end, and if this threatened the civic culture of traditional landed society, after 1798 such niceties appeared irrelevant in the face of the beast summoned from beyond the known political world by the success of the French Revolution.[8]

While the loss of much of a North American empire clarified the limits of British imperial power during the eighteenth century, the ability of the British state to survive that loss displayed remarkable resilience, based on the state's ability to tap the elaborate world and wealth of British finance as it grew from 1688.[9] The British state was built on money which enabled it to finance ever more complex military campaigns based essentially on the need to prevent the emergence of a dominant European power in the form of France, but which had the unexpected effect – unexpected, that is, to the British 'gentlemanly elite' – of first engaging Britain in prolonged imperial conflict with France overseas, and then compensating for persistent defeat in continental Europe between 1792 and 1812 by seeking victory elsewhere in a way which echoed the imperial basis of the elder Pitt's year of victories in 1759.[10] Finance as the key which allowed this transformation to happen reinforces the importance of 1688 in British history, not for constitutional reasons, but because it brought the British into contact rather than conflict with the Dutch and the culture of imperialism and finance which formed the basis of Dutch economic success during the seventeenth century.[11] The British state, formed under the tutelage of its Dutch king William III and II [of Scotland], would succeed the Netherlands as a Protestant, financial, imperial power and agent of European expansion. It was able to do this because an ethos of landed political power was married to that of financial (but not necessarily industrial) gain in a way that sheds entirely new light on the cultural context of eighteenth-century political patronage.[12]

Historians had long known of the eighteenth-century British 'financial revolution', but recent work has endeavoured to relate the context of this financial revolution to the state, quite deliberately identified as an 'English' state. Why? First and foremost, because this great financial wen of profit and despair was located in London, and the apparatus of the state which fed on this invisible market of money and exchange was centred there, if only on a scale which would be considered modest indeed in modern times.[13] One aspect which could be added to Brewer's work is reference to the banking system which grew up in Scotland during the eighteenth century, not quite independent of the mother market in London – indeed, spawned by a Scot who had emigrated there but who extended his operations to Scotland in the 1690s, William Paterson, founder member of both the long-lived Bank of Scotland in 1695 and also of the briefly active Company of Scotland Trading to the Indies.[14] The failure of one organisation and the survival of the other illustrated the domestic nature of Scottish banking, offering cheap credit through adventurous use of paper money, but not really a banking or financial system able to become part of overseas trade and empire. After the failure of the Darien scheme, banking in Scotland developed along very different lines indeed from the London financial markets, although it continued to provide a disproportionate number of recruits for its personnel.[15] The shift to a society built on finance and commerce rather than land and power was British in the sense that it included key members of the Lowland Scots, Welsh, Protestant Irish and American Colonial political elites who saw land as representing political power, but recognised that the nature of the state that was emerging was founded on commerce and finance; and responded to that positively or negatively.[16] Thus being British over the course of the eighteenth century became less and less a matter of being Protestant and more and more about being Capitalistic before what that term represented had yet been imagined by those exposed to it.

The landed interest were the landowners who paid the land tax, the principal support of the doubling of taxation which occurred after 1688. In fact, the increase in taxation did not actually fall on the landowners. Why? Some, chiefly away from the south-east of England, were able to escape its worst effects. Others were able to pass part or most of the burden on to their tenants. Brewer points out ways the landed class benefited from the financial commercial state through access to salaries from government offices and by cautious participation in financial investment. By the 1740s there were more opposition MPs – not those one would readily think of as sympathetic to financial wealth – than government supporters amongst those with money in the public funds.[17] However, while willingness to hold wealth in the stock market increased over the century, access to public office by the gentry actually increased their snobbery towards trade. So while fewer younger sons of the landed class entered trade directly, more of them invested in it or in the public debt whose interest was paid by a land tax, the true cost of which they increasingly passed on to their tenants, just as the British passed the cost of empire building in India on to the native princes (and their subjects) who came into contact with them.[18] Younger sons of the gentry increased their access to salaried posts attached to the state through the military, bureaucratic government posts, or through the East India Company.

The financial interest, by contrast, was identified with the public debt. It was an interest made up of bankers, investors, speculators and others who 'lived parasitically off the state's need to borrow money to fund its wars'.[19] They underwrote government issues of stocks and they arranged to feed and pay the British army abroad. These were two connected functions, as many of those who made fortunes out of government contracts invested those fortunes in government bonds, ensuring that they were fully subscribed. Most of those active in this market were Whigs in politics, and many of them were Dissenters in religion. They consistently attracted the hostility of the landed interest. These were wealthy men who refused to buy land as the social expectations of the age demanded, and Geoffrey Holmes summarised the ill feeling against them by noting that: 'to many in the landed interest it seemed monstrous that Londoners whose new riches were giving them access to political influence should evade both the heavy taxation and social responsibilities which an extensive landed interest incurred'.[20]

The apotheosis of the policy of debt, of course, were the victories of the Seven Years War, when an amazed British elite found itself in possession, after the peace of Paris, of a world empire, just years after facing setback after setback at the hands of the French. If it seemed a divine victory, it was apparent to all that it was a victory for finance and commerce, economic products of liberty – tangible proof that time was not on the side of the absolutist French state. Having won the Empire, generations of scholars have studied British reaction to the problem of trying to govern it. Some have emphasised political patronage, others a now lost political ideology rooted in the history of Ancient Greece and Rome, and still others were determined to write it out of history as something they did not like; a 'patrician' phenomenon which had nothing to do with the culture of ordinary working people in England.[21] Of these different perspectives, it is that drawn from the Classical World which holds most force in trying to understand the origins of British empire. The so-called first British Empire was as quintessentially English as Sir Walter Raleigh, involving as it did the idea of planting the English overseas on the model of the Mediterannean colonisation by the Greeks and Phoenicians. Read with care, Sir Thomas More's *Utopia* is a manifesto for English colonisation, imbued with a confidence that those who did not recognise the superiority of Utopian culture, and refused the opportunity of assimilation to it, deserved to suffer expropriation in the face of its needs.[22] The centrality of Classical scholarship to Renaissance England ensured that its elite conceived of colonisation as transplantation rather than imperial overlordship. This was implicit when Benjamin Franklin predicted that the American colonies would become a mighty empire in their own right, when Archibald Grant of Monymusk agreed with him, and particularly when the elder Pitt, as Earl of Chatham, declared in the House of Lords that when Parliament ceased to have sovereignty over North America he advised every gentleman in Britain to sell his lands and emigrate to that country. The greater partner in a federation, he declared, would control the less, and render it subordinate.[23]

It was a transplantation of population, but also an expropriation of native peoples, whether it be in Ireland, the West Indies or Virginia. People who were hunter-gatherers, whether Gaelic or Indians, had no rights to the land over which they hunted and gathered. Instead, there was a strong belief that 'only the act of tillage mixed labour with the land', and created the right of ownership, whether as smallholder, agrarian improver or colonial planter.[24] In early English colonisation, it was not personal labour which conferred such a right but power in a feudal sense over such labour. Empire was not necessary to expropriate native peoples, but empire was necessary if the goal was power, conquest and sovereignty rather than emigration and settlement. The American Revolution essentially was fought over the question of whether empire was necessary in the extended English polity represented by the idea of Britain. In an immediate British context, the Irish experienced expropriation (twice: by the Old English during the Middle Ages, and then again by the 'New English' during the Reformation that came to England but not to Ireland), whereas the Welsh and the Scots did not, which may be more a reflection on the fertility of Ireland and the inhospitable environment of Wales and Scotland than an indication of Hibernian lack of 'Britishness'.[25] In an American context it provided a ready-made ideological construct for those who had ceased to regard themselves as British to cheerfully and self-righteously eliminate those who lived in the wilderness but had no right to possess it. Those who carried out this process were then themselves American in the tradition of Thomas More's Utopian culture.

What the English proto-empire in America spawned, before the middle of the eighteenth century, was an economic system which acted as a system of financial circulation holding distant colonies of settlement in the Western hemisphere together and connecting them to the markets emerging in Amsterdam and London. After 1707 the colonies in one sense became British too, although in time the idea of extending a British identity to them in terms of an imperial state would provoke resistance, and then rebellion.[26] After 1783 Canada and the British West Indies remained as a reminder to more modern British imperialists of what might have been, but the transplanted English and purportedly British American colonial world of the eighteenth century lost its centre and its purpose after 1783. What evolved in this process of transatlantic plantation and loss for those involved in its economy was an extra-European development of the complex financial system first spawned by William III's incorporation of England into his war effort against France after 1689. This would provide the decisive basis for the creation or re-creation of British empire in Asia after 1783.[27] The key word is 'decisive', for the link between east and west in the British Empire continued to be central until 1815. As Adam Smith predicted in 1776, British trade to independent America grew after 1783 rather than declined.[28] Jeffersonian Republicans hoped to make the United States an Empire of Liberty, but it still drew its supplies from what was no longer a mother country as it faced west and south in the North American continent, and ultimately north, which led in 1812 to a renewed clash between Britain and the United States over the issue of whether there would be any British America at all.[29] As a result of that conflict it was 1815, rather than 1783, which marked the real end of a comprehensive British role on the North American continent, and it was no coincidence that this development coincided with British victory in Europe and the security it provided for its Asiatic empire.

In an important study of London colonial merchants and financiers we can see this process at work in some detail. A substantial number (ten out of twenty-three) of the financiers featuring in the work of David Hancock were Scots. The others were divided between origins in provincial England or London. This contrast with the figures for London merchants' origins overall given by Hancock, of whom 80 per cent were English and only 5 per cent were Scots. His merchants were outsiders by and large, attracted to London by the opportunities offered by being at the centre of a state which was increasingly becoming an empire, a metropolis poised between overseas and inland trade.[30] How did their trading interests survive the break-up of the first British Empire? For some, it marked the occasion to retire from trade, to join the landed elite at a higher social level than that of the decayed gentry from which many of the merchants studied by Hancock sprang. For others, the opportunities of India beckoned as British influence expanded there, investing in ships, lending money to the East India Company, and sending goods to India as freight on East India Company ships. Scots like Richard Oswald or Alexander Grant used connections in the East India Company known as 'husbands' to obtain space on East India Company vessels preparing for their outward voyages, and they often used fellow Scots like Andrew Moffat or Laurence Dundas, known to them from days before they lived in London, as their partners in making these arrangements to trade privately through the medium of the company. Other trading connections took them, or at least their money, to Africa, where the exotic juxtaposition of British and imperial influences can be seen in the game of golf played on Bance (or Bunce) Island off the coast of Sierra Leone, described by a friend of Linnaeus who was on a visit to Africa in 1773. As the players struck their balls towards each of the two holes on 'the course', their play epitomised the overseas trade which so changed Britain in the course of the eighteenth century as more and more of its commercial and political interests were led further and further abroad. The players were dressed in Indian cotton, attended by African caddies dressed, if that is the word, in tartan loincloths made from woollen material manufactured in Glasgow. They were in Africa to buy slaves to take to America.[31] Their presence demonstrated how four continents were united by trade centred on the financial and mercantile expertise of London.

In this outward movement the Scots were important. The crisis with the American colonies coincided with their determination to assert an equal role within the Union, rooted in historical ideas about the concept of Britain which Scots had been developing from the time of the Reformation.[32] These intellectual ideas became imperial when the area under the authority of the British Crown expanded overseas. If the Anglo- Irish looked to the American colonies for an example of how to assert their rights in relation to authority rooted in an imperial crown, a significant and articulate number of Scots realised that Franklin was right about the fabulous wealth to be made from the American continent, and viewed it as essential that the 'British' state, under a new constitution built upon imperial authority in London, keep control of that continent and that wealth. This was what the Union of Scotland and England had been about, in their eyes; the surrender of sovereignty to a larger state which would tap the potential wealth of the polite and commercial society that represented the end of history and the final state of civilisation.[33] They lost. The Scots became notorious as a Loyalist nation in America, despite the fact that there was considerable popular sympathy for the Americans in Scotland itself. What had been unimaginable by Scots like Adam Ferguson, Professor of Moral Philosophy at the University of Edinburgh and sometime secretary to the peace commission sent by the North ministry to negotiate with the Americans in 1778, was that their dream of greater glory would be realised in Asia rather than on the *tabula rasa* they imagined America to be. To them a British empire in Asia was impossible and would bring about corruption and decay.[34] Their student, Henry Dundas, swept aside their niceties with the vigour and ruthlessness of a successful Scottish advocate in possession of a brief for a wealthy client, at a cost which became apparent only after 1815 in terms of increased social conflict and dislocation.[35] At the time of the American crisis the loss of America and the growing influence of the Scots entrenched the unity of Crown and Parliament at the centre of empire.

Some English commentators such as Josiah Tucker, Dean of Gloucester Cathedral, felt that the loss of America thus represented a positive good for England and for Britain. Tucker realised that if America was going to become a fabulous continental empire, its subjugation of Britain and England was inevitable.[36] Tucker argued, like a good ancient Athenian, that Britain had to become independent of its colonies before they outgrew it, since otherwise the Empire would be ruled by those in the provinces rather than the metropolis, and by a people in which slave-owning was well established, which augured ill for the future of British liberty. Both Tucker and Samuel Johnson were acutely aware of a truth that still haunts Americans today – the words of liberty and freedom sound hollow in the mouths of those who live on the labour of others. Tucker called for a British Declaration of Independence from America; for him 'the heart of the American problem for Britain was less the maintenance of imperial control than the preservation of essentially English institutions which the claims of empire were calling into question'. If the Americans invoked the authority of John Locke, Tucker emphasised Locke's authorship of the feudal as well as colonial *Fundamental Constitution of Carolina*, and his possible involvement in Monmouth's rebellion of 1685 in order to present him as an advocate of both slavery and rebellion, like the American colonists themselves.

The reaction of the British elite to the failure of the Americans to participate in Britain marks the end of the so-called First British Empire, which was in fact neither truly British nor a true empire. The Classical analogy was to the Greek dispersal of population about the Mediterranean, and especially to the foreign shores of Asia Minor, rather than the Roman Augustan Empire, which Adam Ferguson held out as a source of civic virture and commercial security.[37] Harold Macmillan once famously remarked that the postwar British would become Greece to America's Rome, the older civilisation tempering and teaching the wealthier but less sophisticated junior.[38] But to the emerging British elite who would coalesce around the younger Pitt, the Americans had to go because they were like so many Greek city-states, forever quarrelling amongst themselves and able to unify only to defeat external threat rather than achieve order and wealth in their own society. When the Americans proved these critics wrong in that crucial year in European history, 1789, it would be the American who had come to model himself on the political career of the younger Pitt, Alexander Hamilton, who would be able to draw on the ideology of British union to bring about the birth of an American state which, ironically, became imperial in the hands of his own arch-enemy, the self-styled revolutionary, Jefferson.[39] It was Jefferson who would purchase the vast wilderness of Louisiana from Napoleon to keep the British out of the centre of the American continent, determined to use the opportunity to perpetuate the politics of settlement in opposition to social and economic development dependent on commercial and financial wealth.[40]

6

PERIPHERAL NATIONS? SCOTLAND, IRELAND, WALES AND PROVINCIAL ENGLAND

The 'four-nations' idea of British history was first advanced in John Pocock's prophetic article published in 1972.[1] It has taken some time to evoke a response. One influential attempt was written by Hugh Kearney and originated in the salutary discipline of attempting to teach British history to American students, but it only since the publication of Linda Colley's widely read study, *Britons*, that sustained discussion about the ideas Pocock advanced twenty-five years ago has begun to take place.[2] Pocock's work since the publication of his article has played a key role in the development of modern Scottish historiography by encouraging the study of Scottish political thought in relation to an English tradition, and in a recent essay he has called for more work on Ireland.[3] That Wales has thus far escaped his attention can only be due to the limitation of time and space on the human intellect, but Geraint Jenkins has produced work on Welsh culture in the eighteenth century that has a genuinely bilingual grasp of the popular and elite cultural response in Wales to European cultural movements of the eighteenth century.[4] At the centre of Pocock's concern for British history is a recognition of the national distinctiveness at work on the intellectual traditions of all four countries. There has been doubt expressed over whether it is useful to study the histories of four nations equally when one of them was so manifestly more populous and wealthy (and hence superior?) than the others; or alternatively, from an Irish or Scottish perspective, suspicions have been expressed that the entire phenomenon is just a device by non-national historians (i.e. English and Americans) to undermine emerging nationalist historiography in Ireland or Scotland.[5] These suspicions include a fear that interest in British history is bound to have an elitist agenda which will subvert the success of social historians in broadening historical research over the past three decades to include the lives and culture of working people in the past.[6] All of these perspectives share the standpoint of critics of the idea of European history as a non-national endeavour. Either European history is seen as an excuse for elevating the history of England, France, Germany and Russia over that of the rest of the peoples of Europe, or it is seen as an elitist exercise in the balance of power through diplomatic history, or it is seen as the intellectual history of an elite united most by their monopoly of available wealth and hegemony (a popular word) over a popular culture which was, by definition, local and regional rather than 'European'.[7]

Where recent work by social and economic historians offers very valuable insight on the growth of interest in British history is when their emphasis moves towards ideas of region and locality as a framework for historical research superior to the use of essentially political units like counties, provinces or nations. Within the period 1660–1832 there has been a renewed interest in the origins and nature of the industrial revolution.[8] Work by Professor Pat Hudson and Dr Maxine Berg has, to quote a joint article they published in 1990, 'rehabilitated' the industrial revolution.[9] Nothing is less suitable to four-nations treatment and, in contrast, more British than the idea of the 'industrial revolution'. Industrialisation brought areas of Britain into modernity, in some cases extremely abruptly, yet left other areas comparatively untouched, continuing to experience a social structure with strong bonds of continuity to the type of landed elite who benefited from the Revolution of 1688 and experienced the trauma of imperial crisis between 1776 and 1798.

Nowhere did this economic revolution (in an eighteenth-century rather than a twentieth-century sense of the word) and its consequent social dislocation occur on a national basis. In England it was the textile manufactures of Lancashire, Cheshire and Yorkshire and the 'toy trades' of Birmingham which first experienced this change. In Scotland it was the area around Glasgow. In Ireland, at a slightly later period, Belfast became detached economically from the rest of Ireland by its participation in the new economy. It is an interesting question whether the economic development of Belfast reinforced existing social divisions in Ireland which were sectarian in nature, or whether it proved to be the origin of them. Even later, in Wales, industrialisation opened up a national division between an industrial South-east and a rural (and more predominantly Welsh-speaking) North; the first participating in an imperial economy and the second remaining part of a separate and traditional world based on agriculture. It is no wonder that economic and social historians have been interested in the ideas of region and locality rather than nationalism and ethnicity.[10]

There does appear to be a case to argue that these changes were spread to the west of Scotland and the north of Ireland by English entrepreneurs looking for new sources of labour and water power. They turned to existing areas where textile manufacture was well established by hand and where wages were low, although there were factors relating to the Union existing since 1707 and the social interaction this had generated which led mill-owners from the North of England to favour the West of Scotland over the North-east of Ireland.[11] Why would textile traders from the North of England turn to Scotland and Ireland rather than East Anglia and Devon? Surely the phenomenon must be rooted in Atlantic trade. Although Bristol was a great Atlantic emporium, it did not share the advantages in 'turnaround' on Atlantic voyages which northern ports had long enjoyed due to their closer proximity to Atlantic trade routes, nor was it as close to the new expanding English area of textile manufacture as Liverpool.[12] Glasgow and Belfast shared the Atlantic advantage and could participate in textile industrialisation once they were able to begin manufacture in their own right, with help from Lancashire and Yorkshire.[13] In this sense the first industrial revolution was much more genuinely British than the first British Empire! However, this British aspect of the industrial revolution, largely unnoticed by historians, was a result of regional interchange rather than the development of a new inter-British economic region.[14] Northern Ireland, the west of Scotland and northern England all became highly individualistic regions within their own countries and, as such, altered the course of each nation's history, just as South Wales would alter the history of Wales when it emerged as a distinctive economic area by the end of the eighteenth century.

One reason the industrial north of England came to perceive itself as English, albeit in opposition to the other of what Disraeli later described as two nations, was the result of the transportation revolution concomitant on the industrial revolution. The canal network which began in the 1760s would link the potteries and metal workshops of the Midlands to the North, and both regions to London, in a way which created an economic manufacturing area of interrelated regions which came to specialise in particular economic activities. However, through the canals, all of these areas had access nationally to the ports of Liverpool, Hull, Bristol and London.[15] Scotland, Wales and Ireland were excluded from this, although their experience differed in that Scotland experienced a wave of canal construction, succeeded by the railway, which laid the basis for the concentration of population and economy in the country in a narrow central belt, with developed transportation and defined urban areas. Taken together, they formed almost as large a conurbation in relation to the rest of the country as London did in relation to England.[16]

To a certain extent, therefore, industrialisation created regionalisation in all 'four nations' of Britain, but perhaps with greatest effect in England. No one could argue that regionalisation was the product of the industrial revolution, but the transformation of the nature of regionalisation was part of the impact of the move to new ways of working and living. The new economy created distinctive industrial areas in place of many different but economically and hence socially similar rural hierarchical communities, whether at the parish and village level beloved of the early modern social historian, or the county level, which reflected the hegemonic influence of the landowning gentry. The areas of textile manufacture were similar to those of the past, but altered their technology and structure of work for reasons we do not yet fully understand. One possibility is that this development occurred in response to the availability of tangible wealth accessible through providing textiles for the endlessly expanding markets of the Western hemisphere. Once they were linked to the South Midlands and London by canal, however, English regional economies became less 'Atlantic' and more English.[17] It also made them more provincial in a cultural sense than the three peripheral nations would ever be. Why? First, Scotland, Ireland and Wales all shared in a Celtic history and civilisation which might provoke varying reactions amongst their inhabitants but ensured that a significant part of the national culture of each nation, even at the height of assimilation, remained foreign to the English tradition. This did not make these areas peripheral in any other than the invented construct that was Britain. The pre-industrial history of the North and Midlands of England was one of subjugation to a centralising monarchy which did incorporate the Welsh politically in the sixteenth century, but only on a political level. The 'otherness' of the Welsh people was apparent to all in their language and its survival over time. Unlike Ireland, there was little in the way of plantation, although during the eighteenth century there would be complaints over the declining commitment to Welsh culture by the gentry, and the acquisition of Welsh estates by non-Welsh landowners, either by marriage or purchase.[18] Thus the assimilation of Wales 'succeeded' in the eighteenth century at gentry level, without reference to assimilation to England at any other level than the state and the law (in the limited sense that each operated before 1832).

This was also true of the North and Midlands of England, but industrialisation changed that, no matter how hard modern English social historians try to locate a popular national tradition in the community. Provincial England became directly linked to London in a more direct way than Scotland, Ireland and even Wales, although Prys Morgan has shown that important elements of modern Welsh culture, society and identity were rooted in the accessibility of London to the Welsh from the eighteenth century onwards and the opportunity of Welsh people in the metropolis to generate wealth which could be used to reaffirm a Welsh cultural identity.[19] In Ireland and Scotland the Gaelic language for part of the population, a distinctive national religion for almost all, and national institutions at elite level, all distanced the nation from the stronger, more populous and wealthier dominant English national element in Great Britain. Where the two countries diverged was in the manner in which the landowning elite in each country came to interpret language and religion in terms of cultural identity and their own Celtic tradition.[20]

Yet to follow Samuel Johnson in rejecting the idea of the provinces as anything but a dependent area on London is too simplistic, and closely mirrors the attitude of a self-regarding metropolitan elite. Johnson was, after all, a provincial Midlands boy grown to manhood in a metropolis which liberated him by making possible a literary life unsustainable elsewhere in Britain at the time. Pat Hudson has pointed out that during the eighteenth century there was 'a growing identification among all social groups with the economic, social and political interests of their region'.[21] The middle class formed a regional identity based on shared urban centres where clubs and societies, like the Lunar Society of Birmingham, met to discuss the issues of the day and recent scientific discoveries and speculations.[22] The working class, expressing its opposition to food shortages and conscription, focused its protest on local elites and presented issues in a local way. There was a British patriotism, but there were also regional political movements, particularly before the 1830s, whether it be the Yorkshire Association at gentry level or more popular movements concentrating on grain shortages, high taxation, and the introduction of machines in textile manufacture.[23] To a surprising degree, British patriotism during times of war was expressed within existing local customs and regional traditions, partly to ensure that popular opposition to the state did not unite as an alternative to the existing order, as had happened in France between 1789 and 1793.[24]

There is now a considerable literature regarding English regional politics from 1763 to 1793 which establishes that it was concerned with opposition to national government, but operated within an intensely regional context. There are interesting links of continuity between the popular Jacobitism manifested in Britain earlier in the century and the extra-parliamentary radicalism which emerged after 1763 that provided the basis for political opposition on a popular level in England. This was an opposition in politics, which operated in a devolved and dynamic manner that represented the antithesis of the politics of the Hanoverian state. Both political movements were joined by a local and regional dynamic which transcended the ideological opposition of each to the other and emphasised the degree to which each of them, in different circumstances, acted as a vehicle for cultural and political independence from London.[25] We now know much about the political life of Newcastle and Norwich during the eighteenth century and how each was affected by national politics, while at the same time reacting to national trends in ways that indicated the existence of a distinctive regional culture. Norwich, for example, with a long tradition of contact with former emigrants to New England, contained few inhabitants interested in expressing any support for the British effort to retain its mainland American colonies in the 1770s and 1780s. This formed an intensely regionalised response to a very national issue. Similarly the 1745 Jacobite rebellion, which never touched Norwich directly, proved to be the issue which consolidated Whig ascendancy in East Anglia by allowing the local Whigs to appropriate as their own the patriotic credit associated with defeat of the rebellion. Thus a very national crisis had a very local effect on public life. Later opposition to ministerial politics in the 1760s and 1770s followed a national pattern in the involvement of professionals, merchants, shopkeepers and craftsmen who were not directly represented in parliament, but 'seized the initiative in the name of the people in order to state their own claims in national affairs'.[26] In relation to the American issue, for example, opponents of that war linked this to domestic considerations just as much as the elite did, albeit from a contrasting perspective; one side emphasising anarchy and popular faction, the other corruption and tyranny on the part of the political elite.

In Birmingham during the grain riots of 1766 a regional political elite reacted to a crisis which at least appeared to be associated with economic change by searching for means by which traditional social values could be defended. One means of doing this was through emphasising the continuity of new urban relationships with old country origins in a way which later readers of George Eliot's novel *Silas Marner* would find familiar. It was not just skilled workers who felt threatened, but the masters of the small workshops which characterised the 'toy trade' of Birmingham. As larger firms began to seek economies of scale and moved into production as well as marketing, 'lesser masters felt themselves threatened in much the same way as did the small landowner confronted by enclosure and the engrossing tenant farmer'.[27] John Money has argued that the idea of 'luxury' was rehabilitated in the aftermath of the grain riots of 1766 'as a provider of employment and a guarantor of the interdependence of the different ranks of society'. Thus the buckle and button manufacture of the Birmingham 'toy' trades were explicitly linked to the role of these items in the fashion adopted by gentlemen who adopted this form of dress, demonstrating the interdependence of different ranks of society. This appealed 'to the region's collective sense of pride in its own past experience', in response to radical ideas which proposed an abrupt break with past history and past practice that would negate the sense of community which had evolved historically in the region. In a period of obvious change at an accelerating pace, radical politics were about social continuity rather than polical change for any reason other than to defend those in traditional economic occupations from the repercussions of the economic revolution which encroached on this particular region.

If the middling sort were not yet the middle class, their urban culture became a means of altering both gentry and plebeian culture. The middle class were not yet aware that they had an identity separate from the traditional labouring class in countryside and town, from whom they had detached themselves, and the landed class with whom they wished to identify their interests. As the urban population grew, those who flourished within it took possession of traditional elite culture and made it accessible to an increasing number of people in a growing number of 'regional centres and provincial capitals' such as York, Northampton and Norwich, which acted as cultural frontiers between traditional elite culture, popular tradition and a new commercial culture based on leisure, print, and social interaction in public places and on public occasions.[28] It was a culture which would have an impact on emerging centres such as Birmingham and Manchester, which differed in social composition by being dominated by a working population rather than one whose principal occupation was leisure. The new business and manufacturing classes of the industrialising regions of Britain nevertheless increasingly shared a commercial culture to which earned income gave them as ready access as those dependent on sinecures, inheritance and rent.[29]

There is now evidence that elite culture itself in Britain became divided between an emerging 'national' and by definition British society, and an alternative communal and provincial culture which respected tradition rather than adopted a sceptical attitude towards it.[30] A new elite which, to a certain extent, reinvented itself in the guise of its predecessors separated itself from tradition and popular culture in a self-conscious attempt to justify and defend its privileged status. Yet at the same time it sponsored an expansion of its culture to include more people, not fewer, while still fundamentally excluding the majority of the working population.[31] Those who were in the middle had a choice. They were people who existed in greater numbers in England (and latterly Lowland Scotland and eastern Ireland) than elsewhere in Europe. These were people who did not fit into a model of the *ancien régime*. They were people who might have had access to enough wealth to aspire to participation in a metropolitan culture dependent on commerce, wealth and leisure, yet would not be so detached from local and traditional culture that they could no longer comprehend it. Several scholars have introduced the considerable authority of Jürgen Habermas into the debate, who more than three decades ago began to consider bourgeois culture in terms of intellectual as well as physical space, as part of the neo-Marxist reassessment of European history.[32] Use of cultural space would be one way to interpret the importance of the coffee-house culture which supported *The Tatler* and *The Spectator*, allowing them, as literary enterprises, to achieve a measure of critical detachment from both elite and traditional culture.[33] The urban square and cathedral precinct gave physical expression to this new phenomenon while also becoming the habitat of the people who personified it.[34] Nationality did not insulate the Welsh, Scots and Irish from the centralising cultural influence of London. The choices facing the elites in these countries became particularly acute because there was an added national dimension faced by those who could engage with or oppose the expansion of what had previously been associated with the English elite, but now represented British wealth, liberty, commerce and empire.[35]

There were thus important similarities between cultural tensions operating within Britain after 1763 and the conflict which was beginning to emerge between metropolitan authority and local elites in Ireland, the West Indies, and British North America.[36] Ultimately Ireland would become assimilated into the British metropolitan model after 1801 for more than a century; the West Indies would become an area of economic desolation through the peculiarities of British emancipation of slavery within the Empire, and British North America would be reinvented in twain as the United States and Canada.

Traditional 'communal–provincial' British culture became an important element in developments in British North America from about 1748, after the end of what Europeans referred to as the War of Austrian Succession.[37] One result of the war was to make obvious the peripheral interest of government in London in the British North American colonies, as illustrated by the return of the French North American fortress of Louisburg to France in 1748, with its implicit threat to anglophone colonies bordering French Canada. Subjection to the interests of metropolitan authority and deference to its interests raised colonial interest in asserting the integrity of their emerging society as part of the British state. The example of the Union of Scotland and England provided the Americans (and the Irish and West Indians) with an example of an attempted solution to the problem of engaging with and assimilating the expansion of elite culture and the encroaching financial demands of incipient state formation on an imperial level. The idea of provincial independence which developed in Scotland during the eighteenth century was taken to America and became part of the justification for the American colonists' defence of their traditional rights as Englishmen, to the point that despite the definition of Scots as foreigners, they contributed to Americans' growing independent political identity.[38] This process can be seen most clearly in the cases of Scots who became members of the American revolutionary elite, such as John Witherspoon and James Wilson. They and others like them came from a lowland Presbyterian culture of small landowners and tenant farmers who had opposed the union with England. They had lacked the strength to stop the Union because their society was so deeply divided between Presbyterian and Episcopalian religious traditions that it lacked the ability to defend a shared traditional polity against union with the British metropolis.[39] Where they were able to collude, as different cultural traditions, was in creating a British provincial culture which would influence subsequent developments in Ireland and the West Indies as well as America.

The career of John Witherspoon represents this culture; Witherspoon was East Lothian born and educated at Edinburgh, but by the time he emigrated to New Jersey in 1767 he had become very much part of a distinctive West of Scotland culture centred on the expanding commerce of Glasgow, and in particular its close connection with and established ties to the British colonies in North America, a connection that had an evangelical and religious as well as a commercial element to it. After 1763, as regional culture in the west of Scotland experienced postwar extension of metropolitan authority and reacted to English prejudice, some members of that society believed that provincial integrity might be maintained overseas in America in a manner becoming impossible within Britain itself. In other words, an alternative to assimilation to modern British national culture was emigration to a place where distance from metropolitan authority would help maintain provincial autonomy. Witherspoon did not just take charge of an American college at Princeton, he became involved in extensive emigration schemes and supported a group of fellow emigrants, who became important in the American campaign to preserve provincial autonomy, ultimately by declaring independence. For Witherspoon, this involved tranferring ideas of provincial autonomy within greater Britain from the West of Scotland to America.[40]

How typical was this experience? The colonies in the American South provided a forum for a very different group of expatriate Scots, eager to serve metropolitan imperial authority and indeed, in the process, making the southern colonies into laboratories for a new kind of imperial power where the Crown and the landowner rather than the settler would hold influence and dominate events. There were a remarkable number of Scots appointed as royal officials in the American southern colonies, even before the Bute ministry's appointments of Scots (and seemingly only Scots) to the governorships of the colonies of East and West Florida gained from the Spanish by the peace of 1763. These appointments were greeted with righteous indignation by the Wilkite opposition as 'Scotch jobbery', but earlier appointments, particularly the group of Scots appointed to positions in the Carolinas between 1730 and 1750, played a role in arguing for greater royal control of the American colonies. The Duke of Newcastle's use of the term 'salutary neglect' to describe the Crown's American policy was employed in correspondence with one of these governors, Gabriel Johnston, who for twenty years represented royal authority in impoverished and underdeveloped colonial North Carolina with little, if any, support from London.[41] It was Johnston and his largely Scottish allies, however, who envisaged the potential for settlement in the southern colonies which came to fruition after 1763. His successor as governor of North Carolina in 1753, Arthur Dobbs, was an Ulsterman from Carrickfergus.[42] Sir William Johnston, also of Protestant Irish origin, would become lord of much of the upstate New York frontier in the period leading to the American Revolution as a Royal Commissioner for Indian Affairs.[43]

By broadening the area of consideration in British history during the eighteenth century to include British North America, therefore, the perspective on British history which relegates the geographical periphery of Britain to something approximate to that status in cultural terms becomes redundant.[44] In mainland Britain, there were industrialising areas in Ireland, Scotland and Wales as well as England by 1800, just as there were areas in all four countries which remained largely untouched by the industrial revolution. There were parts of the societies of all four nations who responded to the intellectual currents of the Enlightenment, just as there were areas in all four nations which remained resistant to or remote from its assimilating dynamic. The American colonies did not industrialise by 1800, but their economy had already reached a point where it acquired a momentum of its own which helped fuel their exit from the incipient empire.[45]

Positing a metropolitan monolithic England and an equally monolithic but subordinate 'Celtic fringe' of dependent nations does not really accurately convey what happened to Britain during the eighteenth century. There were parts of England which were more thoroughly colonised, by the end of the eighteenth century, than any sugar island in the West Indies. Regions of England such as the East Midlands regressed to the status of rural backwaters, even while parts of Wales and Ireland became central to the imperial economy. This became part of the power of the idea of Britain, in that it transcended traditional 'four-nations' national, political and cultural identities in favour of a new imperial identity, which was founded on commerce, polite culture, leisure and the wealth to enjoy it, as well as public service and the extension of government authority under the Crown in defence of property and the liberty of those who held it. Britons would never, never, never be slaves, but an English farm labourer or an industrial mechanic might become just as much a slave as a Jamaican sugar worker or the subjects of a decadent Asiatic despot. That is what the idea of Britain came to mean during the course of the eighteenth century, and its history includes the effect it had on those it excluded as well as those who reinvented themselves within its framework.

7

CULTURAL POLITICS: NATIONAL CULTURE IN A METROPOLITAN STATE

Is it possible to write of a British culture for the eighteenth century? What would that culture consist of? Was there a British Enlightenment? Or do we, by using such a term, conflate the commercial and imperial with the intellectual in a way that doesn't really advance our understanding of any of these areas? There has been a long-standing division in the thinking of historians of eighteenth-century Britain regarding the best way of furthering our exploration of it. Studies of government, politics and culture often emphasise the activities of the landed elite; studies of social and economic history since the 1960s, on the other hand, have broken important new ground in trying to extend our knowledge regarding other groups in British society, following the inspirational example of the work of E. P. Thompson.[1]

Discussions of eighteenth-century culture invariably involve the use of the term and the idea of 'the Enlightenment' as a European or international movement which characterised the culture of the day. Notoriously difficult to comprehend by students new to the period, originally the Enlightenment was discussed as a canon of ideas, largely French in origin, whereby the monolithic authority of continental absolutism was challenged by liberal thinkers who favoured freedom of speech and the advancement of learning based on reason and science. Although often thought of as part of European rather than British history, it is significant that each of the three most recent textbooks in English on the subject use an English illustration on their cover, two taken from paintings by Joseph Wright of Derby, whose work expressed an English culture at once provincial and enlightened, and the third from a popular print of Newton conducting an optical experiment.[2] All are English, all involve the use of images representing scientific experiment, and all use the visual representation of light to illustrate the advancement of knowledge. All three illustrations also emphasise not just scientific experiment, but scientific experiment as public display. They present science as entertainment as well as popular education for a middling class with more money, more leisure and more interest in science and culture than it had previously.

In fact, as Dorinda Outram concludes in a recent short study of the Enlightenment, 'the Enlightenment was much better at creating new relationships amongst elites, and bringing sections of elites together in the new forms of sociability centring on ideas, than it was in reaching out to lower social classes'.[3] In many ways this was a period when members of the elite in St Petersburg and Paris had more in common with each other than either had in common with the peasants who worked on their estates. The peasants and the old elite shared a localised and traditional culture specific to a particular geography, while the new elite of professionals and landowners were participating in a common culture across state and regional boundaries. While this is true, it leaves out what was changing over the course of the century as more people had access to elite culture, and in the process detached themselves from what had preceded it. An example of a non-elite social group who did have ready access to aspects of Enlightenment culture was the large servant class of the eighteenth century, of which an example in art, as Outram points out, would be Beaumarchais's character

Figaro. An excellent example from the real world which would relate to this popular aspect of the Enlightenment in a British context would be the *Memoirs of an Eighteenth-Century Footman* published by John Macdonald, a Scottish Highlander and professional servant who worked for no less than twenty-seven different masters and reached Bombay and Paris in his travels. His life as a working man does not fit the stereotype of the benighted Highlander passively victimised by commercial rents and absentee landlords.[4]

It was the town and city which served as the social setting for the Enlightenment, not as a canon of ideas, but as a social phenomenon incorporating the changes wrought by financial and commercial profit, the leisure they created and the markets involving leisure and learning they brought about. The English elite (and those elsewhere in Britain and its colonies who shared in their culture) accelerated their withdrawal from traditional culture as a means of confirming their elite status. This process became bound up with the idea of being British; an identity open to Scots, Irish, the Welsh and to members of colonial societies in a way that Englishness, which emphasised ethnicity, did not. The long-term result, as Peter Borsay has written, was that a widening cultural gap emerged between polite society and the majority of ordinary people, and with it the transformation of an inclusive traditional culture into an exclusive popular one'.[5] The cultural and leisure activities of the town during the eighteenth century became a means of the elite, landed and commercial, effecting their withdrawal from their traditional culture, whether in London, English provincial towns, Ireland, Jamaica, Bombay or Philadelphia. The expanding urban sector of society, while still incorporating a minority of the population, helped change the nature of elite pastimes and incorporate more people into elite activity at any of several levels. This expanded area of activity provided a means for those with ambition to rise in society, even as it brought traditional culture under increasing pressure. One way of thinking about the Enlightenment is to see it as 'in part a campaign to reveal to the gentry the error of plebeian ways'. Just what was being offered as an alternative can be deduced from Peter Borsay's study of the provincial town in England, which emphasises five aspects of the urban culture developing in the period in relation to space, literacy, language, leisure and time.

Space involved a move away from the local customs and practices of traditional culture towards imitation of external models in London and Paris. The names of London pleasure gardens were used for equivalent parks in English provincial towns, as in the 'Vauxhall Gardens' of Bath and Birmingham, and the 'New Ranelagh Gardens' of Newcastle and Norwich. Newspapers and local presses expanded the uses of literacy in this culture. Although it has been notoriously difficult to determine who had access to the medium, it had to involve those, even at its most popular level, with money to buy access to print, whether it be the price of a penny broadsheet and chapbook, or the equivalent of a year's wages earned by a working man necessary to buy a quarto edition of Smith, Gibbon, Swift or Pennant. Of course, once bought, print could be read aloud, and this made it available to those still part of traditional oral culture. The impact of the works of Tom Paine, for example, came from their ability to speak to those who were part of both traditional and Enlightenment culture. Smith and Gibbon, on the other hand, wrote works which were not read aloud in taverns or churches, although to many of the gentlemen possessing their works ownership symbolised loyalty to an ideology, rather than actual engagement with it through literally reading them!

Literacy was related to what was happening to the use of language in elite culture. The culture of print expanded dramatically in its sophistication and the gap between different kinds of printed literature grew, whether it be that between a chapbook and a quarto in size and bulk, or that between a devotional tract and the pornography which was beginning to find its way into print in terms of content. This reinforced the growing gap between 'traditional culture, with its oral and local character', which supported diversity in dialect and syntax, from the move towards a standardised language that in English was symbolised by the publication of John-son's *Dictionary of the English Language* (1755). This was pre-sent also in Welsh, Irish and Scots Gaelic with the compilation and publication of dictionaries and etymologies.[6] The 'polite' thus began to cultivate communication through standardised 'received' English, while those denied access to polite culture or those who chose not to assimilate to it 'continued to articulate their multiplicity of regional accents and words', independent from elite culture but isolated from each other.[7]

This division extended to the relationship between literacy and leisure. An emphasis on literature drew the 'polite' mem-bers of society away from the fair, the county races, cock-fighting and other traditional leisure activities towards assem-bly rooms, coffee houses and bookshops. The third Duke of Argyll, sitting in Gavin Hamilton's bookshop in Edinburgh in 1757, perfectly illustrated this gap when he pointed to a gallows in the square opposite and speculated, in a polite manner, as to whether it was destined to be used on one of the Highlanders who came from his estates to live in Edin-burgh, proceeding to engage Hamilton in conversation as to whether all Highlanders were thieves and deserved hanging, or if this was an individual characteristic: ' "Mr. Hamilton," says he, "is not that fellow there one of my countrymen?" "No." said I, "he is not one of your countrymen, he is a Lochyell [Lochiel] man." "Well, well," said the Duke, "that is Argyleshire, that is in my country; there are many there more than that fellow who deserve to be hanged." '[8]

The growing division between those who believed in magic and witchcraft and those who had adopted an uncritical faith, often just as uninformed, in science and reason, also served to set up a barrier between those who subscribed to Enlight-enment culture and those who remained true to oral tradi-tion. Time began to be organised socially in different ways, both in work and leisure. Whereas the historic calendar was divided at December (Christmas) and late June (Midsummer) into ritualistic and secular halves, the new calendar was sepa-rated at roughly October and April, into winter and summer seasons, and the populace at large felt robbed of eleven days by the elite.[9] Nowhere did this clash in the urbanised world of the Enlightenment appear more acute than in the changing world of medicine, with its agenda of scientific experiment and, it now seems, elite control over new areas of social life which had been inaccessible to professionals in traditional culture. Mary Fissell has pointed out that 'historians of British hospitals have focused on their role in polite culture, with various provincial cities emulating one another's new foundations. But analyses of Continental institutions suggest that hospitals also served as sites for the negotiation and mediation of power by local elites.'[10] Infirmaries became centres of moral reform for the deserving poor as well as disseminators of medical knowledge and care, and their construction symbolised the power of the landed elite every bit as much as a country house. Doctors achieved increased authority from the hospital setting, negotiating a shift from a benefactor/client relationship ruled by patronage to a practitioner/patient relationship which was more remote and 'professional', although also available to a greater proportion of the population. Doctors acquired more power as vernacular medicine became 'a mode of expression suitable only for the plebeians'. The body became subject to increased policing in a manner similar to the extension of social control and state power. Although poor patients were successful in using institutions for ends never intended by their benefactors, infirmary surgeons obtained increased access to patients' bodies through institutional control. Medical training became necessary to 'read' illness, thus robbing the patient of his or her understanding of their illness and in some cases 'ownership of themselves'.[11]

This physical appropriation of the poor by enlightened medical culture can be seen in a Bristol case of 1761, in which the son of a collier from Kingswood had been brought to the infirmary suffering from a head injury, which he did not survive. Later that night the hospital surgeon, John Castelman, was awakened at home by the angry shouts of the boy's father, who had opened his son's coffin on collecting it from the institution, only to find that the body lacked its head. Castelman hurried to the infirmary while the angry man waited in his home, 'returning with the head in a sack', enabling it to be reunited with the rest of its corporeal remains.[12] Similarly, the famous Edinburgh scandal of 1828 in which a respected lecturer of anatomy, Robert Knox, was found to have been purchasing cadavers from two murderers of Irish birth, Burke and Hare, caused a sensation. The Irishmen had improved upon an existing trade in cadavers by murdering the living to meet the demand for corpses, preying upon easy victims amongst the appalling slums which had appeared in Edinburgh by the early nineteenth century. The case unleashed a popular hysteria, which combined fears about the elitist nature of Enlightenment culture with resentment at the onset of substantial Irish emigration to Scotland, and the perceived threat this represented to traditional Scottish culture.[13] Science and reason appeared to have brought in their wake corruption and palpable evil rather than promised improvement. Throughout the eighteenth and early nineteenth centuries the cavalier manner in which subjects were sought for dissection by the medical community in Britain indicated an attitude towards the mass of society every bit as detached as the head taken from the Kingswood collier's dead son. This attitude of social detachment from traditional society and 'the lower orders' increased over time. One illustration of this is the contrast between Alexander Morgan, who practised as a Bristol surgeon in the eighteenth century after training as an apprentice, incorporating the patient's experience as well as his own observations in recording his case notes, whereas evidence from the early nineteenth century in the form of notes by James Bedingfield, an apothecary who worked at Bristol infirmary, reveals a willingness to make moral as well as medical diagnosis of patients. Mary Townsend, for example, appears in his case notes as 'aged thirty years, of a dark complexion, disagreeable Mulatto features and emaciated form'. She also, Bedingfield added ominously, 'led a very dissipated life'.[14]

This very individualistic sense of detachment and superiority has been claimed by Alan Macfarlane as the basis of a
distinctive English culture which was exceptional 'not only
from that of peoples in Asia and Eastern Europe, but also in
all probability from the Celtic and Continental countries of
the same period...a society in which almost every aspect of
the culture was diametrically opposed to that of the sur-
rounding nations'.[15] To Macfarlane, the essence of Englishness was living in 'a country where the individual has been
more important than the group and the hierarchy of ranks
has not been closed' from at least the time of the Middle
Ages. That very individuality was rooted in an acquisitiveness
which Macfarlane illustrates by coolly claiming Adam Smith
as working in 'an anglicised tradition'![16] The English
individualism embodied 'a vast set of individualistic attitudes
and rights' which were 'very old, very durable, and highly
idiosyncratic', as illustrated by the exceptional nature of
English colonisation abroad, where 'the only areas that had
never had peasantries at all were those colonised by
England [sic]: Australia, New Zealand, Canada and North
America'.[17]

In contrast, Gerald Newman states that 'the English quest
for national identity began around 1750 and was substantially
complete by 1830'.[18] But in his book much English 'sincerity'
and 'moral independence', which he derives from literary
sources as marking the hallmark of the English identity,
derive from sources such as *The Vicar of Wakefield*, written
by the Irishman Oliver Goldsmith, or the emphatically 'four-
nations' British novel *Humphry Clinker* written by Tobias
Smollett, a Scot. Both these works are intrinsically different
from the novels of Fanny Burney, another of Newman's
sources, in ways which demonstrate that Newman is writing
about an emerging sense of British civilisation and decency
rather than about an English national identity.[19] Newman's
treatment of James Watt illustrates his confusion over English
and British nationality. Watt is described as 'the pioneer of
English engineering'. He is discussed, along with Josiah
Wedgwood, as examples of meritocratic 'sincerity' that

embodied Newman's ideas of English identity. Watt, for example, declined a baronetcy in later life out of hostility to the idea of aristocracy, which, for Newman, was an example of his sincerity as an Englishman. Yet Newman records that Watt was happy to live in Birmingham, and refused an offer to work in Russia because he did not want to leave his country, by which he presumably meant Britain. He also declared later in life that if his patented improvements to Newcomen's steam-engine meant anything, he hoped that 'if I merit it some of my countrymen, inspired by the *Amor Patriae* may say: *Hoc a Scota factum frut* [this was made by a Scot]'.[20] The nationalism Newman perceives in Watt is his participation in the new modern construction of Britishness in a way which did not exclude his traditional national identity as a Scot. This was the period in which the figure of John Bull came to symbolize England, standing in awkward contradistinction to Britannia, who came to represent the common-sense political economy of the voting public. John Bull as a representative character of Englishness was an invention of the Scots, despite the English qualities of 'independence, courage, patriotism and stoicism' often attributed to the him.[21] The original point was to highlight English insularity. 'Some of the John Bulls cannot believe that such a body of men could be raised in so short a space', Andrew Fletcher (grand-nephew of the Scottish patriot) reported from London to his father in 1757, when Highland regiments were first raised for the British war effort during the Seven Years War.[22] This Scottish image was taken up by the Wilkites as an assertive badge of Englishness and non-Britishness, quite the reverse of what motivated James Watt, and from that point in the 1760s the character developed into the image of decent 'little-England' village modesty it has continued to represent to the present day.

Another perspective on Englishness during the eighteenth century has been put forward in the form of the idea of an English confessional state founded on the Anglican Church. While it is clear that the strength of the Anglican tradition during the eighteenth century had been underestimated by a generation of historians with primary interests in social, political and economic change, that does not negate the fact that England, and by extension Britain, was different from the rest of Europe in the large proportion of its population which was participating in a commercial economy, and who consequently might be seen as an incipient middle class.[23] In this debate there are interesting resonances of the reaction to Sean Connolly's efforts to analyse eighteenth-century Ireland as part of the European *ancien régime* rather than as an English 'colony'.[24] It is clear that both elements are present and that the debate is over which to give precedence; continuity or change. Similarly, if exceptionalism and change are to be emphasised rather than the continuity represented by the confessional state, is it to be looked for in an English or a British context?

Just as it can be stated that the idea of a British or an English Enlightenment is elusive because the French Enlightenment consisted of an admiration for the English Constitution and a desire to propagate its perceived virtues elsewhere, so it can be stated that the English had no need to genuinely engage with the idea of Britishness, because implicit in the entire concept was the value of the English Constitution, as elaborated after 1688, in safeguarding the rights of the individual, securing individual possession of property, and thereby unleashing the cultural spirit of scientific experiment and the economic spirit of commerce and finance, which formed the foundation of British success in its wars with France and the acquisition of its overseas empire.[25] In many ways the Scottish Enlightenment was thus similar to the French Enlightenment and the Enlightenment as an international movement, because it was founded on an admiration for the liberty and commerce made possible by the English Constitution and economy. John Robertson, in writing about Franco Venturi's work, defines Venturi's concern with Enlightenment cosmopolitanism and patriotism as rooted in a political economy which is constructed on the premise that 'rulers and writers' should renounce 'any aspiration to hegemony over others, whether in politics, in religion or in ideas', and that patriotism thus consisted in encouraging general improvement rather than an assertion of superiority over others.[26] This forms a very useful framework for an understanding of the Scottish Enlightenment, in which Nicholas Phillipson's early studies based on Edinburgh have been complemented by his subsequent work on Hume, by substantial studies of the leaders of the Moderate clergy of the Church of Scotland by Richard Sher, and the political issue of extending the English Militia Laws of 1757 to Scotland by John Robertson.[27] More recent work has extended the study of the urban context of the Enlightenment in Scotland, but not, as yet, its influence in the smaller urban centres which attracted the attention of Peter Borsay in England.[28] The picture which emerges is one of a group of professionals and merchants active in the principal regional urban centres of Edinburgh, Glasgow and Aberdeen, with Edinburgh continuing to perform some of the cultural functions of a national capital for Scotland, just as it does today. As a movement, the Enlightenment in Scotland was utterly convinced of the need to modernise on the model of England, without conceding subordination to it. That is what the negotiated union of 1707 was all about. Like the Enlightenment anywhere, it was located in a particular elite group which deliberately detached itself from vernacular society, both of the Gaelic-speaking Highlands, the Jacobite and Episcopalian Lowland culture of the North-east of Scotland, and the intensely Presbyterian Scottish regional culture found within and south of the Tay and Clyde river valleys.[29]

The Scottish Enlightenment was emphatically part of a British Enlightenment, led by generations of a middle class which perceived the creation of Britain in a way similar to those in the late twentieth century, who look to the creation of a united Europe as a panacea for many modern problems through the creation of an expanded market and polity. It was a national or a regional movement (both terms carry connotations even in the present, so to exclude either is, in effect, to make a political statement) very much within the model of cosmopolitanism and patriotism pursued by

Venturi.[30] It had a national aspect in that the Scottish middle class did not wish to concede hegemony to the English, but it also had lively regional and local urban capitals. It was built on the professional institutions of a legal system and a church which were different from that of England and were used in a way unavailable to the Welsh and the Irish to keep significant English intrusion into Scotland to a minimum. This was an inheritance of the Covenanting Wars, when Cromwell conquered Scotland, but discovered just how poor it was and just how expensive it was to garrison, and it was a legacy of the parliamentary Union which neutralised Scottish aggression without diverting English wealth away from war with France until the peace of 1713.[31] Colin Kidd has published work recently which has demonstrated how this Enlightenment culture incorporated a rewriting of Scottish history that emphasised Britishness, and obliterated the Gaelic/Celtic element in Scottish historical culture as well as the long political/dynastic tradition of an independent Scottish kingship which went back to the Dark Ages.[32] By no means all Scots accepted this rewritten history, as the continued popularity of the legend of William Wallace and Robert Bruce demonstrated, but the urban enlightened commercial middle classes did, and it made them British more thoroughly than the English themselves, as they proved in both America and India during the eighteenth century.[33] Within the British Isles, friction persisted between Scots and English. In 1778 a shocked Horace Walpole reported an outburst by Henry Dundas in London, when the then Lord Advocate, 'broke out into an invective against the English. He said that any ten Scots could beat any ten English: and if there were any competititon, he was, and would avow himself, a Scot.'[34] Effigies of John Wilkes were burned on public occasions in Scotland well into the nineteenth century.[35] This even extended to Ireland, but on the Continent and overseas the use of English by the Scots gave them access to trade and preferment on a scale unimaginable to their country, if it had been conquered by the English again, or even if it had retained its independence.

The Welsh had their language but they also reinvented themselves during the eighteenth century. Prys Morgan has argued that the Welsh lost confidence in themselves during the seventeenth century, quoting the Welsh lexicographer Thomas Jones in 1688, in a passage published in a significantly titled book, *The British Language in Its Lustre*; 'To languages as well as Dominions...theer is an appointed time;.... And thus it hath pleased the Almighty to deal with us the Brittains [i.e. the Welsh]; for these many ages hath eclipsed our Power, and corrupted our Language, and almost blotted us out of the Books of Records.'[36] During the eighteenth century the gentry in Wales detached themselves from traditional Welsh culture, Anglicised themselves, and began to participate in the society of the British landed class in a way which made it perfectly plausible for Tobias Smollett to make the 'British' narrative voice of his novel *Humphry Clinker* the Welsh squire Matthew Bramble. There were also important groups of Welshmen in London; Anglicised, participating in commercial society, but eager to demonstrate their memory of their origins to themselves and its interest to those amongst whom they were living. Welsh gentry like Lewis Morris and his brothers in Anglesey, or the Anglican vicars in Wales, who realised that the old ways were passing before the onset not just of a new economy, but the evangelical Christianity which appeared to be part of it, and also colourful originals such as the unforgettable Iolo Morganwg (Neddy from Glamorgan), whose name in English was Edward Williams, a laudanum addict and stonemason who reinvented both the idea of the Welsh bard and of druidic custom, and in a mist of sentiment and drug-induced hallucination created the modern romantic symbol of traditional Welsh culture, the eisteddfodau, in the very significant year of 1789.[37] If Americans in that year recast their political culture through adopting a written constitution, and France changed its public culture fundamentally through the assault on the Bastille and a revolution, Wales became its modern self through ritualistic song, story and poetry.

Ireland in the eighteenth century, of course, does not fit into a model of Britishness until the Union of 1801. From one perspective it was foreign, and its inhabitants were not Britons in the same sense that the English, Scots and Welsh could so define themselves. When the London Welsh ostentatiously displayed the three ostrich plumes of the Prince of Wales's standard at the ceremonies of the Order of Ancient Britons, this was done to demonstrate the loyalty of the Welsh to the Hanoverian kings, in contrast to the Irish or the Scots.[38] When the Scots gentry demanded a militia it was to demonstrate the value of Scotland's martial tradition to their fellow Britons.[39] Ireland, on the other hand, could be seen as the 'other' on sectarian grounds, of course, because most Irish remained Catholic after the Reformation when most English, Scots and Welsh did not. The Irish as 'other' could also be defined in terms of politics and empire, because Ireland remained a kingdom, given the operation of Poynings' Law, held by the monarch of Great Britain. Even James II, at the head of the Catholic Irish nation in 1689, insisted that he did not hold the Crown of Ireland independently, but as a subordinate crown to that of England. That changed with the Union of 1801, brainchild of the Scot Henry Dundas, as a solution to what was already considered 'an Irish problem', and it marked the end of a distinctive phase of Irish cultural life in which a native Protestant minority pushed the majority of the population to the periphery of national life.[40] Eventually the Protestants of Ireland came to see themselves as inalienably British, as many still do today, but their odyssey mirrored that of many other settler elites in British imperial history and illustrated a legacy of the expansion of Britishness as an identity into empire. There were those who would become incorporated in the idea who would benefit from its opportunities as long as empire lasted, but once its time had passed they would have no significant cultural or political identity distinct from the idea of Britishness. No one has written of an Irish Enlightenment, although there have been those who have written about the 'Protestant Asecendancy' and its 'mind', which included the great Irish

Protestant influences on eighteenth-century British culture; Bishop Berkeley, Dean Swift, Oliver Goldsmith, Richard Brinsley Sheridan and of course, Edmund Burke.[41] Burke stands forth in the eighteenth century not as a representative of the Irish Enlightenment but as a great Irish critic of empire, transfixed by the new Constitution emerging at the end of the eighteenth century, yet convert to its cause when he saw the world of property, commerce and privilege threatened by the French Revolution, and continuing to fascinate because the tensions at work within his own identity mirror so accurately those of all 'Britons' in their era of imperial crisis.[42]

The Anglo-Irish Ascendancy of scientific enquiry and the expansion of the culture of print in Dublin and Belfast in particular fit into the model of Enlightenment activity anywhere in the European world, from the colonies of the Western hemisphere to the Russian Empire to the east, and involved another elite rethinking its culture and questioning the nature of authority, knowledge and political economy. What was distinctive culturally about Ireland in the eighteenth century was that its Protestant elite came to terms with its Gaelic/Celtic history and culture in a rather different way than their social peers in Wales and Scotland, and did so as part of their own emerging national identity as Irish first, and subjects of the British king (or queen) second. Clare O'Halloran and Colin Kidd have recovered this historical and antiquarian debate.[43] The Scottish poems of Ossian by Macpherson, based on Gaelic tradition, helped develop new attitudes towards the Gaelic past by Protestant as well as Catholic writers in Ireland, which by the 1780s contributed to a positive reassessment of the role of Gaelic culture in Irish history and cultural identity. The new involvement of Irish Protestant writers on Gaelic literature and history, which began in earnest in the 1780s when the Royal Irish Academy was founded, can be seen as part of this. The success of Macpherson's poems gave those who wished to present Irish Gaelic culture positively the material to do so, although they achieved this by ignoring Macpherson's attempt to argue that Gaelic culture originated in the Scottish High-lands, and emphasised the intrinsic literary merit of the poems, as for example in Joseph Walker's *Historical Memoirs of the Irish Bards*.[44] Walker quoted from the Ossian poems liberally in his text, while in his footnotes he hinted at the unreliability of Macpherson, in an attempt to detach the poetry from their translator's and editor's agenda of relating them to a cultural condition of primitive though noble sav-agery. Thus the influence of Ossianic poetry may have helped influence the Protestant-dominated Trinity College Dublin and the Royal Irish Academy to begin the work of collection of Gaelic manuscripts and transcriptions of oral tradition, although translation skills to deal with this material were not developed properly until many years later.[45]

The willingness to accept Gaelic culture in Ireland as civil rather than savage had its roots in a moderate Catholic Enlightenment, dedicated to winning toleration and repeal of the penal laws, and this attracted moderate Protestant support during the 1780s as Protestants asserted their Irish-ness in relation to England. Although the violence of 1798 in Ireland limited further developments at the time of union with Britain, the effect and example of interest in Ireland's Celtic civilization which transcended sectarian boundaries would provide a model for the future of Irish scholarship.[46] In Scotland, by contrast, by the middle of the eighteenth century non-commercial cultures were defined as backward and destined to disappear. William Robertson and other Scottish writers saw the Gaelic Highlands of Scotland as a violent tribal society much like that of North American Indians. There was a pronounced difference in Scottish culture between a view of the Gaels of Antiquity and the Highlander of the present. 'Enlightened Scots argued that the past was a foreign country; that the mental world of primitive man, including one's own ethnic and national forebears, and hence by extension the primitive institutions of one's nation, were far removed conceptually from the concerns of civilized, commercial modernity.' Thus the Irish, in the words of Colin Kidd, 'traversed the quicksand of

Enlightenment, with important repercussions for the maintenance of a "non-British" Irish identity even after the imposition of parliamentary union on Ireland in 1801'.[47] The construction of Irishness during the nineteenth century would be on modern lines of European romanticism, in contrast to those of the other British nationalities, but with the crucial exception of the industrialised sectarian society of the north around Belfast, where the positive view of Gaelic culture never took root and a very different sense of mission and superiority in relation to the rest of Ireland remained entrenched. This was a settler society in a way in which the rest of Ireland under the 'Ascendancy' was not, and the continuous contact and emigratory stream from Ulster to the American colonies and states of the Middle Atlantic and New England regions demonstrated their affinity with and close relationship to settler societies which displaced native peoples rather than ruled over them.[48]

Thus there was a British Enlightenment, because it was a movement about the expansion of culture and the realisation of human achievement, founded on an admiration of the personal liberty and security possible in the commercial societies of Holland and England by the late seventeenth century, re-exported and revised a generation later by continental intellectuals as part of their own struggle against Absolutist government. It involved receptiveness to English influences and ideas, although not subservience to them. In adopting the English (or should one say Dutch) precedent, native elite groups made them their own, just as similar groups do today in the Third World when they adopt Western precedents and examples. What is important to identify, however, is that first, Anglicised elites became influential and powerful and even semi-independent, but never obliterated the culture from which they had been recruited. This was obviously a much more complicated process in Ireland than it was in Scotland and Wales, but important similarities remain. Second, in adopting Enlightenment culture, native elites made it their own in a way which contributed to the construction of Britishness during the eighteenth century, bringing into existence a cultural edifice which made it possible for the British state to sustain the Asiatic Empire which would bring it fabulous wealth during the nineteenth century.

8

THE AMERICAN REVOLUTION AND THE ORIGINS OF THE SECOND BRITISH EMPIRE

The American War of Independence was about America's place in the new British Empire secured by the Peace of Paris in 1763. Britain became the dominant power in North America, including the West Indies, and as such, for the first time in history, could in turn be perceived in Europe as a powerful country of the first rank. When a challenge to British imperial authority arose amongst the population of the mainland British colonies in North America, it became revolutionary when it took the form of an assertion of the rights of the citizen against the authority of central government and, in particular, the authority of hereditary monarchy. Given that victory for the American settler colonists was secured by the intervention of the army and navy of a European hereditary monarchy in the form of France, this aspect of the conflict can be obscured, but as Gordon Wood has stated:

> The republican revolution was the greatest utopian movement in American history. The revolutionaries aimed at nothing less than a reconstitution of American society. They hoped to destroy the bonds holding together the older monarchical

society – kinship, patriarchy, and patronage – and to put in their place new social bonds of love, respect, and consent. They sought to construct a society and governments based on virture and disinterested public leadership and to set in motion a moral movement that would eventually be felt around the globe.[1]

If this idealistic movement was able finally to repulse British authority with the help of France, we should not forget that the authority of the French monarchy was undermined only six years after the Americans secured their independence in 1783. The French King was executed by the representatives of his people in 1793. It was the Marquis de Lafayette, the most famous of the French volunteers who fought with the Americans during their revolution, who led the Parisian national guard which took the French royal family from Versailles to Paris in 1789, forcing them to leave but saving their lives from the mob whose actions they anticipated. 'There goes Cromwell', muttered one courtier at Versailles when Lafayette entered the palace on his way to meet with the king. 'Cromwell' Lafayette answered back, 'would not have come unarmed.'[2] The incident illustrated just how much British, or perhaps merely English, history the French political nation had in mind as its own polity unravelled in 1789 and after. The ideas and issues implicit in the American Revolution and its English predecessor were not stopped by the Channel or by a linguistic frontier. They had become part of European history and culture generally.

Empire and freedom, or in more conventional eighteenth-century language, property and liberty: these were the two crucial issues at stake in the American Revolution and the creation of the second British Empire. While it is true that Americans drew on a powerful tradition of English Protestant dissent in their rejection of British imperial authority, nevertheless the importance of their war for empire lay in the very material question of who would benefit from the economic development of the North American continent. Alexander Hamilton stated it in the first Federalist essay in support of a centralised American government, as an issue concerning 'the fate of an empire, in many respects, the most interesting in the world'.[3] When Hamilton wrote of empire, it was an American rather than a British one he had in mind. His remarks had been anticipated by those in a letter from Benjamin Franklin to the Scottish judge Lord Kames in 1767, in which he commented on the idea of an incorporating union between America and Britain:

> Scotland and Ireland are differently circumstanced. Confined by the sea, they can scarcely increase in numbers, wealth and strength, so as to overbalance England. But America, an immense territory, favoured by Nature with all advantages of climate, soil, great navigable rivers, and lakes, must become a great country, populous and mighty; and will, in a less time than is generally conceived, be able to shake off any shackles that may be imposed on her, and perhaps place them on the imposers.[4]

English writers such as Josiah Tucker came to very similar conclusions at the time conflict actually broke out between the colonies and Britain, and argued that no attempt to retain the American Empire should be made, lest in future Britain itself be rendered insignificant by the scale and wealth of its colonies.[5]

Out of the materialism basic in Franklin's observations arose the idealistic common-sense assertion of the rights of man and the idea of a democratic society and a democratic state, in which the spiritual egalitarianism of English, Scottish or other British Protestant religious dissent would be translated into an immediate doctrine of the liberty to pursue the accumulation of property equally. It was this which Tom Paine expressed in 1776 when he published *Common Sense*, with its identification of 'the cause of America' as 'in a great measure the cause of all mankind'. American working people never accepted the classical republican ideology of the gentry, or at least that part of it that asserted that commerce was corrupt, but artisans were quick to see that taxation on their small-scale commerce could only benefit the elite.[6] American revolutionary ideology might seek ways to limit extremities of wealth, but only to ensure that more people had the opportunity to accumulate it, as seen, for example, in the pamphlet literature published in Philadelphia in 1775.[7] This was classic Jeffersonian republicanism as it developed as an ideology after 1783.

Despite this important international, universalist aspect to the American Revolution, it also obviously involved conflict over the issue of what Britain would become, partly in terms of empire, and partly in terms of geographical area, as Benjamin Franklin made clear in his journalism before 1775. The exchange between Franklin and Kames quoted above was also significant in that it involved American and Scottish Britons exchanging ideas about the state that were literally incomprehensible to those bound up in the traditional language of English liberty. Franklin elsewhere in his letter mentioned his love of Britain and did not entirely dismiss the idea of an incorporating union, an idea which would be advanced seriously in America as late as 1775 by Joseph Galloway of Pennsylvania during the First Continental Congress.[8] In terms of what Britain came to mean and came to be, the American Revolution was crucial, because it saw the exit of Americans such as Franklin to begin a process of reinvention as 'Americans', on a basis which was initially premised on race – only those who had been European could become American, although they did not have to be British – but which, eventually, through the crucible of another war fourscore and some years later, would be definitively expanded in a way which has not yet, at the end of the twentieth century, reached its limits.[9]

On the other hand, the Scots, during the war, would complete a process which had begun during the previous war with France from 1756 to 1763, a process which members of their political class termed 'completing the union'. The Scots would not just 'out English the English' during these years in which the Scottish Enlightenment reached its apogee, but would become more British than any other British nation, and become identified as a nation particularly important in the military, administrative and emigrant elements of the Empire.[10] As would become apparent by the end of the century, only some Scots included themselves in this equation, and they were disproportionately drawn from 'the people above' and the professional classes left to man the parish pump – or pulpit – in the wake of the departure of the wealthier nobility for the more affluent parts of England.[11] There were others, such as the volunteer Peter Laurie, discussed by Linda Colley, or James Watt the engineer, as discussed by Gerald Newman, but it is important to remember that, although Scots came to be associated with Stuart despotism and loyalty to the monarchy during the American Revolution (all but three of the Scottish counties sent loyal addresses to the King, as did the majority of parliamentary burghs), this was a perception of the Scots adopted chiefly by Americans and their sympathisers in England.[12] It was rooted in English dislike, indeed hatred, for the foreign intrusion to England represented by the brief political success of the third Earl of Bute, and the more sustained judicial eminence of Lord Mansfield as Chief Justice of the Court of King's Bench.[13]

There were a significant number of Scots who were sympathetic to the American cause, but very few of them were from the Scottish elite. Rather, they were largely from the Presbyterian community of the Scottish Lowlands from which John Witherspoon and James Wilson had emigrated to America to become prominent in the American cause. John Erskine, one of the ministers of Edinburgh, published a pamphlet in 1769 under the title 'Shall I go to war with my American Brethren?' It was republished in 1776 to coincide with the publication of other pamphlets by Erskine on the American conflict.[14] Profoundly sympathetic to the predicament of a provincial community when faced with expanding and intrusive metropolitan power, Erskine's publications were only an indication of much wider Scottish Presbyterian sympathy for the American cause. There were others in Edinburgh, probably drawing on the same Presbyterian traditions, who saw an analogy in American activity and their own attempts to broaden the base of political activity in the city. Representatives of the artisan community in Edinburgh, determined to assert their independence of burgh oligarchy, met in a 'Congress' in 1777, after the outbreak of war in America. Members of the Congress adopted the names of American patriots. Charles Dallas of the Wrights called himself Samuel Adams, Peter Bowie became John Hancock, and a merchant named James Stodart was referred to as George Washington. A pamphlet appeared in Edinburgh under the title 'Common Sense', although its moderate contents would hardly have earned the approval of Thomas Paine. Later, in 1781, the politician who served as the city's MP was eulogised by the Lord Provost of Edinburgh as 'the man who established our independence'.[15]

To artisans and tenant farmers, and even in some cases journeymen craftsmen and literate farmworkers, events in America raised new possibilities. Gwyn Williams wrote that 'politics in Wales began with the American Revolution', meaning specifically that the first political text to find its way into the Welsh language was a pamphlet on the American Question.[16] In England the radical John Cartwright, drawing on the tradition of the English Civil War, published a pamphlet on political rights under the title 'Take your Choice!', which advocated universal manhood suffrage and denied the hereditary principle.[17] Its outlook, and those of the many other publications published in sympathy with the American cause, indicate a readership interested in politics which was very different from those who were intended to read Adam Smith's *Wealth of Nations*, published, like Cartwright's pamphlet, in 1776, but in an expensive quarto edition priced beyond the means of most of the population. Thus although religion was still dominant in political questions, there was an element of social divisiveness arising in both Britain and America during the 1770s, well illustrated by the episode reported in one of the trials that followed the otherwise sectarian Gordon Riots in London of 1780. George Rudé noticed testimony before one of the quarter-sessions concerning a barge builder in East Lane, Bermondsey who, upon being told at one point during the riots that the house he was threatening to pull down was not owned by a Papist, replied that 'Protestant or not, no gentleman need be possessed of more than £1,000 a year, that is enough for any gentleman to live upon', and proceeded with the attack upon the dwelling of what was a too obviously prosperous, albeit Protestant, iron manufacturer.[18] This single exchange can be related to the debate over the 'moral economy'. Edward Thompson discerned in the grain riots of the eighteenth century he studied, and the debate over inflation in wartime Philadelphia examined by Gary Nash. Political economy, or 'police', as it was sometimes referred to in a more neutral way during the eighteenth century, was not the sole preserve of the landed elite in either Britain or America.[19]

Thus the effect of the American Revolution on British political thinking was to undermine the idea of virtual representation in such a way that British politics would never be the same again. The American precedent set an example for both the radical and reform movements which emerged so strongly at the time of the French Revolution, and which would continue to dominate the political agenda after the war with France finally ended in 1815. Acceptance of the idea of virtual representation depended on a sense of community which encompassed those who did not participate in the political process. Although there were politics of protest before the American Revolution in various parts of Britain which demonstrated fully that there were those who did not feel represented by the political regime, the American revolt occurred in an atmosphere of domestic political crisis in which the radical Wilkite politics of the 1760s and 1770s, the American resistance to political authority, and the economic difficulties which led to widespread grain riots and emigration, were all part of a single crisis which affected America and Britain equally as part of the same polity and essentially the same society.[20] To many Englishmen, the government appeared to be 'systematically establishing despotic control in America as a preliminary stage in its long-range plan for imposing an authoritarian regime in Britain. Once this initial object had been achieved, it would exploit America as a source of patronage and as a base from which further attacks could be made on the constitution at home.'[21] In harbouring these fears, English radical Whigs in the eighteenth century feared the monarchy's policy in America in much the same manner that their seventeenth-century predecessors had viewed the activity of Tyrconnell and the government of James II in Ireland between 1685 and 1689. Once a politically conscious class perceived the British Parliament as serving interests which were directed at extending control over them rather than representing them, and extension of tax certainly could be perceived in this manner, then virtual representation was a dead concept amongst all but 'the people above'. It would take the French Revolution and a new kind of external threat to revive it. Americans ceased to think of themselves as Englishmen, as many of them would put it, because they did not want to become part of an incorporating 'British' empire or kingdom.[22]

From the perspective of the landed elite, political radicalism and rioting in England, Protestant unrest in Ireland and Scotland, unprecedented levels of emigration from all three kingdoms in the years leading up to its forcible cessation in 1776, and the economic difficulties of the times, all led to a sense of acute crisis which threatened the very basis of civil society. One issue which appeared to demonstrate this to politicians more than any other was the sectarian one of Catholic Relief. It is difficult for a secular radical of any age – and there were already some active in the eighteenth century – to understand or admit that those who believed in the rights of true Englishmen, in liberty and property, and who were sympathetic to the idea of a national right to the pursuit of property and happiness, would simultaneously refuse to see Roman Catholics as human beings entitled to the basic right to worship freely as their conscience directed them, let along aspire to equality under the law and access to political rights.[23] Here the sectarianism of the past did indeed intersect with the radical critique of the regime which was emerging in urban centres all over Britain and America. This was partly at the centre of the American resistance to British authority when it became clear that the government in 1774, with its Quebec Act, intended to tolerate and recognise the religion, language and culture of the French colonists who had become British subjects. In addition, of course, by annexing the Ohio River Valley to Quebec rather than the several existing British colonies to the east, the British government was restating the policy adopted at the time of the Peace of Paris in 1763, despite subsequent concessions, of attempting to limit and control westward expansion of the largely English-speaking settler population, larger by far than the French of Quebec or all the Indian tribes put together. And, of course, American colonists might with some justification fear that the non-representative nature of the government proposed for Quebec would extend the power of the Crown. This was not just the fear in America. In Parliament 'many opposition speakers greeted with incredulity... assertions that the Canadians did not desire an elected assembly or trials by jury in civil cases'.[24] The governor who reported this to the ministry, it was asserted, had been seduced by the absolutist ways of the French in which he had become enmeshed after taking up his post.

Much of the opposition in England to the government's American policy was provincial and regional, and much of it involved dissenters from the state Church. 'The dissenting interest' meant that politically conscious opinion in England was divided over the American war to an extent which has in the past often been underestimated.[25] From the perspective of 'dissent', the Americans were defending liberties hard won for all Englishmen during the Civil Wars and Commonwealth, while the government, with its purportedly Scottish influence, favoured Catholics in Quebec and Ireland as well as native American savages in its imperial policy. Success in this policy would bode ill for the future of the dissenting community in England, and in Scotland and Ireland there were many Presbyterians who drew the same conclusion.

The explosion of popular dissent in the Gordon Riots in London in 1780 drew on this pro-American feeling, although the specific issue was emancipation of Catholics in England rather than what was happening in America. Catholic emancipation in England, however, was tied to the government's need for Catholic manpower to feed the American war effort. It was during the American war that large-scale enlistment of Irish Roman Catholic recruits occurred, despite the fact that it was illegal for Roman Catholics to serve in the army.[26] We have seen how intense feeling had been about Roman Catholics in the army of James II and VII, his use of Irish soldiers, and the use to which he was suspected of intending to put them. This historical memory was part of the dissenting tradition, but it was also part of the historical memory of 1688 as a political rather than a sectarian event, and part of the justification upon which the new political regime had been erected. The Gordon Riots, spectacularly violent as they were, were not the only expression of opposition to Catholic emancipation in Britain. They had been preceded in Scotland by outbreaks of a similar nature which had defeated the efforts of the chief law officer of the Crown in Scotland, the Lord Advocate, to contain them. That Lord Advocate was Henry Dundas, perhaps the most vilified, and successful, political manager in Scottish politics of the eighteenth century. No matter what his political skills at management, he was unable to contain popular violence against the idea of religious toleration for Roman Catholics, and he had to convince the government that it was impossible to bring forward a bill for Scotland. The population would not accept it, and had demonstrated the extent of its reaction through both organised political activity and serious rioting in Glasgow and Edinburgh. In Edinburgh Dundas's former teacher and Principal of the University of Edinburgh, William Robertson, the most prominent and influential Church of Scotland minister of his generation, received death threats on account of his support for Roman Catholic Relief, one of which reminded him of the fate of Archbishop Sharp, the head of the Restoration Church of Scotland assassinated by Presbyterian zealots in 1679. In the event violence was wreaked on his house in George Square in the area south of the burgh, which was sacked by the mob. A shaken Robertson had taken his family to seek refuge in Edinburgh Castle, and never returned to an important role in affairs of the Scots Church. Nor did he regain that confidence in public activity which had made him a leading figure of the Scottish Enlightenment. The house and library of the Roman Catholic Bishop of Edinburgh in the centre of the town was also sacked. James Boswell was an eye-witness. 'It hurt me to see a large book, perhaps some venerable manuscript, come flaming out at one of the windows. One of the mob cried, "They" (i.e., the papists) "burnt us. We'll burn them." Another cried, "Think what they did to our worthy forefathers."[27] He returned home to find his child's Italian music teacher hiding in his house for fear of the mob.

It was parliamentary discussion of proposed compensation to Catholics whose property had been damaged during the Scottish riots which had first given Lord George Gordon a chance to put himself at the head of opposition to Roman Catholic Relief, attacking Henry Dundas and ironically asking ministers in the House of Commons if the government intended to send troops to subdue the Scots as it had done against the Americans.[28] In Scotland John Erskine, author of 'Shall I go to War with my American brother?', was opposed to violence against Catholics, but published an account of the General Assembly of the Church of Scotland debate over Roman Catholic Relief. He counted 356 separate petitions or resolutions against the proposal in Scotland. An elaborate publication appeared in Edinburgh in 1780 which collected as many of these declarations as the editors could gather, probably through the efforts of 'the Edinburgh Friends of the Protestant Interest', and several elaborately bound copies were sent to Lord George Gordon in London.[29] Defeat of Catholic Relief led those who had opposed it to make another attempt to pass a resolution in the General Assembly in Scotland against the right of the Crown or landowners to present ministers to parishes. Thus, although Scotland was perceived in England as an area where support for the war was particularly strong, Catholic Relief was defeated, despite its purpose as a device to help raise Roman Catholic troops in the Scottish Highlands there for the American war. Military recruitment generally in Scotland was poor during the war. There was no shortage of Scottish officers willing to fight the Americans, but a distinct lack of enthusiasm amongst those who might have been enlisted as ordinary soldiers.[30] Opposition against Roman Catholic relief was not presented as opposition to the war, but it certainly drew on anti-government feeling there which was radical as well as sectarian.

In Ireland the idea of Roman Catholic Relief of course carried more resonance than elsewhere in the British kingdoms, given that it involved the great majority of the population. In addition it coincided with the efflorescence of Protestant Irish nationalism, which drew on the analogy of the American Congress in advocating complete legislative devolution for Ireland within the Empire. Lord Midleton, an Irish peer, wrote to an English correspondent from Cork in 1775 that 'we are all Americans here except such as are attached securely to the castle or are papists'.[31] He was right. It is interesting, however, that neither he nor the historian who quoted him so approvingly mentioned that the phrase 'we are all' indicated, at most, 30 per cent of the population of Ireland in contrast to the 70 per cent or more who in religion were 'Papist'. It was the leaders of this community, self-made men like John Keogh, who had acquired wealth and some social status associated with wealth as the Irish economy began to grow during the eighteenth century, who took the opportunity of the war to approach the British government and advance the case of the Roman Catholic population of Ireland as loyal subjects of the Crown who deserved relief from at least some of the laws which limited their rights to practise their religion.[32] It was the Irish Roman Catholic community which had first encouraged the North ministry to think of Roman Catholic relief as a means of expanding military recruitment in Ireland.[33] Such legislation in a British context as opposed to a strictly Irish one would be less contentious, or so the North ministry thought, and could be presented as a general enlightened measure in favour of toleration rather than as a device to expedite recruitment for an imperial war.

The prospect of increased numbers of Roman Catholics in the army, when legally there should not have been any at all, alarmed Irish Protestants and increased their sympathy for the American cause. When an administration supporter in the Irish House of Commons argued that enlistment of Roman Catholics for the army meant that 'it was better to export papists than Protestants', another MP replied that 'if papists were trained as soldiers they would be the more dangerous'.[34] There are clear parallels with the mentality of the West Indian slave-owning elite towards their slaves during the same period.[35] Others saw the issue in more constitutional terms. It was impossible, argued some Irish Protestant MPs (all Irish MPs were Protestants, as Catholics were forbidden under the penal laws to sit in Parliament), to agree that America was in rebellion without accepting that the British Parliament had the right to vote taxes on Ireland. Charles Lucas, an MP whose radical credentials went back to the 1740s, warned other MPs that by supporting a British war on the American colonies, 'you are putting a sword in the hands of the British minister which when he has got, he will cut the throats of your American brethren and when that is done, he will turn it against ourselves'.[36]

As the war progressed, and particularly after it broadened to a war with France and Spain as well as the American colonies, the Irish Parliament became more assertive in advancing its rights to independence of action, emboldened by the absence of government troops all sent away to fight the war. This general confidence owed much to the raising of semi-private 'volunteer' regiments amongst the Protestant community that personified the independent military capacity of the Irish Protestants, particularly in Ulster and Leinster, and particularly visible in Belfast and Dublin. Burdened by a war which was going badly, increasingly convinced that the Irish Protestant community and its volunteers just might rebel, the North ministry conceded substantial economic concessions to Ireland in 1780. There was even some talk of a union. On both sides of the Irish Sea, Ireland's importance to the Empire was proclaimed. The Duke of Richmond gave a speech in the British House of Lords in which he declared that 'all local distinctions were creatures of prejudice... Ireland and England were in fact the same nation and people', yet by 'same nation', which Ireland did he mean?[37]

This was the 'parliament of Grattan', as Henry Grattan led the Irish Protestants to assert their identity and their nationhood within the Empire, modelling his political conduct on Chatham and his policy, if policy is what we can call an assertion of national identity. In this vision there was a place, it seemed, for all Irishmen, even the 70 per cent who were Catholics. It was never said, however, in the fluent and inspiring speeches of Grattan to his Protestant fellow MPs, that what was being asserted was that there was a place in Ireland for the many only if they knew what their place was to be, and that place was not to be in the parliament chambers on St Stephen's Green or the glittering, enlightened, polite society of Georgian Dublin. 'Liberty', said Grattan, 'is a native of the north, translated into the south and now flourishing in every part of the kingdom.'[38] When he stated that liberty was a native of the North, he meant that its origins in Ireland were in 1688, in the defence of Londonderry and Enniskillen, and that from these acorns of resistance to Stuart despotism a native Irish constitutional oak had grown. He was adamant that Irish nationality was rooted in British (and really English) history, just as the American colonists were defending traditional English liberties in a new world against a ministerial government diverted by the distractions of imperial administration. Only in the provinces of the Empire had the libertarian freedom at the root of the 1688 Constitution been preserved, and only provincial assemblies like those of the Americans or the Irish Parliament could preserve these liberties from a ministry and crown which could so easily corrupt an imperial parliament in London. 'This nation', Grattan declared, 'is connected with

England not only by allegiance to the crown but by liberty – the crown is one great point of unity, but Magna Charta is greater – we could get a king anywhere but England is the only country from which we could get a constitution.'[39]

When the British Parliament repealed the so-called Irish Declaratory Act of 1720, passed in the reign of George I to assert the right of the English Parliament to legislate for Ireland, the Irish House of Commons responded by voting an address which asserted its determination as a legislature 'to stand or fall with the British nation' – and then voted authorisation of £100,000 towards raising men for the navy, and empowered the government to withdraw 5000 troops from Ireland for general service.[40] Given the general euphoria in Ireland on the great strides its Parliament was taking in acquiring an independent role in Irish affairs, Catholic Irish expectations of relief were justifiably high. Henry Grattan had, after all, referred to Ireland as one nation, albeit an Anglicised one. 'We are free, we are united, persecution is dead,' he declared, 'the Protestant religion is the child of the constitution – the Presbyterian is the father – the Roman Catholic is not an enemy to it.'[41] This, however, was a device to win the last bit of freedom for the Irish Parliament from England by securing repeal of the Declaratory Act and renunciation by the British of any right to legislate for Ireland. 'The opposition of the patriots [to Catholic Relief] in 1778 could be represented as a refusal to accept dictation from England;' Maureen Wall has observed, 'but support for Catholic relief in 1782 was to be used to demonstrate to England that the whole population of Ireland, irrespective of creed, was united behind the demand for an independent parliament.'[42] Grattan and Charlemont (one of the most eminent of the leaders of the military 'volunteer' movement) carefully planned the Dungannon assembly of volunteers to include the resolution 'that as men and as Irish men, as Christians and as Protestants, we rejoice in the relaxation of the penal laws against our Roman Catholic fellow-subjects, and that we conceive the measure to be fraught with the happiest consequences to the union and prosperity of the inhabitants of Ireland'.[43] Yet Grattan never intended to give equal political rights to Catholics in Ireland. He believed in English liberty and Magna Carta, he believed in the Church of Ireland, he believed in reason and enlightenment, and he believed in extending religious toleration to the Roman Catholic population of Ireland until such time as they were assimilated to the culture and civilisation of the Protestant Ascendancy. He no doubt believed that the inherently superior culture whose politics he represented would eventually incorporate the enthusiasm of Protestant dissent as well.

Thus Irish Catholics obtained substantial concessions as part of their inclusion in the programme for Irish legislative devolution. The Catholic elite recovered their property rights and the Catholic Church was allowed to embark on a programme of Church and school building which expanded its influence and presence as an institution in Irish life. Catholics 'were expected to make an immediate return by providing recruits for the armed forces', which of course were British, not Irish.[44] The £100 000 voted by the Irish Parliament for the war effort after British repeal of the Irish Declaratory Act was meant to enable the navy to enlist 20 000 seamen in Ireland. The expectation was that these men would be recruited from the Catholic population. They certainly were not going to come from the elite regiments of largely Protestant 'volunteers'. Like the Scots before them during the Seven Years War, Ireland became a reserve of manpower for the imperial army and navy during the war from 1775 to 1783, a war which, of course, was not just with the Congress of the American Colonies, but with the monarchies of France and Spain as well. It was a sign of things to come. John Pocock has commented that 'a North Briton was a Scotsman committed to a restatement of English culture in such terms that it would become British and that Scotsmen would make their own way in it'.[45] The same might be said of Henry Grattan and the Protestant country Whigs of Ireland in their desire to become 'West Britons' through inclusion in British political culture.[46]

Like the Scots before them, once the idea of a Protestant, libertarian, commercial and propertied Britain was embraced, the next rational step for those within the circle was incorporation with the metroplitan model for their polity.

9

WAR AND THE NATION, 1793–1815: BRITISH IDENTITY AND THE NEW EMPIRE

There is a division in the historiography of Britain during the long period of warfare and conflict with revolutionary France between 1793 and the final end of war in Europe with the Allied victory over Napoleon at Waterloo in 1815. On the one hand there are histories of the British state, celebrating its survival during long years of defeat at the hands of the French, as well as ultimate victory and security in status as a dominant European power in a 'Concert of Europe' founded at the Congress of Vienna. These were also years in which Britain acquired a substantial overseas empire which, as with that won in 1763, made Great Britain truly a world power. On the other hand, from a domestic perspective, success abroad masked civil division within, both between the traditional ruling class and a new emerging group of people with a political consciousness who were of artisan and middle-class background, although of course the language of class did not yet exist. The issue here was the rights of man as enshrined in the words of Thomas Paine. There have been relatively few attempts by historians to relate each of these perspectives to the other.

There was also another level of division within Britain, which was of course national, in that the experience of

Ireland in particular was different in this period, as it was in all other periods of 'British' history. Indeed, it is only with the Union of the Irish and the British Parliaments in 1801 that Ireland could in any formal sense be considered British, which indeed was the point of the Irish Union: to neutralise and incorporate Ireland in 1801 as effectively as Scotland appeared to have been incorporated in the British state over the course of the eighteenth century.[1] There were significant differences in the Welsh and Scottish experience of these years as well, complicated by social and regional conflicts within each nation. One could also argue that the English experience was not just one of class and political conflict, but also of region in relation to what the British state was coming to represent, which is a theme that will be explored in the final chapter of this book.

Let us start by considering the success of the state, at one time the subject of popular literature in the form of Arthur Bryant's histories, which struck such a chord with a British reading public who had immediate experience of the setbacks and seemingly ultimate success of the Second World War. Ronald Hutton has remarked how the word 'England' in Bryant's books is employed with all the talismanic force of a mantra.[2] Later historians became preoccupied with Parliament and political process, perhaps because it seemed that enough history had been written of foreign policy and Empire. At the end of the twentieth century historians have returned to Britain's experience of war and empire and reunited the domestic history of these years with the history of the state and the Empire. Patrick O'Brien's work on state finance, for example, has brought the history of the state and the state's success in financing war back to the centre of historiographical concern for this period. In doing so he has revived some of the points made by generations of admirers of the Younger Pitt. Pitt may have dropped his early interest in Reform and stooped to repression in his dealings with those who advocated an extension of the franchise, but he succeeded triumphantly in the arcane field of tax reform – hardly an area likely to attract popular fervour and support. Certainly, Britain's ability to finance more than twenty years of war against France was not solely due to Pitt's financial genius. It owed much to the coincidence of the existence of a financial class with long experience of raising loans and making money out of government expenditure, and a government that could draw on equally long experience of using their services. O'Brien considers Pitt 'the greatest Chancellor of the age', but emphasises that it was not so much Pitt's genius as the threat to private property (and public credit) posed by revolutionary France which persuaded Parliament to translate into law 'their oft-proclaimed principle that Englishmen should contribute to the needs of the state in accordance with their ability to pay'.[3] The expense of the war with France was colossal, and Pitt had to depart from traditional British government financial practice, in areas additional to his creation of an income tax, as part of the extraordinary effort he made to devise means to finance continuous struggle with France[4] – an effort which quite literally killed him. From 1798, if not before, the war with France was fought with revenue raised from taxes as opposed to borrowed money. This in itself marked a departure from the government financial policies chronicled by Dickson and Brewer. There was a shift off the gold standard as well, and, despite the danger of inflation, the economy continued to grow and respond to the demands of war, with beneficial effects for farmers, industrialists and international merchants. The move off the gold standard also helped the government and its associated financial system meet 'additional demands for liquidity occasioned by bad harvests or the exigencies of commercial warfare and enemy blockades'.[5] It is clear that the Napoleonic war years marked the apogee of the state financial system which had begun with the wars against the French state of Louis XIV, and that this achievement, rather than the famous battles of the Nile, Trafalgar and Waterloo, made ultimate victory over France possible. The postwar depression was rooted in the failures of the Liverpool administration to manage the move from a wartime economy after more than two decades of growth, but postwar failure should not obscure what the creation of that wartime economy had accomplished, which was really the successful prevention of a military dictatorship not just in France but over all of Europe, rather than defeat of the French Revolution itself. As Linda Colley has pointed out, no one, in Britain at least, idealised Napoleon as the songbird of liberty until he was safely put away on St Helena.[6]

Another product of the long struggle with France, however, was consolidation of the British financial state on an imperial basis. This is most obvious in relation to India, but there were also developments in the West Indies, where the military campaigns of the 1790s were orchestrated from London by Henry Dundas as Pitt's Secretary of State for War. Dogged by persistent setbacks and high mortality, they would appear to represent just as much a failure as contemporary British military efforts in Holland, but these costly campaigns enabled Britain to retain, and indeed to dominate, control of the lucrative West Indian trade with Europe. British trade expanded during the wars with France, and the West Indian trade in sugar, coffee and cotton was important to this expansion.[7] Britain's efforts to keep the neutral Americans from sharing in the financial gain implicit in the end of continental Europe's direct access to the West Indies would eventually cause the 1812–15 revival of war between the Americans and the British.

The British war effort and the British state increased in strength because of its efforts in the West Indies. First, income from taxation rose. How did this development relate to the West Indies? Sugar taxes went up under Pitt, and the new income tax of 1799 made it possible to tap the wealth made from colonial trade, so theoretically domestic taxation was drawing upon essentially colonial wealth. Second, the 'Caribbean-led trade boom' helped boost government credit. If the British had lost their West Indian trade, they would have lost the ability to sustain their credit on the London financial markets. The success of the British expeditions to the West Indies in maintaining British superiority there, although it came at the cost of a military mortality rate which could only be described as catastrophic, 'enabled Pitt to ride out the financial crisis which his high borrowing had helped cause in 1797'. This survival enabled the government to borrow even more between 1798 and 1802, 'and to do so on less disadvantageous terms'.[8] Government credit expanded on the back of commercial security. This was commercial security built on secure overseas trade with the West Indies, but it also came on the backs of the tens of thousands of dead British soldiers and sailors whose lives were lost in these campaigns.

While in many ways the remains of the first Empire were defended and consolidated in the West Indies, although at such a high cost, the creation of a new Britain was really taking place in India, where Britain had already recovered from setbacks suffered at the hands of the French between 1780 and 1783. From 1798 onwards, however, under the stimulus of Richard Wellesley and his successors as Governor-General, a genuinely new centre of British power would expand as inexorably over the Indian subcontinent as the might of Napoleonic France extended over all continental Europe. Christopher Bayly has synthesised his own work and that of many other scholars of British India to provide an overview of this period of British imperialism in India. The difference between the activities of the British state in India, complicated as it was by its relationship to the East India Company, and its activities in the Western hemisphere, was that after the renewal of the struggle with a new kind of French polity in 1793 there began what Bayly has called 'a heightened sense of national mission' and 'a new emphasis on the legitimacy of British authority in India' which was part of the sense of struggle for national survival implicit in these wars.[9] They were national in the sense that the elite which dominated the British state could see clearly that its existence was at stake and that there was a real possibility that the order established in 1688, based on an equipoise of landed and financial wealth, could be overwhelmed. Thus the maintenance of commercial hegemony in the East Indies was seen as being as vital for the survival of the state as preservation of older interests in the West Indies. In the event, success in the East would obscure the failures in the West and compensate for what became in effect the lost continent of Europe, by creating an Asiatic continental Empire dominated by the British state and administered in its interests, and larger in scale than Europe itself.

The emphasis on the legitimacy of the British rule in India was a means of reinforcing permanent status in a period of uncertainty and defeat. Richard Wellesley, Lord Mornington, as Governor-General in India, strove to attach 'an uncompromisingly regal status' to his office as agent of the monarch of Great Britain. There was also an appeal to the Indian tradition of Mughal sovereignty adapted to the needs of finding a way to place increasing British authority over the continent. Most Indian rulers had in history owed allegiance to a Mughal emperor who could be represented as giving way to a new overlord in the person of the British monarch. Indian local rulers, nawabs, nizams and others, could be accommodated by importing a British schema of the allegiance of country gentry to central monarchical authority, in which Indian rulers did not share sovereignty but were subject to it.[10] In addition, it was a model of government which, in fact, conceded much autonomy in administration and police to local landowners. Wellesley emphasised that Britain was in India by right of conquest. Its expansion was justified by its military success, and the size of the East India armies during the French Revolutionary and Napoleonic wars more than doubled in size, from 90 000 soldiers to more than 200 000. Did Wellesley's origins as an Irish Protestant landowner influence his outlook, policy and emphasis on the right of conquest as its justification for imperial policy? The connection cannot be directly established, but intriguing similarities in approach can be detected. Although Wellesley was successful in expanding British influence in India during his years there, he was not successful in reducing its cost or the debt necessary to pay for it, which contributed to what

Bayly terms 'the harder edge of British empire-building after 1798', as a solution to these pressures was sought in further expansion.[11] This was a development not unlike that affecting the parallel European continental expansionism of the militarily successful Napoleonic state, which had its own financial problems.

Thus the basis of British expansionism in India was an incorporating policy which drew on British precedent. Tipu Sultan of Mysore headed resistance to the British by refusing to be drawn into the British network of subsidiary alliances in which Indian rulers promised some of their revenue to pay for East India Company troops to support their authority. Tipu sought to pay for his own army. He also declared himself an emperor in his own right rather than trying to place himself within the authority of the old Mughal emperor, thus countering British claims to succeed Mughal absolute sovereignty, as well as rejecting any claim for overlordship on the part of the British Crown.

Were there similarities between previous English attitudes towards subordinate monarchies in Britain? There was a ruthless imposition of the 'rule of law', the assertion of the paramount status of the British, and the sanctity of regular payments of revenue to British authorities, but on the other hand there were real limits to how much beyond this the British could choose to go. 'The British needed magnate intermediaries', Bayly has argued, 'to collect the revenue and keep the peace', especially after the East India Company's finances became mired in debt after 1800.[12] The political culture of the British encouraged them 'to leave in place a neutered form of Indian kingship' once the paramount position of the East India Company was firmly established. 'Out of this ambivalence the British fashioned their policy towards princely states and rural magnates.' Utter subjection and conquest on a Cromwellian model did not mark British policy in India, in other words, rather there was an attempt to co-opt local elites to achieve a stable political system within which commercial profit on advantageous terms could be pursued.

Thus the 'Second British Empire' had been created in the crucible of war, revolt and the international ideological challenge of Republican France.[13] As noted above, the sense of wonder at what had been won parallels in many ways the sentiments expressed in the writings of some of the British elite after the Peace of Paris in 1763. Patrick Colquhoun, in a treatise on the British Empire published in 1815, the year of the Peace, calculated that in 1750 the population of the British dominions, including the American colonies, had been 12.5 million persons at most. His calculation for the population of the British Empire in 1815 was 61 million. Christopher Bayly's analysis of Colquhoun's claims increases the estimate to approximately 200 million people under the authority of the British Empire by 1820; 'Certainly it must have represented about 26 per cent of the total world population'.[14] Why had it happened? Bayly's argument is that 'the British empire from 1780 to 1830 (and in some areas beyond) represented not simply a hiatus between irresistible waves of liberal reform, but a series of attempts to establish overseas despotisms which mirrored in many ways the politics of neo-absolutism and the Holy Alliance of contemporary Europe'.[15] It was an empire built upon the idea of a landed elite which incorporated a sense of 'racial subordination'. In establishing this empire the landed elites of England and Wales, Scotland and Ireland united not just in their patriotism but in their determination to support the survival of the state, and in so doing they created an intercontinental empire to oppose Napoleon's continental dominance in Europe. After 1815 possession of an absolutist empire gave the British state something in common with the absolutist European monarchies with whom it found itself in alliance, and with whom it shared an interest in preserving the status quo.

This empire was won by reinforcing the English landed class with soldiers, merchants and administrators of empire from the Irish Protestant community and the landed class of Scotland. 'The hard men of the peripheries' were brought in 'to the support of the [English] centre'.[16] Some contemporaries referred to a 'British Empire in Europe' in relation to the British Isles as a whole, harking back to an earlier idea of a British imperial crown which was English. From the time of the Union of 1707 there were Scottish landowners who called for 'compleating the Union'. This was now accomplished for the landed class of Scotland under the leadership of the Younger Pitt's chief lieutenant (or henchman, in the eyes of some), Henry Dundas of Melville, upon whose advice Pitt extended the principle of incorporating union to Ireland in 1801. Thus one can argue that a 'British imperial tradition which had been developed in Scotland and Ireland' would later be 'exported in modified form to the Cape, the Mediterranean and North America'.[17] From one perspective, the Irish equivalents of Dundas were Richard Wellesley and his brother Arthur, later Duke of Wellington, never as consummate as politicians as Dundas the Scottish lawyer, but military men who brought the military and the civil together in the style of imperial government they developed in India, which was another form of extension of state authority within Britain and Ireland into a larger ambit of operation.

There were ties between these Irish and Scottish elites, although never complete integration. Wellington denied his Irishness by stating that 'just because one was born in a stable didn't make one a horse', but Scottish border families had long had links with Ulster, as did many of the small landowners and tacksmen of Kintyre, Knapdale and adjacent islands in Argyll in the south-west Highlands.[18] The connection between the Dundas family of Scotland and that of the Irish Earl of Moira is an example. Moira served as Commander-in-Chief of the army in Scotland, and others of his family served in London and India.[19] Families like the Dundases and the Moiras, or the Elliots of Minto in the Scottish borders and the Stewarts of Castlereagh in Ulster, represented a continuation of the kind of British gentry nationalism which developed over the eighteenth century, originating in the wars against Louis XIV, consolidated in the war for empire from 1756 to 1763, and reaching its definition during the years of war with France after 1793. It drew on the cosmopolitanism of the Enlightenment, but by the end of the century became a vehicle for anglophone nationalism built on the idea that a culture which constructively employed the wealth created by commerce and finance represented not just modernity, but civilisation itself.

The culture of the landed elite in the widest sense became genuinely British by the beginning of the nineteenth century. Most of the gentry became 'polite and commercial' wherever their lands lay in Britain and Ireland, and as a result became the basis of a culture which represented a minority of people of landed wealth, professional status or commercial stature who came to perceive themselves as 'the nation', which in turn has encouraged the use of the term 'political nation' by historians writing about British parliamentary politics of the eighteenth century.[20] The gentry of Wales had, by the end of the eighteenth century, become Anglicised, even if they espoused a new kind of particularism within their Britishness which expressed a sense of being Welsh and being British too.[21] The gentry of Scotland reached their apotheosis of Britishness during the French wars, with Sir Walter Scott as the amanuensis of their sense of history and their new identity. It was an identity which represented a continuation of the Scottish Enlightenment, but with more of a legal and political (and conservative) edge to it than the prevailing academic and clerical ethos that had preceded it. Its militarism helped Scott romanticise Scottish history in the light of later British imperial success.[22]

The period of the French wars, of course, was an epoch in which the Protestant nation of Ireland saw its dreams of Irishness dashed upon the rocks of revolution and sectarianism. The Ascendancy imploded into political union with Great Britain as a talisman of its historical identity and indeed, its hopes for survival as a distinctive community and culture. By 1815 the gamble must have seemed worth it. Britain emerged triumphant, with an Anglo-Irishman at the head of the allied army that defeated Napoleon and one of the architects of the Irish Union, Castlereagh, constructing a Concert of Europe at Vienna to safeguard the old European Order forever. If the idea had a limited history, it may still be said to have had its time for the people who embraced it, many with genuine reluctance, in 1801. It must be remembered that much of the manpower which was mobilised to fight the Napoleonic wars for Britain was not only Irish but Irish Catholic. As Bayly has noted, 'as the need for manpower increased after 1787, all regiments were allowed to recruit in Ireland and after 1793 Catholics were allowed to take lower commissions in the British army'. By 1780 there were three East India Company recruiting stations in Ireland, two drawing from the south and central areas of the country. In 1815 as much as 50 per cent of all the military forces of the British Crown may have been Irish in origin.[23]

This was reflected in the approach of post-union Irish government to the majority of the population and to Irish nationalism. Wellesley in Ireland tried to work towards Catholic Emancipation, as Pitt and Dundas had done in their move for incorporating union, although this they had to postpone due to the determination of the King, who refused to be persuaded by Dundas's arguments, and thus shared an identity of purpose with the rioters of 1778–80 against Roman Catholic Relief. The idea was to persuade the Catholic gentry and merchant classes 'into the imperial project'.[24] Irish Protestant interest in ancient Celtic Ireland as part of a shared Irish history which both Catholic and Protestant could claim became part of this endeavour. The nature of the Irish landowning class as essentially alien to the peasantry set it apart and did make it 'colonial' in a way that other landed elites in Britain were not. Perhaps in that sense Ireland in the eighteenth century was indeed more an Atlantic colony than a part of a Britain that included Wales, Scotland and England, let alone really a part of ancien-régime Europe.[25] Much depends on whether to emphasise class or ethnicity. If class; a landowner is a landowner is a landowner, and an Irish one is not very different from any other.[26] If ethnicity, or if sectarian, the Irish landowners could not claim community with those who lived on their land in the same way that a Welsh gentleman, Scots laird or English squire could.[27] In this bleak equation, Celticism came to obscure rather than qualify such loyalties and identities, and the debate over its relevance was gentry-dominated.

The question which Linda Colley successfully raised in her book *Britons* was the extent to which it is possible to look beyond the emerging sense of Britishness among the gentry and consider British patriotism in a popular sense. Indeed, such patriotism became an aspect of popular culture in the early nineteenth century which had not found its way into the charismatic image of a people, and a popular culture created by modern social historians anxious to recover a people's history divorced from the history of the British state.[28] First, there is the phenomenon of popular royalism. How was it that George III ceased to be the hostile proponent of the royal prerogative and the butt of American and English Wilkite hostility and became, almost literally concurrently, both the personification of a paternalistic and beneficent squire, and a John Bull-like figure who became one of a number of important symbols of British patriotism? George III represented a patrician class which successfully reinvented itself between 1763 and 1815, overcoming defeat in America and revolution in France by conceiving of a national public whose interests were served by the monarchy and the political nation.[29] Monarchy became symbolic of Britain as a conservative and imperial nation in which the individual liberties of the subject were safeguarded in a way possible neither in an absolutist monarchy or a revolutionary regime. While the Crown was not absolutist, its survival demonstrated the existence of strong bulwarks against the excesses of revolution. While Parliament was not democratic, its existence demonstrated the existence of strong bulwarks against the exercise of arbitrary power.

The new patriotic culture allowed a place for women in a popular sense that had not been available to them before, at least to such an extent. The Duchess of Devonshire became notorious amongst all classes for her activity in the Westminster election of 1784. By the time of the celebration of the peace of 1814 in Taunton, Somerset, the parade which marked the occasion featured the members of six female friendly societies.[30] Their active involvement in politics and ritual is in stark contrast to the traditional female role in popular protest, standing up to agents of authority, daring them to use violence against women in asserting their power, sometimes at considerable cost, as the [Scottish] women beaten up by English calvary at Ravensheugh in East Lothian found out to their cost in 1760.[31] Just as the age was moving towards the cult of domesticity, in which women were seen by moralistic writers as custodians of civilisation at home, untrammelled by the immediate demands of commerce and with the leisure to attend to the important task of educating children as future members of society, public patriotism offered women a way out of the private world which was closing in around them. It offered them access to part at least of public life and represents what is still a hidden history of the period, in which women campaigning for the emancipation of slaves realised just how constrained people of their gender had become in the midst of revolutionary change.[32]

Colley has also used the data on the vast militia and volunteer movement which arose in Britain to argue that the large numbers of men willing to fight proves the extent of popular British patriotism. The detailed returns submitted in response to the Defence of the Realm Act of 1798, compiled by constables and schoolmasters all over Britain, served as a rudimentary census of who was, and who was not, prepared to fight for Britain and the state in that most critical of years, 1798. To interpret them in this way is to accept, of course, that men would answer truthfully the constables and schoolmasters who confronted them with this question. The responses varied from region to region and from county to county. Insular counties like Norfolk responded less well than counties such as Kent, faced with an immediate threat. Industrialised and urbanised areas would be more aware of national questions and have a sense of external threat to the working of the national economy, although there was an exception. Yorkshire was a populous county where only 20 per cent of the population was willing to volunteer for possible service, and it was Yorkshire which provided much of the evidence for mass alienation during the Napoleonic Wars employed in Edward Thompson's *Making of the English Working Class*.[33]

Thompson's response to this point was to appeal to 'testimony', not of faith but of alienation throughout England during the war years, as available in legal evidence. He had to concede, however, that during the war against Napoleon, 'at any time between 1803 and about 1810 the Colley thesis is probably right', partly because of the betrayal of revolutionary principles by the Napoleonic regime as it turned itself into an empire and turned the last head of the first French Republic into an emperor.[34] In this respect, Thompson's critique of Colley's book revives the issue his own book raised thirty years before. Did the well-documented radicalism and opposition to the state all over Britain during the 1790s disappear absolutely after the renewal of war against France in 1803? Did those who enlisted in the cause of the British state against the empire of Napoleon turn their backs on the ideas of Tom Paine and the *Rights of Man*? When working people began again to support agitation for an extension of the political franchise after the conclusion of the peace at Vienna in 1815, had they forgotten all that had happened twenty years previously? Thompson argued that there was a tradition which was remembered and his argument that it need not contradict an analysis of British patriotism is convincing. There can be, he admitted, a sense of nation and a sense of different class. 'After all,' he wrote, 'English, Scottish and Welsh reformers and Chartists managed to work together, and the most prominent British Chartist leader, Fergus O'Connor, was an Irishman.'[35] 'There are times when the patriot must also be a revolutionary', Thompson also wrote, but it is important to remember that when British working people asserted their political rights after 1815, it was as Britons; as fellow members of a nation which had contributed to victory in a long and bloody war in partnership with rather than submissive to the propertied Englishmen whose lives and liberties they now wished to share. But when they did so, the empire which came about as a result of that war did not form part of their deliberations because it had not been what it became during the heady days of the *Rights of Man* in 1792. It is also important to remember that the limited political reform which came in 1832 came not just with Catholic Relief, but Catholic Emancipation in England and Wales, Scotland and Ireland. If political reform attracted working-class support in 1832, Catholic Emancipation did not, except amongst Irish Catholics wherever they were in Britain when it was enacted in 1829. Patriotism, class and sectarianism all continued to provide concurrent, if not always conflicting, loyalties in Britain after 1815.[36]

It is ironic that the 'success' of the French wars in integrating divergent nationalities and groups into the concept of a British nation came about in conflict with a centralised militaristic state which was the first in history to practise something like total mobilisation of its resources, even if it paled in comparison with the kind of mobilisation witnessed in the twentieth century. This centralisation within Britain became the basis for building a more permanent imperial order. It also became the basis for a racist ideology which in the Empire, particularly but not exclusively in India, mirrored domestic class tensions in Britain itself. More people were sharing in commercial culture. More people were Britons, but most people still were not. And what is more, there came to be a very tangible fear of those who were not Britons both in Britain and Ireland and in the Empire abroad. Henry Dundas, discussing the Scottish volunteer regiments of yeomanry with his friend the Duke of Buccleuch during the war, remarked that of course these regiments would remain embodied after the Peace, because they would be needed to maintain order amongst the population of the expanding industrial cities.[37] It was a prophecy of Peterloo. This was the terrible legacy of victory in the Napoleonic Wars, and it set the scene for the confrontation, conflict and aggression which marked much of the postwar period.

10

EMPIRE AND ITS DISCONTENTS: ENGLISH NATIONALISM AND THE IMPERIAL STATE

Nationalism in any guise is an elusive concept, but in the case of the English it is particularly difficult, as recent debate over the nature of the European Community has demonstrated. The tradition of imperial expansion in a British framework from the time of the Middle Ages has left the English identity blurred, and blurred in such a way that the majority of the population are unable to express their cultural identity in anything other than loyalty to an abstract state whose genuine interests coincide with those of only a very small minority of the population. Much of this situation is rooted in the national experience of war against Napoleonic France, which taught many people to be Britons, but the phenomenon of English patriotism being expressed in British terms is also part of what was learned by so many during those long years of war, and is perhaps now in most need of study.

There has been an enormous amount of very valuable research carried out over the past thirty years on the history of English and British radicalism, galvanised by the brilliance of Edward Thompson's book, *The Making of the English*

Working Class and later articles such as 'The Moral Economy of the English Crowd in the Eighteenth Century'. His work embodied a commitment to popular history and the value of the history of working people which still exerts a power all its own over many readers. His perspective was adamantly English, rooted in a deeply held belief in the integrity and autonomy of English cultural and national experience among the population as a whole that had little or nothing to do with the state and the Empire. Famously, in his preface to *The Making of the English Working Class*, he distanced himself as much from other British nationalities, working-class or not, in a manner which influenced the outlook of a generation of social historians:

> Finally, a note of apology to Scottish and Welsh readers. I have neglected these histories, not out of chauvinism, but out of respect. It is because class is a cultural as much as an economic formation that I have been cautious as to generalizing beyond English experience. (I have considered the Irish, not in Ireland, but as immigrants to England.) The Scottish record, in particular, is quite as dramatic, and as tormented, as our own. The Scottish Jacobin agitation was more intense and more heroic. But the Scottish story is significantly different. Calvinism was not the same thing as Methodism, although it is difficult to say which, in the early nineteenth century, was worse. We had no peasantry in England comparable to the Highland migrants. And the popular culture was very different. It is possible, at least until the 1820s, to regard the English and Scottish experiences as distinct, since trade union and political links were impermanent and immature.[1]

Unintentionally, Edward Thompson set up a scholarly equation in which working-class history up until the 1820s was not British, but English, Welsh, Scottish and Irish. He did not go on to distinguish amongst the varieties of Englishness, or to recognise regional variation within English national working-class or popular culture, although in fact much of the evidence on which he based his book related to Yorkshire, gathered during his long years of service as an extra-mural lecturer for the University of Leeds.[2] Thus, although

Thompson was committed to writing the history of working people and their culture, he was doing so on a national basis, and that nation was England. His Englishness is a denial of British imperialism, militarism and power politics, but because its origins are in a national commitment to the dominant element amongst the subjects of a British state, its intended focus is distorted and became more insular than he no doubt intended. As David Eastwood has remarked, it was not so much that Thompson's work focused on England, 'but rather that his reading of English history so often verged on a celebration of English exceptionalism'.[3]

Thompson's famous article, 'The Peculiarities of the English', a long response to the searching critiques of 'British Labourism' published by Perry Anderson and Tom Nairn in the *New Left Review* during the 1970s, wobbled in its use of the national term 'English'. At one point, Thompson wrote of 'Britain' as a *'protestant* country' in which Catholicism had been 'smashed'.[4] He wrote of 'the Enlightenment in Britain' not as a monolithic movement, but as manifesting itself in *'scores* of intellectual enclaves, dispersed over England, Wales and Scotland, which made up for what they lost in cohesion by the multiplicity of initiatives afforded by these many bases . . .' (emphasis in original). Thus a discussion of 'English dissent' includes a discussion of intellectual developments in Edinburgh and Glasgow, and there is a discussion of the impact of the ideas of Adam Smith on the lives of people in England, just as there was in Thompson's article on 'the moral economy'. Thompson discussed the difference between an 'English' Revolution and the French Revolution, yet wrote that 'British' reformism rather than revolution had enabled working people to defend their culture and their way of life against the effects of economic change.[5]

The language of patriotism in the eighteenth century was, as David Eastwood has put it, 'predominantly a language of radicalism' distinct from the older tradition of unquestioning loyalty to the Crown.[6] Thus, after 1790, this language of English patriotism divided into a conservative strand which evolved into an uncritical identification with the newly emergent British state on the part of some people in Britain, including some Irish people. On the other hand a popular radicalism also emerged, committed to obtaining political rights for (male) working people, but developing in such a way that rights for working people became focused on gaining the vote and representation in the British Parliament in London, in a way which conflated British with English political rights.[7] Access to the political Constitution was seen as the means by which working people could safeguard their interests.

The conservative English ideology of the 1790s, expressed most completely of course by the Irishman Edmund Burke, emphasised the glories of the British polity; established order in church and state, social harmony and security of property.[8] Hannah More, begetter of writings thought of by some as 'Burke for beginners' through her *Cheap Repository Tracts*, probably reached more people than Paine.[9] John Reeves's Association for the Preservation of Liberty and Property against Republicans and Levellers became one of the largest political organisations in the country, certainly rivalling any of the reformist associations.[10] These conservative, patriotic writers drew on many of the messages of past English popular radicalism, which was usually concerned with traditional rights and the rights of Englishmen from the Wilkite movement, back through earlier crowds who often expressed Tory or Jacobite sympathies in their opposition to the hegemony of a Whig elite. Now the message to the populace, urban and rural, was clear in a time of war.[11] Although the French Revolution had advanced the cause of equality, it had also brought anarchy, which, in its wake, 'would threaten even the small possessions of the honest labourer'.[12] The British Constitution, for all its flaws, had permitted most people in England to live in peace and security since 1688, and many accepted the logic of Burke, More and Reeves that it would be dangerous to criticise this constitution 'and absolute folly to change it so that it accorded better to the speculative designs of some impractical theorists'.[13]

141

Although this conservative loyalty to the Constitution, the King and the nation became linked with confident British expansionism, part of it involved glorying in a King who, while not English in ancestry, had spent much effort trying to assimilate to the culture of the English squirearchy, and it particularly involved placing value on a constitution which was essentially English. It might now serve a British state, but no one could argue that its emphasis on law and individual liberties came anywhere other than from an English tradition, which had been extended geographically to Wales, Scotland and Ireland (and at one time to America and other colonies).[14] Now reformers were arguing for a different degree of extension, which was social rather than geographical. More English(men) should have access to the benefits of participating in the Constitution. Much of the national feeling in the Wilkite movement had been that it was unfair that the Scots gentry and nobility had access to the benefits of the Constitution when honest English local merchants and artisans did not, and in addition, of course, there was a widespread conviction that the Scots would prove to be the means of reintroducing absolutism by securing disproportionate favour with a German king, who may have gloried in the 'name of Briton' but was certainly not an Englishman.[15] The intention during the reformist and radical years was not to exclude those who were not English but to open the Constitution to universal manhood suffrage, or as near to universal manhood suffrage as one could get. In one sense, postwar political radicalism and reform would be based around the idea that a people who had defended King and Parliament against the threat of French totalitarianism deserved to be included in the political nation and to participate in the Constitution.[16]

More surprising is that the reformist and radical element in British politics and British society that was not completely absorbed in the 'Church and King' patriotism of the majority of the population adopted a kind of English nationalism which, like Edward Thompson himself, countered the universalist ideas of the French Revolution and the Napoleonic state (which was still, in ideology, egalitarian, in that it incorporated the idea of an 'aristocracy of talent'), with an emphasis on English exceptionalism rooted in a tradition of liberty, security of property and Magna Carta. There are two points to make about the Englishness of this movement. The first is that, amongst the diverse groups and individuals out of which English trade unionism and chartism developed, the two movements of reform and 'physical force' illustrate the indigenous and external influences at work on popular ideology in England and Britain.[17] 'Physical force' looked to the example of France and the French Republic; because of its very nature we know less about the movement. There were United Englishmen and United Scotsmen, but they did not use violence as their comrades in Ireland did in 1798. Nor, when radical activity could become more open after 1815, was there ever more than the most minor organised English or Scottish resistance or challenge to the power of the state.[18] When Europe experienced revolutionary activity in the 1820s, 1830 and even later, in 1848, the 'British' experience was to be different, and it was to be different, essentially, because of an English political system which was based on English historical experience of civil war and extended conflict, within Britain, but not beyond it.[19]

The English reformers of the 1790s who gave Pitt's government such pause for thought were reformers and constitutionalists, despite the efforts of the conservatives to portray them as traitors. They did not wish to overthrow King and Parliament, but to extend representation in Parliament and confirm it in its powers. Although many, if not most, of those involved with English and British reform had sympathised with the American and French revolutions, the crucible of politics and political debate between 1784 and 1798 concentrated their minds on what it was they admired in their own British political tradition. At least, this became the only avenue which continued to be open to reformers, once war with France meant that admiration for republican government could be presented as treason to the monarchy. What is striking about many of the artisan leaders of the reform societies in the 1790s was that they refused to give up political activity completely after war broke out.[20] Their acquittals in the face of government prosecution indicated that their confidence in the constitutional nature of their activity was not entirely misplaced, but under the remorseless pressure of Loyalist propaganda and argument their platform had to be presented as British, and because it was a political platform based on universal suffrage and reform of Parliament, the version of Britishness which was presented was one of the extension of English liberties to more parts of Britain as well as to more Englishmen. The nature of the British campaign against the slave trade and, ultimately, for the abolition of slavery in the British Empire, grew out of this concern to extend the benefits of 'Britishness' to more and more people who lived under British rule, even beyond the British Isles and in the Empire.[21] This would become a central tenet of 'British reformism' which sought to improve and reform rather than to overthrow the hierarchies with which it had to deal.

Many of the reformers personified the changing nature of Britain at this time as the idea of what it presented became more accessible to more people through the culture of the printing press, whether it be letterpress or caricature, book or broadside; and also as more people from different parts of Britain moved around it, particularly to London, of course. The traffic was almost always but never quite one-way, from the periphery towards the economic, demographic and urban centre that was London. Richard Price was Welsh, but his fame was achieved as a dissenting minister in London. Iolo Morganwg, or Edward Williams, in his anglophone incarnation, co-operated with Richard Price in an electoral campaign of 1789 in Glamorgan centred on the idea of political reform, bringing political issues from London to Wales. Later the eisteddfodau would become Iolo's way of creating a popular Welsh identity which may not have given more Welshmen political rights, but as Prys Morgan has demonstrated, restored a sense of continuity in Welsh culture during a period of very rapid change.[22]

John Jebb was an Irishman. Hardly an artisan, but a graduate of Trinity College Dublin and Cambridge, who became a Unitarian and a medical doctor when he could find no charge as a minister. Although he died young in 1786, his ideology is typical of the movement. 'Equal representation, sessional Parliaments, and the universal right of suffrage are alone worthy of an Englishman's regard', he wrote. Although not born an Englishman, he came to see his liberty bound up in becoming one, almost in the sense that disappointed reformers sought to become American when they emigrated to the English-speaking republic during the 1790s.[23] Thomas Hardy was originally from Stirlingshire, although he was a Londoner by the time he became so active in the London Corresponding Society.[24] Thomas Spence, a real radical in his proposals for land reform, may have been a Newcastle man born and bred, but he was the son of Scots parents and the parishioner for many years of a dynamic Scots minister active in Newcastle.[25] Both Hardy and Spence make an interesting contrast with Peter Laurie, whom Linda Colley has instanced as a model of the patriotic volunteer during the wars with Napoleon. Born and bred in East Lothian in Scotland, he became too closely involved with radical politics while working as a printer's apprentice in Edinburgh, and left for London, where he became a member of a regiment of volunteers. He capitalised upon his military contacts eventually to acquire contracts for his saddlery business to supply East India Company regiments, and became a true Briton in the guise of a Director of the East India Company and a Lord Mayor of London.[26] John Binns, of the London Corresponding Society, had been born in Dublin and was a London plumber who later became associated with the United Irishmen, like his compatriot Colonel Edward Despard, the half-pay officer executed for treason in 1803. It is interesting that these Irishmen should be drawn into more radical activity by the turn of the century while the Scots, by and large, were not.[27]

Why was this? During the 1790s reform and radical activity in Scotland itself did not become nationalistic, but was confirmed in its commitment to 'British' liberties. John Brims has argued a case that probably has a context elsewhere in Britain as well, although the religious aspect would vary. Those dissatisfied with 'Old Corruption' or 'the Thing', vivid terms which genuinely convey the sense of opposition current amongst the reformers, had to face up to a fundamental division within their own ranks, which was that between those who had adopted the secular ideas of the Enlightenment and saw universal suffrage and freedom of speech as part of the rights of man; and those whose egalitarianism was more deeply rooted in an older religious tradition which Edward Thompson was right to see as originating in the British seventeenth-century revolutions.[28] In the case of Scotland, Brims has shown how this involved invoking the idea of the Scottish covenant with the Deity in pursuit of national salvation through limiting the monarchy's power over the Church.[29] It also involved a very strong religious commitment to individualistic worship and salvation, which, by the eighteenth century if not before, could find secular expression, as, for example, in Thomas Hardy's earlier political activity, or Peter Laurie's equally earnest pursuit of trade and profit.

Thus an appeal to British political rights centred on the symbol of the Parliament in London prevented a confrontation between Painites who shared their mentor's religious views, and compatriots who saw no reason to defer to 'the Thing' in this world but still had the Deity and the next world very much before them. Magna Carta was foreign, it was remote, it was political, and it left the religious settlement of 1688 alone, which is perhaps why one of the key speakers at the Scottish Convention of the Friends of the People in 1793 linked English traditional liberties with the Scottish Claim of Right passed by the Scottish Convention of 1689 (the terms on which the Scottish throne was offered to William and Mary).[30] The Claim of Right mentioned Scottish customs and liberties, but above all it was concerned with safeguarding the Protestant religion in Scotland.[31] In Ireland, no matter how sympathetic enlightened Protestants of Henry

Grattan's Parliament were towards their fellow Irishmen who were Roman Catholic, once sectarian conflict began in the 1790s and manifested itself in atrocities on both sides during the Irish rising of 1798, the only sure (if ultimately limited) way of neutralising the poison was the balm of secular political tradition sought through union with Great Britain. Only thus could the Protestant Irish preserve an arena for their Irishness in which confrontation with Catholicism would not dominate politics. Or not, that is, until O'Connell brought Catholic Emancipation irresistibly to the postwar political agenda and altered the very nature of the state after 1829.[32]

In this sense 1798, or the period 1797–1800, did become a defining moment in what Britain was to be. The French landing at Fishguard in Wales in 1797 led to panic on the financial markets in London. It was summarised disarmingly by Gwyn Williams as 'when the [French] Directory under the cover of its Irish campaign dumped a gaggle of criminals led by a paranoid American' on the innocent Welsh.[33] One repercussion of this was that it led to a calling to account of those Welsh who had become part of the movement for reform. There was no room for the Godless in Wales, 'the devout in Merthyr had their boot-nails stamped in a TP so as to trample the infidel Paine underfoot', but there was room for Methodism, more so than in England.[34] While the curate in Anglesey whose reports of 'hordes of Methodists...over-running North Wales' and 'descanting on the Rights of Man' no doubt exaggerated, historians of the Welsh culture are as one in recording that the spirit of much of the nation changed under the impact of Methodism.[35] British political reform kept Methodism out of the political equation while keeping God in men's lives, and if that has been the despair of modern social historians, it was the making of a way to meet and transcend the tortuous trek to a modern economy which was starting over much of Britain, and certainly in Wales at that time.[36]

This brings us back to a consideration of the concept of Englishness in its peculiar, rather than its political, sense. If an imperial British state was being formed, if it was incorporating as citizens part of the populations of Scotland, Wales and Ireland as immigrants or agents, if the rights of an English-man were being proffered in contradistinction to the novel and uncertain modern promises of the Rights of Man, what remained to the working Englishman? Something more than cricket and morris dancing, but perhaps less than what can really be described as a national identity. David Rollison's study of the Vale of Stroud presents an economic locality as a genuine social organism free of nationalism, sectarianism and, given the ability of people to go about their business, free of the hierarchy represented by the county community of the gentry and some of the nobility.[37] Our understanding of this is increased when individuals' lives can be seen to personify aspects of history on a broader plane. One of the working Englishmen of these years whose life can perhaps bring us closer to the Englishness of working life, and to the roots of the persistent English identity we find living on in the life and history of Edward Thompson, is the Northamp-tonshire poet John Clare.

From one perspective Clare is just another colonised peas-ant poet, like Samuel Duck from Wiltshire, or Robert Burns, or even Iolo Morganwg. His access to print and his participa-tion in the world of print ultimately detached him from his people and his real life and left him with nothing. Clare died in the Northampton Asylum for the insane, still writing poetry to the end, but less and less sure of who he was or where he was, and less and less aware of anything other than what he wrote on the page. Clare has thus presented literary scholars with far more problems of interpretative identity than a poet laureate like Southey, or the other poets of the period who found their way into the national literary canon, like Wordsworth and Shelley. Clare was part of his locality, but his detachment from national affairs as a local poet lim-ited his audience in the new literary market-place of print.[38] His poem 'The Flitting' is an elegy for a move of only three miles in distance, but infinite in its sense of severance from the village of his birth. National affairs did intrude, as Clare's poetry on enclosure makes all too clear, particularly when the extent to which these poems were reworked by his publishers and middle-class patrons is revealed. Clare's poetry was published in London for 'polite' bourgeois consumption. Little if any of it was read by his friends and workmates near Peterborough. So 'those who most fully shared his language and understood the sources from which his poetry was derived ...as well as local knowledge, popular radical politics and ways of thinking' were least likely to read his work.[39] The ploughman who wrote poetry became a kind of English noble savage, a sentimental primitive whose Englishness was as remote from that of Southey as the culture of a Tahitian, and with every bit as much to fear from metropolitan attention.

In that sense, from a literary perspective, Clare was not 'authentic', but he was in other ways. His voice found its way into print, and like a slave testimony, it bore witness to millions of other working lives whose details are unrecorded. At one point Clare writes of the 'dull and obstinate class from whence I struggled into light', detaching himself, at least for his readership, from his origins.[40] Throughout Clare's poetry, access to the land and proximity to nature loom large in a way which links him to other very English poets, while contrasting with the manner in which his poems on enclosure cut him off from them. It is this ambiguity in his identity which perhaps makes his Englishness so current, despite its location in a lost rural world. Shelley, Southey and Wordsworth produced a coherent canonical English literature which, at the last resort, excluded people like Clare. His experience has been described as 'regional, partial, self-fractured and fracturing'. What could be more postmodern? What could more accurately reflect the cultural state of the dispossessed as they were moved off the land and moved into the towns? Clare literally ended up in an 'asylum'. For how many others of his generation was a move to the town similarly an act of displacement, if not of literal incarceration?[41]

Jeanette Neeson's work on enclosure and common right focuses on Clare's county, and complements its careful use of parish records with the testimony of Clare's poetry.

Comparing Clare to Thomas Bewick and others, Neeson observes that 'no other sources get as close to peasants who left no wills, for whom no inventories were drawn up, who had few family papers.... That there were so few who came so close to the peasantry is the strongest testimony of all to its isolation in the later eighteenth century.'[42] Clare has provided testimony for those whose access to the land was limited, but vital to their sense of identity as well as their livelihood. Four acres of good land, a unit of such diminution as to be scandalous in the eye of an agricultural improver, was enough to support a family of four in Northamptonshire during the 1790s, according to a report to the Board of Agriculture. Those who petitioned against enclosure schemes were ' "the cottagers, the mechanic, and inferior shop-keepers," the small masters, innkeepers and butchers who used land in their trades; and they were the better-off of the artisans who combined a trade with stock-keeping or subsistance farming – almost half of the weavers and combers in Kilsby occupied land and cottages at enclosure'.[43] 'Enclosure', Dr Neeson has written, 'had a terrible but instructive visibility' to the poor.[44] It made clear who was to gain and who was to lose from the new British order. It made clear who would become a Briton and who would remain a peasant, and thus lose almost any identity at all in a modern commercial society.

This visibility of the social divisions which were being introduced in those areas that underwent enclosure during the eighteenth century in England tells us something about Englishness at the time. If Englishness was built upon an extraordinarily strong sense of exceptionalism, the rapid agrarian change chronicled by Neeson, the famine during the 1790s studied by Roger Wells, and the industrial conflict which attracted the attention of Edward Thompson, might have contributed to a popular sense of loss of tradition coincident with the emergence of the new militarism. State militarism spawned a patriotism which coincided with the moral certainty of a self-proclaimed British elite that was expanding in numbers outwards to empire, and also down the social scale to include shopkeepers, tenant farmers and soldiers.[45]

Englishness on this reading had ceded its imperial connotations to the political, imperial and ultimately sectarian concept of Britain, reducing men like John Clare to the status of aborigines, or excluding them from Britishness as thoroughly as if they were residing in the West of Ireland or the mountains of North Wales, and reducing their dialect to the status of Welsh or Gaelic, 'outside and below', in relation to English as lingua franca of empire. The idea of Britain became a means of imagining modernity for millions of people of many nationalities who learned how to become part of it and to use it to advance their interests. Some of them were English. Many of them were not. All of them detached themselves from tradition and distanced themselves from other people in their society and other peoples in the Empire.

In an age when romantic nationalism captured the imagination of many in Europe, Britishness preserved political continuity with identities that were built on institutions. This embodied an ideology constructed around the endeavour to perfect institutions of Crown, Parliament, and the rule of law. It was, above all else, an institutional identity rather than a cultural one, which genuinely does make Crown and Parliament uniquely British, founded as they are on the premise that good institutions ensure a good society. The idea of Britain has everything to do with a preoccupation with establishing the precise location of sovereignty in society, which inescapably made it a constitutional concept. That is why it has come to occupy the attention of people in Britain at the end of the twentieth century, as they contemplate the prospect of a new constitution and an incorporating union with Europe of a very different nature from its anglocentric British predecessor. Does a British History really have relevance for most people living in England, Scotland, Wales and Northern Ireland, and given the special status of the latter, the Republic of Eire as well? The war to retain the Falkland Islands in 1982 indicated that it had. Increasing European integration indicates that it does not. For modern Britons contemplating their history there may be some relevance in the words of the black American writer

James Baldwin: 'Know whence you came, there really is no limit to where you can go.'[46] It is because the future is so important that the study of genuine British history should continue to receive the attention it has attracted in recent years.

NOTES AND REFERENCES

1 INTRODUCTION: REGION AND LOCALITY

1. David Cannadine, 'British History as a "New Subject": Politics, Perspectives and Prospects' in Alexander Grant and Keith Stringer, eds., *Uniting the Kingdom? The Making of British History* (1995), p. 15.

2. A. J. P. Taylor, *English History, 1914–1945* (1965), pp. v–vi; John Pocock, 'Conclusion: Contingency, Identity, Sovereignty' in Grant and Stringer, eds., *Uniting the Kingdom?*, pp. 297, 301; Cannadine, 'British History', p. 17.

3. Pocock, 'Conclusion', pp. 297, 301.

4. T. O. Lloyd, *The British Empire, 1558–1995*, 2nd edn. (1996), p.viii.

5. Pocock, 'Conclusion', p. 297.

6. Cannadine, 'British History,' p. 26; Edward Thompson, 'The Peculiarities of the English' in Thompson, *The Poverty of Theory and Other Essays* (1978), pp. 35–91; Thompson, *The Making of the English Working Class* (1963).

7. In addition to the volume of essays edited by Grant and Stringer, recent collections include R. G. Asch, ed., *Three* [sic] *Nations: A Common History? England, Scotland, Ireland and British History* c.*1600–1920* (Bochum, 1993); Steven G. Ellis and Sarah Barber, eds., *Conquest and Union: Fashioning a British State 1485–1725* (1995); Brendan Bradshaw and John Morrill, eds., *The British Problem*, c.*1534–1707* (1996); and Murray Pittock has just published a literary study, *Inventing and Resisting Britain: Cultural Identities in Britain and Ireland, 1685–1789* (1997).

8. Geoffrey Barrow, *Feudal Britain: The Completion of the Medieval Kingdoms, 1066–1314* (1956); Barrow, *Robert the Bruce and the Community of the Realm of Scotland* (first published 1965, 3rd edn. 1988).

9. J. C. Beckett, *The Making of Modern Ireland 1603–1923* (1966), chapter 4, 'The War of the Three Kingdoms'.

10. E.g. R. R. Davies, *Domination and Conquest: The Experience of Ireland, Scotland and Wales 1100–1300* (1990); Robin Frame, *The Political Development of the British Isles 1100–1400* (1990); Conrad Russell, *The Fall and Rise of the British Monarchies* (1991); Keith Robbins, *Nineteenth-Century Britain: Integration and Diversity* (1988).

11. E.g. Linda Colley, *Britons: Forging the Nation 1707–1837* (1992); Colin Kidd, *Subverting Scotland's Past: Scottish Whig Historians and the Creation of an Anglo- British Identity, 1689–c.1830* (1993).

12. William Ferguson, *Scotland's Relations with England: A Survey to 1707* (1977, reissued 1994), p. v.

13. N. T. Phillipson, 'Politics, Politeness and the Anglicisation of Early Eighteenth-Century Scottish Culture' in Roger Mason, ed., *Scotland and England 1286–1815* (1987), pp. 226–46; N. T. Phillipson, 'Politics and Politeness in the Reigns of Anne and the Early Hanoverians' in J. G. A. Pocock, ed., *The Varieties of British Political Thought* (1993), pp. 211–45.

14. Thus contrast the approach in William Ferguson, *Scotland: 1689 to the Present* (1968) with T. C. Smout, *A History of the Scottish People, 1560–1830* (1969).

15. Colley, *Britons*, pp. 237–375.

16. Linda Colley, 'Britishness and Otherness: An Argument', *Journal of British Studies*, 31 (1992), pp. 309–29.

17. Michael Broers, *Europe Under Napoleon 1799–1815* (1996), pp. 24–233.

18. Maldwyn Jones, *The Limits of Liberty: American History 1607–1992*, 2nd edn. (1995); Robert Gildea, *Barricades and Borders: Europe 1800–1914* (1987), pp. 57–66.

19. Michael Fry, *The Dundas Despotism* (1992), pp. 235–8.

20. J. G. A. Pocock, 'British History: A Plea for a New Subject', *Journal of Modern History*, 47 (1975), pp. 614–16.

21. Pocock, 'Conclusion', p. 301.

22. David Marquand, 'How United is the Modern United Kingdom?' in Grant and Stringer, eds., *Uniting the Kingdom?*, p. 284.

23. Cannadine, 'British History', p. 25.

24. David Rollison, *The Local Origins of Modern Society: Gloucestershire 1500–1800* (1992), pp. 21–63; and his paper, 'Exploding England', given at the 'Conflict and Change in English Communities and Regions' symposium at the University of

Liverpool, 27–28 March 1995, as well as points made at that conference by its co-organiser, Dr Andy Wood, now of the University of East Anglia; and a paper by Jess Edwards of the University of Sussex given at a conference at Nene College, Northampton in November 1994.

25. David Eastwood, *Government and Community in the English Provinces, 1700–1870* (1997), chapter 1, 'English Exceptionalism' and chapter 4, 'County Communities and Patterns of Power'.
26. Rollison, *Local Origins*, p. 21.
27. *Ibid.*, p. 15. Charles Phythian-Adams, 'Introduction: An Agenda for English Local History' in Phythian-Adams, ed., *Societies, Cultures and Kinship 1580–1850: Cultural Provinces and English Local History* (1993), pp. 1–23.
28. Adrian Randall and Andrew Charlesworth, eds., *Markets, Market Culture and Popular Protest in Eighteenth-Century Britain and Ireland* (1996), chapter 1.
29. *Ibid.*, pp. 17–18.
30. Dror Wahrman, 'National Society, Communal Culture: An Argument About the Recent Historiography of Eighteenth-Century Britain', *Social History*, 17 (1992), pp. 43–72; E. P. Thompson, *Customs in Common* (1991); Peter Linebaugh, *The London Hanged* (1991).
31. Ian Mowat, *Easter Ross: The Double Frontier, 1750–1850* (1981), pp. 153–5.
32. Ian Adams, 'The Agents of Agricultural Change' in M. Parry and T. Slater, eds., *The Making of the Scottish Countryside* (1980), p. 173.
33. As interviewed by David Dabydeen of the University of Warwick in the Open University programme, 'Equiano and the Noble Savage', part of OU course A206: The Enlightenment.
34. Pocock, 'Conclusion', p. 299.
35. Christopher A. Bayly, *Imperial Meridian: The British Empire and the World 1780–1830* (1989); John Brewer, *The Sinews of Power: War, Money and the English State 1688–1783* (1989); Patrick K. O'Brien, 'The Political Economy of British Taxation, 1660–1815', *Economic History Review*, 41 (1988), pp. 1–32; O'Brien and P. A. Hunt, 'The Rise of a Fiscal State in England, 1485–1815', *Historical Research*, 66 (1993), pp. 155, 163, 168, 170.
36. This is the missing aspect in the valuable studies of Newcastle political culture during the eighteenth century in Thomas Knox, 'Popular Politics and Provincial Radicalism: Newcastle-upon

Tyne, 1769–85', *Albion*, 11 (1979), pp. 224–41; and Kathleen Wilson, *The Sense of the People: Politics, Culture and Imperialism in England, 1715–1785* (1995), pp. 315–75.

37. Colley, *Britons*, p. 7.
38. Thompson, *Customs in Common*, p. 267.
39. H. T. Dickinson, *The Politics of the People in Eighteenth-Century Britain* (1995), pp. 221–86.
40. P. K. O'Brien, 'Public Finance in the Wars with France 1793–1815' in H. T. Dickinson, ed., *Britain and the French Revolution, 1789–1815* (1989), pp. 165–87.
41. Thompson, *Making*, pp. 781–915.
42. J. C .D. Clark, *English Society, 1688–1832: Ideology, Social Structure and Political Practice During the Ancien Regime* (1985).
43. To paraphrase Giuseppe Tomasi di Lampedusa, *The Leopard*, translated by A. Colquhoun, revised edn. (1961), p. 29.

2 THE STUART MONARCHY AND THE IDEA OF BRITAIN

1. Jenny Wormald, *Court, Kirk and Community: Scotland 1470–1625* (1981), p. 191.
2. Arthur H. Williamson, *Scottish National Consciousness in the Age of James VI* (1979) is a difficult but rewarding book which should be read by anyone interested in the origins of the ideology of Britain. Access to the dense text of the book can be made easier by reading Williamson's essay, 'Scotland, Antichrist and the Invention of Great Britain' in John Dwyer *et al.*, eds., *New Perspectives on the Politics and Culture of Early Modern Scotland* (1982), pp. 34–58; also see Williamson, 'George Buchanan, Civic Virtue and Commerce: European Imperialism and its Sixteenth-Century Critics', *Scottish Historical Review*, 75 (1996), pp. 20–37.
3. Bruce Galloway, *The Union of England and Scotland 1603–1608* (1986); Galloway and B. Levack, eds., *The Jacobean Union: Six Tracts of 1604* (Scottish History Society, 1985); Jenny Wormald, 'James VI, James I and the Identity of Britain' in Brendan Bradshaw and John Morrill, eds., *The British Problem c.1534–1707* (1966). Compare the focus of the essays in Roger A. Mason, ed., *Scots and Britons: Scottish Political Thought and the Union of 1603* (1994) with Mason, 'Introduction' in J. Dwyer *et al.*, eds., *New Perspectives*.
4. Steven G. Ellis, 'Tudor State Formation and the Shaping of the British Isles' in Ellis and Sarah Barber, eds., *Conquest*

and Union: Fashioning a British State 1485–1725 (1995); pp. 40–63; B. Bradshaw, 'The Tudor Reformation and Revolution in Wales and Ireland: The Origins of the British Problem' in Bradshaw and Morrill, eds., *The British Problem*, pp. 39–65.

5. Ciaran Brady, 'Comparable Histories?: Tudor Reform in Wales and Ireland' in Ellis and Barber, eds., *Conquest and Union*, pp. 77–80. For a Scottish perspective see Brian Levack, *The Formation of the British State: England, Scotland and the Union 1603–1707* (1987), p. 21.

6. Nicholas Canny, 'Identity Formation in Ireland: The Emergence of the Anglo-Irish' in Canny and A. Pagden, eds., *Colonial Identity in the Atlantic World 1500–1800* (1987), p. 160; Roy F. Foster, *Modern Ireland 1600–1972* (1988), pp. 60–5; M. Perceval-Maxwell, *The Scottish Migration to Ulster in the Reign of James I* (1973); M. MacCarthy-Morrogh, *The Munster Plantation: English Migration to Southern Ireland 1583–1641* (1986).

7. J. C. Beckett, *The Making of Modern Ireland 1603–1923* (1966), p. 82; John Morrill, 'The Fashioning of Britain' in Ellis and Barber, eds., *Conquest and Union*, pp. 28–33.

8. Conrad Russell, 'The British Problem and the English Civil War', *History*, 72 (1987), p. 397. His subsequent account is in *The Fall and Rise of the British Monarchies* (1991), chapter 2, 'The British Problem and the Scottish National Covenant', pp. 71–146.

9. Daniel Szechi, *The Jacobites: Britain and Europe 1688–1788* (1994); S. J. Connolly, 'Varieties of Britishness: Ireland, Scotland and Wales in the Hanoverian State' in Alexander Grant and Keith Stringer, eds., *Uniting the Kingdom? The Making of British History* (1995), pp. 193–207.

10. John Robertson, 'Empire and Union: Two Concepts of the Early Modern European Political Order' in Robertson, ed., *A Union for Empire: Political Thought and the Union of 1707* (1995), p. 34; Frances D. Dow, *Cromwellian Scotland 1651–1660* (1979); William Ferguson, *Scotland's Relations with England: A Survey to 1707* (1977), pp. 135–41.

11. Dow, *Cromwellian Scotland*; Lesley M. Smith, 'Scotland and Cromwell: A Study in Early Modern Government' (University of Oxford D.Phil. thesis, 1980); T. C. Barnard, *Cromwellian Ireland* (1973) and Ronald Hutton, *The British Republic 1649–1660* (1990).

12. John Robertson, 'An Elusive Sovereignty: The Course of the Union Debate in Scotland 1698–1707' in Robertson, ed., *Union*, pp. 198–227.

13. William Ferguson, 'Imperial Crowns: A Neglected Facet of the Background to the Treaty of Union of 1707', *Scottish Historical Review*, 53 (1974), pp. 22–44.

14. T. C. Barnard, 'Settling and Unsettling Ireland, 1649–1688' in Jane Ohlmeyer, ed., *From Independence to Occupation* (1995), pp. 265–91.

15. Ronald Hutton, *Charles the Second: King of England, Scotland and Ireland* (1989), p. 352.
    Hutton's biography is particularly good at capturing the British aspect of Charles's reign.

16. *Ibid.*, pp. 299, 324.

17. *Ibid.*, p. 380.

18. T. C. Barnard, 'Scotland and Ireland in the Later Stewart Monarchy' in Ellis and Barber, eds., *Conquest and Union*, pp. 250–75; Hutton, *Charles*, p. 299.

19. Hutton, *Charles*, pp. 141–2, 171–2; Michael Lynch, *Scotland: A New History* (1991), pp. 287–90.

20. John Patrick, 'A Union Broken: Restoration Politics in Scotland' in Jenny Wormald, ed., *Scotland Revisited* (1991); Roy W. Lennox, 'Lauderdale and Scotland: A Study in Restoration Politics and Administration 1660–1682' (University of Columbia Ph.D. thesis, 1977).

21. Hugh Ouston, 'York in Edinburgh: James VII and the Patronage of Learning in Scotland, 1679–1688' in J. Dwyer *et al.*, eds., *New Perspectives*, pp. 133–55; S. Bruce and S. Yearley, 'The Social Construction of Tradition: The Restoration Portraits and the Kings of Scotland' in D. McCrone *et al.*, eds., *The Making of Scotland: Nation, Culture and Social Change* (1989), pp. 175–88.

22. Julia Buckroyd, *Church and State in Scotland 1661–1681* (1980); Ronald Lee, 'Government and Politics in Scotland, 1661–1681' (University of Glasgow Ph.D. thesis, 1995).

23. Hutton, *Charles*, p. 299.

24. Barnard, 'Scotland and Ireland' in Ellis and Barber, eds., *Conquest and Union*, pp. 250–75.

25. Williamson, 'Scotland', in Dwyer *et al.*, eds., *New Perspectives*, pp. 35, 42–4, 49.

26. Gordon Donaldson, *James V–VII* (1965), p. 198; *Oxford Dictionary of Quotations*, 4th edn. (1992), p. 362, citing W. Barlow, *Sum and Substence of the Conference* (1604), p. 82.

27. This paragraph is based on Hutton, *Charles*, as informed by reference to Levack, *Formation*, pp. 132–3; Richard Tompson, *The Atlantic Archipelago: A Political History of the British Isles* (1986), pp. 220–6; J. G. Simms, 'The Restoration' in T. Moody *et al.*, eds., *New History of Ireland*, Vol. III (1976), pp. 420–53; and T. C. Barnard, 'Scotland and Ireland in the later Stewart Monarchy' in Ellis and Barber, eds., *Conquest and Union*, p. 263.

28. Quoted in Ferguson, *Scotland's Relations with England*, p. 131.

29. J. C. Beckett, 'The Irish Viceroyalty in the Restoration Period', *Transactions of the Royal Historical Society*, 5th ser., 20 (1970), pp. 53–72; Daniel Szechi and David Hayton, 'John Bull's Other Kingdoms: Scotland and Ireland' in C. Jones, ed., *Britain in the First Age of Party 1680–1750* (1987), pp. 262–3.

30. Barnard, 'Scotland and Ireland' in Ellis and Barber, eds., *Conquest and Union*, pp. 250–75.

31. Jim Smyth, 'The Communities of Ireland and the British State, 1660–1707' in Bradshaw and Morrill, eds., *The British Problem*, p. 256; S. J. Connolly, *Religion, Law and Power: The Making of Protestant Ireland 1660–1760* (1992), pp. 19–20.

32. Connolly, *Religion*, p. 27, citing letters by Colonel Edward Vernon of 1663 and Ormond of 1666.

33. Barnard, 'Scotland and Ireland' in Ellis and Barber, eds., *Conquest and Union*, p. 272; Connolly, *Religion*, p. 27.

34. Connolly, *Religion*, pp. 27, 162, 164.

35. Szechi and Hayton, 'John Bull's' in Jones, ed., *Britain*, p. 261.

36. Beckett, *Making of Modern Ireland*, pp. 134–4.

37. Hutton, *Charles*, pp. 150–1.

38. *Ibid.*, p. 181.

39. Tim Harris, *Politics Under the Later Stuarts* (1993), p. 66.

40. *Ibid*, p. 67.

41. Hutton, *Charles*, p. 182.

42. Szechi and Hayton, 'John Bull's', in Jones, ed., *Britain*, p. 242; Allan Macinnes, 'The First Scottish Tories?', *Scottish Historical Review*, 67 (1988), pp. 56–66.

43. Buckroyd, *Church and State*, pp. 78–89, 118–20, 132–5.

44. Ferguson, *Scotland's Relations with England*, p. 147.

45. Buckroyd, *Church and State*, pp. 78–89, 103–8, 118–20, 132–5; Hutton, *Charles*, pp. 267, 350–1.

46. Hutton, *Charles*, pp. 387–8; Buckroyd, *Church and State*, pp. 132–3.

47. Allan Macinnes, 'Repression and Conciliation: the Highland Dimension 1660–1688', *Scottish Historical Review*, 65 (1986),

pp. 167–95; Hugh Ouston, 'York in Edinburgh', in Dwyer *et al.*, eds., *New Perspectives*, pp. 133–5.

48. Lynch, *Scotland*, p. 296.
49. Ferguson, *Scotland's Relations with England*, pp. 153–4; Hutton, *Charles*, p. 268; E. Hughes, 'The Negotiation for a Commercial Union between England and Scotland in 1668', *Scottish Historical Review*, 24 (1927), pp. 30–47.
50. Ferguson, *Scotland's Relations with England*, pp. 155–6.
51. Levack, *Formation*, pp. 72, 94–5, 99, 101; Alexander Murdoch, 'The Advocates, the Law and the Nation in Early Modern Scotland' in Wilfred Prest, ed., *Lawyers in Early Modern Europe and America* (1981), pp. 147–51.

3   JAMES LOSES THE KINGDOMS: THE REVOLUTIONS OF 1688 IN THEIR
BRITISH CONTEXT

1. Ronald Hutton, *Charles the Second: King of England, Scotland and Ireland* (1989), pp. 355–6; 425–8.
2. Allan I. Macinnes, 'Repression and Conciliation: The Highland Dimension 1660–1688', *Scottish Historical Review*, 65 (1986), p. 189; T. C. Barnard, 'Scotland and Ireland in the Later Stewart Monarchy' in S. Ellis and S. Barber, eds., *Conquest and Union: Fashioning a British State 1485–1725* (1995), pp. 273–5; John Miller, 'The Earl of Tyrconnel [*sic*] and James II's Irish Policy 1685–1688', *Historical Journal*, 20 (1977), pp. 803–23.
3. J. R. Jones, *The Revolution of 1688 in England* (1972), p. 305.
4. Michael Lynch, *Scotland: A New History* (1992 edn.), pp. 295–7.
5. Hugh Ouston, 'York in Edinburgh', in John Dwyer *et al.*, eds., *New Perspectives on the Politics and Culture of Early Modern Scotland* (1982), pp. 135–6, 143; Lynch, *Scotland*, pp. 296–7.
6. John Childs, *The Army, James II and the Glorious Revolution* (1980), p. 184.
7. J. G. Simms, *Jacobite Ireland 1685–91* (1969).
8. Quoted in S. J. Connolly, *Religion, Law and Power: The Making of Protestant Ireland 1660–1760* (1992), p. 34.
9. *Ibid.*, p. 39. Also see p. 34.
10. Childs, *The Army, James II*, pp. 57–8.
11. Miller, 'Tyrconnel', pp. 808–9, 815, 819–22.
12. Quoted in Childs, *The Army, James II*, p. 58.
13. Jonathan Israel, 'The Dutch Role in the Glorious Revolution' in Israel, ed., *The Anglo–Dutch Moment* (1991), pp. 105–62.

14. Quoted in Hutton, *Charles*, p. 346.
15. Rodger Cunningham, *Apples on the Flood: The Southern Mountain Experience* (1987), chapter 3, which provides the book with its title; Thomas Bartlett, *The Fall and Rise of the Irish Nation* (1992), which by choice does not fully explore the British aspects of Catholic emancipation as an issue; T. M. Devine, *Clanship to Crofters' War* (1994); Allan Macinnes, *Clanship, Commerce and the House of Stuart 1603–1788* (1996).
16. David Hayton, 'The Williamite Revolution in Ireland, 1688–91' in Israel, ed., *Anglo–Dutch Moment*, p. 186, citing the fact that this point underlines the contrasting efforts of J. C. D. Clark, *Revolution and Rebellion* (1986) and John Brewer, *The Sinews of Power: War, Money and the English State 1688–1783* (1989).
17. The content of this paragraph is based on my reading of Roy Porter, *The Enlightenment* (1990), and 'The Enlightenment in England' in Porter and M. Teich, eds., *The Enlightenment in National Context* (1981), C. B. A. Behrens, *The Ancien Regime* (1967), pp. 9–24; Behrens, *Society, Government and Enlightenment: The Experiences of Eighteenth-Century France and Prussia* (1985), pp. 152–205.
18. See H. T. Dickinson, 'How Revolutionary was the "Glorious Revolution" of 1688?', *British Journal for Eighteenth-Century Studies*, 11 (1988), pp. 125–42.
19. Quoted in John Pocock, 'The Significance of 1688' in Robert Beddard, ed., *The Revolutions of 1688* (1991), p. 271, citing Gilbert Burnet, *History of His Own Time*. I found the relevant passage on p. 500 of the 1875 edition.
20. William Ferguson, *Scotland: 1689 to the Present* (1968), pp. 5–6; William Ferguson, *Scotland's Relations with England: A Survey to 1707* (1977), p. 172.
21. Dickinson, 'How Revolutionary', p. 127.
22. *Ibid.*, p. 132. See pp. 134–5 in relation to the other points made in this paragraph.
23. See Edmund Morgan, *Inventing the People: The Rise of Popular Sovereignty in England and America* (1988); H. T. Dickinson, 'The Rights of Man – from John Locke to Tom Paine' in Owen Dudley Edwards and George Shepperson, eds., *Scotland, Europe and the American Revolution* (1976), pp. 38–48; Peter Burke, *Popular Culture in Early Modern Europe*, revised edn. (1994), pp. 3–22.
24. Thomas Perry, *Public Opinion, Propaganda and Politics in Eighteenth-Century England* (1962); Nicholas Rogers, 'Crowd and

People in the Gordon Riots' in Eckhart Hellmuth, ed., *The Transformation of Political Culture* (1990), pp. 39–56.

25. National Library of Scotland, Saltoun Papers, Sir James Carnegie, MP to Andrew Fletcher, Lord Milton of the Court of Session in Scotland, 16 March 1742.

26. Quoted in Alexander J. Murdoch, 'Politics and the People in the Burgh of Dumfries, 1758–1760', *Scottish Historical Review*, 70 (1991), p. 159.

27. Clive Behagg, 'Custom, Wealth and the Continuity of Small Scale Production', a paper given at the 'Conflict and Change in English Communities and Regions' conference at the University of Liverpool, 27–28 March 1995, citing the Galton Papers in the Birmingham Reference Library.

28. Tristram Clarke, 'The Scottish Episcopalians 1688–1720' (University of Edinburgh Ph.D. thesis, 1987), chapter 1; Gordon Schochet, 'From Persecution to Toleration' in J.R. Jones, ed., *Liberty Secured? Britain Before and After 1688* (1992), p. 123.

29. Tristram Clarke, 'The Williamite Episcopalians and the Glorious Revolution in Scotland', *Records of the Scottish Church History Society*, 24 (1992), pp. 33–52.

30. Ferguson, *Scotland*, pp. 7–9. Ferguson's shrewd point is not really followed up in essays by Bruce Lenman on the Revolution of 1688 in Scotland: 'The Scottish Nobility and The Revolution of 1688–1690' in Beddard, ed., *Revolutions of 1688* and 'The Poverty of Political Theory in the Scottish Revolution of 1688–1690' in Lois Schwoerer, ed., *The Revolution of 1688–1689* (1992); nor by Ian B. Cowan, 'The Reluctant Revolutionaries: Scotland in 1688' in E. Cruickshanks, ed., *By Force or Default? The Revolutions of 1688–1689* (1989).

31. P. W. J. Riley, *King William and the Scottish Politicians* (1979); see the different framework of analysis offered in John Robertson, 'An Elusive Sovereignty: The Course of the Union Debate in Scotland 1698–1707' in Robertson, ed., *A Union for Empire: Political Thought and the Union of 1707* (1995), pp. 198–227.

32. Hayton, 'Williamite Revolution' in Israel, ed., *Anglo-Dutch Moment*, p. 186.

33. Colin Kidd, 'Religious Realignment' in Robertson, ed., *Union for Empire*, pp. 159, 166; Kidd, *Subverting Scotland's Past: Scottish Whig Historians and the Creation of an Anglo-British Identity, 1689– c.1830* (1993) pp. 67–9; *Dictionary of National Biography* entries for William Carstares and William Dunlop; Robert

Emerson, 'Scottish Cultural Change' in Robertson, ed., *Union*, p. 136.

34. Richard B. Sher, '1688 and 1788: William Robertson on Revolution in Britain and France' in Paul Dukes and John Dunkley, eds., *Culture and Revolution* (1990), pp. 98–109.

35. Paul Hopkins, *Glencoe and the End of the Highland War* (1986), p. 488.

36. Connolly, *Religion*, p. 35.

37. J. G. Simms, *The Williamite Confiscation in Ireland 1690–1703* (1956), p. 22.

38. Quoted in Hayton, 'Williamite Revolution' in Israel, ed., *Anglo-Dutch Moment*, p. 191.

39. *Ibid.*, p. 198.

40. Connolly, *Religion*, pp. 198, 217, referring to Boswell, *Life of Johnson*, ed. R. Chapman (1970 edn.), p. 423.

41. Simms, *Williamite*, p. 160.

42. Hayton, 'Williamite Revolution' in Israel, ed., *Anglo-Dutch Moment*, p. 201, with its acknowledgement to Professor Thomas Bartlett in note 50.

43. *Ibid.*, p. 213.

4 THE UNION OF ENGLAND AND SCOTLAND AND THE DEVELOPMENT
OF THE HANOVERIAN STATE

1. Geoffrey Holmes, *The Making of a Great Power: Late Stuart and Early Georgian Britain 1660–1722* (1993), pp. 195–321.

2. Holmes, *Making*, pp. 350–66; Tristram Clarke, 'The Scottish Episcopalians 1688–1720' (University of Edinburgh Ph.D. thesis, 1987), chapter one; Colin Kidd, 'Religious Realignment' in John Robertson, ed., *A Union for Empire: Political Thought and the Union of 1707* (1995), pp. 145–68.

3. P. W. J. Riley, *King William and the Scottish Politicians* (1979), pp. 1–10.

4. Andrew Fletcher, *Speeches by a Member of Parliament which began at Edinburgh the 6th of May, 1703* (1703), pp. 8–9. See John Robertson, 'An Elusive Sovereignty: The course of the Union Debate in Scotland 1698–1707' in Robertson, ed., *Union*, p. 204.

5. Rosalind Mitchison and Leah Leneman, *Sexuality and Social Control: Scotland 1660–1780* (1989), p. 36.

6. J. G. Simms, *William Molyneux of Dublin 1656–1698*, ed. P. H. Kelly (1982), p. 106.

7. On the 'Old English' see Aidan Clarke, *The Old English in Ireland 1624–1642* (1966) and S. J. Connolly, *Religion, Law and Power: The Making of Protestant Ireland 1660–1760* (1992), pp. 6–7, 12, 114–18.

8. Edmund Morgan, *Inventing the People: The Rise of Popular Sovereignty in England and America* (1988), pp. 267–73; John C. Miller, *The Wolf by the Ears: Thomas Jefferson and Slavery* (1977).

9. H. T. Dickinson, *The Politics of the People in Eighteenth-Century Britain* (1995), which refutes J. C. D. Clark, *English Society, 1688–1832: Ideology, Social Structure and Political Practice During the Ancien Regime* (1985), pp. 19–20.

10. See for example, 'The Moral Economy Reviewed' in E. P. Thompson, *Customs in Common* (1991), pp. 259–351.

11. Riley, *King William*, p. 10.

12. Daniel Szechi and David Hayton, 'John Bull's Other Kingdoms: Scotland and Ireland' in C. Jones, ed., *Britain in the First Age of Party 1680–1750* (1987), p. 247.

13. *Ibid.*, p. 248, quoting from H. L. Snyder, ed., *The Marlborough Godolphin Correspondence* (1975), Vol. I, p. 359.

14. William Ferguson, *Scotland's Relations with England: A Survey to 1707* (1977), p. 186.

15. Bruce Lenman, *The Jacobite Risings in Britain 1689–1746* (1980), pp. 50–106.

16. Ferguson, *Scotland's*, p. 258.

17. Marinell Ash, 'William Wallace and Robert the Bruce: The Life and Death of a National Myth' in Raphael Samuel and Paul Thompson, eds., *The Myths We Live By* (1990), pp. 83–94.

18. Ferguson, *Scotland's*, p. 201.

19. Riley, *King William*, pp. 4, 53–5, 65; Riley, *The Union of England and Scotland* (1978), pp. 10, 25, 63, 165; Bruce Lenman, *The Jacobite Clans of the Great Glen 1650–1784* (1984), pp. 68–70.

20. Kidd, 'Religious Realignment' in Robertson, ed., *Union*, pp. 166–8.

21. Quoted in Chris Whatley, *'Bought and Sold for English Gold'? Explaining the Union of 1707* (1994), p. 28.

22. *Ibid.*, p. 46.

23. T. C. Smout, 'The Burgh of Montrose and the Union of 1707 – A Document', *Scottish Historical Review*, 66 (1987), p. 184.

24. Whatley, *Bought and Sold*, p. 45.

25. This is debated well in a classic exchange: T. C. Smout, 'Scotland and England: Is Dependency a Symptom or a Cause of

Underdevelopment?' and Immanuel Wallerstein, 'One Man's Meat: The Scottish Great Leap Forward', both published in *Review*, Vol. 3, Part 4 (Spring 1980), pp. 601–40. *Review* is published by the Fernand Braudel Center for the Study of Economics, Historical Systems and Civilisations at the State University of New York, Binghamton.

26. Daniel Defoe, *A History of the Union Between England and Scotland: With a Collection of Original Papers Relating Thereto, to which is prefixed a life of Daniel De Foe by George Chalmers* (1786).

27. Simms, *Molyneux*, p. 105.

28. William Ferguson, 'Imperial Crowns: A Neglected Facet of the Background to the Treaty of Union of 1707', *Scottish Historical Review*, 53 (1974), pp. 24–30, 36–8; Ferguson, 'Introduction' to James Anderson, 'An Historical Essay Shewing That the Crown and Kingdom of Scotland, Is Imperial and Independent' in W. M. Gordon, ed., *The Stair Society Miscellany Three* (1992), pp. 1–27.

29. Simms, Molyneux, p. 106.

30. *Ibid.*, p. 115; Jacqueline Hill, 'Ireland without Union: Molyneux and his Legacy' in Robertson, ed., *Union*, p. 289.

31. Jeremy Black, *Convergence or Divergence: Britain and the Continent* (1994), pp. 143–73; J. Robertson, 'Empire and Union: Two concepts of the Early Modern European Political Order' in Robertson, ed., *Union*, pp. 3–36; David Hayton, 'Constitutional Experiments and Political Expediency, 1689–1725' in Steven G. Ellis and Sarah Barber, eds., *Conquest and Union: Fashioning a British State 1485–1725* (1995), pp. 276–305; Daniel Szechi, 'The Hanoverians and Scotland' in M. Greengrass, ed., *Conquest and Coalescence: The Shaping of the State in Early Modern Europe* (1991), pp. 116–33.

32. Colin Kidd, 'North Britishness and the Nature of Eighteenth-Century British Patriotisms', *Historical Journal*, 39 (1996), pp. 361–82; Colin Kidd, *Subverting Scotland's Past: Scottish Whig Historians and the Creation of an Anglo–British Identity, 1689–c. 1830* (1993), pp. 205–16.

33. Colin Kidd, 'Gaelic Antiquity and National Identity in Enlightenment Ireland and Scotland', *English Historical Review*, 109 (1994), pp. 1197–1214.

34. S. J. Connolly, 'Varieties of Britishness: Ireland, Scotland and Wales in the Hanoverian State' in A. Grant and K. Stringer, eds., *Uniting the Kingdom? The Making of British History* (1995), pp. 193–207.

35. P. G. M. Dickson, *The Financial Revolution in England* (1967), pp. 200–4; John Brewer, *The Sinews of Power: War, Money and the English State 1688–1783* (1989), pp. 163–218.
36. Szechi and Hayton, 'John Bull's' in Jones, ed., *Britain*, pp. 254–8, 270–4.
37. Geraint Jenkins, *The Foundations of Modern Wales: Wales 1642–1780* (1987, reissued 1993), pp. 87–172.
38. David Hayton, 'The "Country" Interest and the Party System, 1689–c.1720' in Clyve Jones, ed., *Party and Management in Parliament, 1660–1784* (1984), pp. 37–86; Dickson, *Financial Revolution*, pp. 200–4.
39. Part of this point is implicit in traditional surveys such at Charles Wilson's *England's Apprenticeship* (1965), but the sweep of excitement of it all is conveyed in David Hancock, *Citizens of the World: London Merchants and the Integration of the British Atlantic Community, 1735–1785* (1995).

5 THE IDEA OF BRITAIN AND THE CREATION OF THE FIRST BRITISH EMPIRE

1. Linda Colley, *Britons: Forging the Nation 1707–1837* (1992), pp. 11–100.
2. John Pocock, 'Empire, State and Confederation: The War of American Independence as a Crisis in Multiple Monarchy' in John Robertson, ed., *A Union for Empire: Political Thought and the Union of 1707* (1995), pp. 314–48.
3. P. J. Cain and A. G. Hopkins, *British Imperialism: Innovation and Expansion 1688–1914* (1993), p. 19.
4. Hence the different emphasis between the collection of essays edited by Brendan Bradshaw and John Morrill, *The British Problem, c.1534–1707* (1996) with Colley, *Britons*, or with genuinely British imperial history such as Christopher A. Bayly, *Imperial Meridian: The British Empire and the World 1780–1830* (1989).
5. John M. Simpson made an analogy with this difficulty and the 'nothing is but what is not' quality of Mozart's *Così fan tutte* in 'Who Steered the Gravy Train 1707–1766?' in N. T. Phillipson and Rosalind M. Mitchison, eds., *Scotland in the Age of Improvement* (1970, reissued 1996), p. 48. The relationship of politics and social transformation caused by economic change forms the basis for the studies of John Brewer, *Party Ideology and Popular Politics at the Accession of George III* (1976) and H. T.

Dickinson, *The Politics of the People in Eighteenth-Century Britain* (1995).

6. Roy Porter, 'Georgian Britain: An Ancien Regime?', *British Journal for Eighteenth-Century Studies*, 15 (1992), p. 142.

7. P. J. Corfield, *Power and the Professions in Britain 1700–1850* (1995); Peter Earle, *The Making of the English Middle Class* (1989); Lorna Weatherill, *Consumer Behaviour and Material Culture in Britain 1660–1760* (1988).

8. Paul Langford, *Public Life and the Propertied Englishman 1689–1798* (1991), pp. 582–6.

9. Patrick K. O'Brien, 'The Political Economy of British Taxation, 1660–1815', *Economic History Review*, 41 (1988), pp. 1–32; O'Brien, 'Political Preconditions for Industrial Revolution' in O'Brien and R. Quinault, eds., *The Industrial Revolution and British Society* (1993), pp. 124–55.

10. Bayly, *Imperial Meridian*, pp. 100–32; 164–92.

11. Jonathan Israel, 'The Dutch Role in the Glorious Revolution' in Israel, ed., *The Anglo-Dutch Moment* (1991); Israel, *Dutch Primacy in World Trade, 1585–1740* (1990); Israel, *The Dutch Republic: Its Rise, Greatness, and Fall, 1477–1806* (1995).

12. Charles Wilson, *England's Apprenticeship* (1965); Geoffrey Holmes, *The Making of a Great Power: Late Stuart and Early Georgian Britain 1660–1722* (1993); John Brewer, *The Sinews of Power: War, Money and the English State 1688–1783* (1989), pp. 137–61.

13. Brewer, *Sinews of Power*, pp. 88–134.

14. David Armitage, 'The Scottish Vision of Empire' in Robertson, ed., *Union*, pp. 97–118; Richard Saville, *Bank of Scotland: A History 1695–1995* (1996), pp. 32–8, 73, 84–6.

15. R. H. Campbell, *Scotland Since 1707*, 2nd edn. (1985), pp. 57–63; David Hancock, *Citizens of the World: London Merchants and the Integration of the British Atlantic Community, 1735–1785* (1995), pp. 254–58.

16. Ned Landsman, 'The Provinces and the Empire: Scotland, the American Colonies and the Development of British Provincial Identity' in Lawrence Stone, ed., *An Imperial State at War* (1994), pp. 258–87; Thomas Bartlett, *The Fall and Rise of the Irish Nation* (1992), pp. 66–81; S. J. Connolly, *Religion, Law and Power: The Making of Protestant Ireland 1660–1760* (1992), pp. 41–73; Philip Jenkins, *The Making of a Ruling Class: The Glamorgan Gentry 1640–1790* (1983), pp. 239–71; Allan Macinnes, *Clanship, Commerce and the House of Stuart 1603–1788* (1996), pp. 159–87.

17. Brewer, *Sinews of Power*, p. 204.

18. Christopher A. Bayly, *Indian Society and the Making of the British Empire* (1988), pp. 79–105.
19. Brewer, *Sinews of Power*, p. 206.
20. Geoffrey Holmes, *British Politics in the Age of Anne*, revised edn. (1987), p. li.
21. Sir Lewis Namier, *The Structure of Politics at the Accession of George III*, 2nd edn. (1957); Holmes, *British Politics*; Bernard Bailyn, *The Ideological Origins of the American Revolution* (1967); J. G. A. Pocock, *The Machiavellian Moment* (1975); E. P. Thompson, *Customs in Common* (1991).
22. Sir Thomas More, *Utopia*, ed. E. Surtz and J. H. Hexter (1964), p. 137. See David Armitage, 'Making the Empire British: Scotland in the Atlantic World 1542–1707', *Past and Present*, 155 (May 1997), pp. 34–63, for a valuable study which helps place More's ideas in context.
23. Benjamin Franklin to Henry Home, Lord Kames, 11 April 1767, *The Norton Anthology of American Literature*, 3rd edn. (1989), Vol. I, pp. 394–8; B. Bailyn, *Voyagers to the West* (1986), pp. 436–7, citing the Seafield Papers in the Scottish Record Office; Chatham, quoted in J. G. A. Pocock, '1776: The Revolution Against Parliament' in Pocock, ed., *Three British Revolutions* (1980), p. 276.
24. J. G. A. Pocock, 'A Discourse of Sovereignty' in N. T. Phillipson and Q. Skinner, eds., *Political Discourse in Early Modern Britain* (1993), p. 419.
25. Compare Roy F. Foster, *Modern Ireland, 1600–1972* (1989), pp. 3–166; 195–225; T. C. Smout, *A History of the Scottish People 1560–1830*, revised edn. (1972), pp. 126–45, 261–81, 311–37; Michael Lynch, *Scotland: A New History* (1992), pp. 362–77; Philip Jenkins, *A History of Modern Wales* (1992), pp. 17–80 and p. 418, 'The People Above'.
26. This is the organising concept behind Angus Calder's sprawling and neglected classic, *Revolutionary Empire* (1981).
27. Patrick K. O'Brien and P. A. Hunt, 'The Rise of a Fiscal State in England 1485–1815', *Historical Research*, 66 (1993), pp. 155, 163, 168, 170; Bayly, *Imperial Meridian*, chapters 4, 6 and the Conclusion.
28. Colin Bonwick, *The American Revolution* (1991), p. 234; J. McCusker and R. Menard, *The Economy of British America, 1607–1789* (1985), pp. 371, 376–7.
29. D. Malone and B. Rauch, *Empire of Liberty*, Vol. II (1960), p. 103; Maldwyn Jones, *Limits of Liberty: American History*

1607–1992, 2nd edn. (1995), pp. 79–82, 93–9, 101–11; Joyce Appleby, 'What is Still American in the Political Philosophy of Thomas Jefferson?', *William and Mary Quarterly*, 39 (1982), pp. 287–309, esp. 295, 303; Appleby, *Capitalism and a New State Order* (1984), pp. 88–9.

30. Hancock, *Citizens*, pp. 25–78.

31. *Ibid.*, pp. 1–2, 121.

32. For a negative perspective see Colin Kidd, *Subverting Scotland's Past: Scottish Whig Historians and the Creation of an Anglo-British Identity 1689–c.1830* (1993), pp. 205–16, 268–80. For a different perspective see Bayly, *Imperial Meridian*, pp. 75–99; 133–63.

33. For Ireland see James Kelly, *Prelude to Union: Anglo- Irish Politics in the 1780s* (1992). For Scotland see Calder, *Revolutionary Empire*, pp. 416–25; Landsman, 'The Provinces and the Empire' in Stone, ed., *An Imperial State*, pp. 258–62; Eric Richards, 'Scotland and the Uses of Atlantic Empire' in B. Bailyn and P. Morgan, eds., *Strangers Within the Realm* (1991), p. 67–114.

34. Robert Kent Donovan, *No Popery and Radicalism* (1987), pp. 271–9; Dalphy Fagerstrom, 'The American Revolutionary Movement in Scottish Opinion 1763–1783' (University of Edinburgh Ph.D. thesis, 1951); Jane Fagg, 'Biographical Introduction' in *The Correspondence of Adam Ferguson*, ed. V. Merolle (1995), Vol. I, pp. xlvii–lvi; Stewart J. Brown, ed., *William Robertson and the Expansion of Empire* (1997), especially the essay by Geoffrey Carnell.

35. David J. Brown, 'Henry Dundas and the Government of Scotland' (University of Edinburgh Ph.D. thesis, 1989), pp. 201–2, 232–3; Michael Fry, *The Dundas Despotism* (1992), pp. 217–23.

36. J. G. A. Pocock, 'Political Thought... Part I, The Imperial Crisis' in Pocock, ed., *The Varieties of British Political Thought* (1993), p. 264. The quotations which follow are taken from pp. 278 and 291.

37. Adam Ferguson, *History of the Progress and Termination of the Roman Republic* (1783); Adam Ferguson, *Biographical Sketch, or Memoir, of Lieutenant-Colonel Patrick Ferguson* (1817).

38. John Turner, *Macmillan* (1994), p. 157.

39. Gary Wills, *Explaining America: The Federalist* (1981), pp. 13–23, 190–2; John Robertson, 'Empire', in Robertson, ed., *Union* (1995), p. 36; J. Pocock, 'Empire' in *ibid.*, p. 346.

40. Appleby, 'What is Still American in the Political Philosophy of Thomas Jefferson?', *passim*.

6 PERIPHERAL NATIONS? SCOTLAND, IRELAND, WALES AND PROVINCIAL ENGLAND

1. J. G. A. Pocock, 'British History: A Plea for a New Subject', *Journal of Modern History*, 47 (1975), pp. 601–28.
2. Hugh Kearney, *The British Isles: A History of Four Nations* (1989). See Raphael Samuel, 'British Dimensions: Four Nations History', *History Workshop Journal*, 40 (1995), pp. iii–xxii.
3. J. G. A. Pocock, 'Empire' in John Robertson, ed., *A Union for Empire: Political Thought and the Union of 1707* (1995), pp. 318–48; Pocock, 'Two Kingdoms and Three Histories' in Roger A. Mason, ed., *Scots and Britons: Scottish Political Thought and the Union of 1603* (1994), pp. 293–312.
4. Geraint Jenkins, *The Foundations of Modern Wales: Wales 1642–1780* (1987); Jenkins, *Literature, Religion and Society in Wales, 1660–1730* (1978); J. G. A. Pocock, 'Conclusion' in Alexander Grant and Keith Stringer, eds., *Uniting the Kingdom? The Making of British History* (1995), n. 15.
5. Conrad Russell, 'The British Problem and the English Civil War', *History*, 72 (1987), pp. 395–415; Russell, *The Fall and Rise of the British Monarchies* (1991), chapter 2, 'The British Problem'; Keith Brown, 'British History: A Sceptical Comment' in R. G. Asch, ed., *Three Nations: A Common History? England, Scotland, Ireland and British History c.1600–1920* (1993), pp. 117–27; N. Canny, 'Irish, Scottish and Welsh Responses to Centralisation' in Grant and Stringer, eds., *Uniting the Kingdom?*, pp. 147–69.
6. Samuel, 'British Dimensions'; E. P. Thompson, 'Which Britons?' in Thompson, *Persons and Polemics* (1994).
7. Peter Burke, *Popular Culture in Early Modern Europe*, revised edn. (1994), pp. 3–64; J. Habermas, 'Citizenship and National Identity', *Praxis International*, 12 (1992), pp. 1–19; R. Mackenney, *Sixteenth Century Europe* (1993), pp. 307–9; M. Thompson, 'Ideas of Europe During the French Revolution and Napoleonic Wars', *Journal of the History of Ideas*, 55 (1994), pp. 37–58.
8. P. Hudson, *The Genesis of Industrial Capital* (1986); Hudson, *The Industrial Revolution* (1992); M. Berg, *The Machinery Question* (1980); Berg, *The Age of Manufactures*, 2nd edn (1993).
9. M. Berg and P. Hudson, 'Rehabilitating the Industrial Revolution', *Economic History Review*, 45 (1992), pp. 24–50. Also see

P. K. O'Brien and R. Quinault, eds., *The Industrial Revolution and British Society* (1993), pp. 1–30.

10. Hudson, *Industrial Revolution*, chapter 4, 'Regions and Industries', pp. 101–32; Hudson, 'Land, the Social Structure and Industry in Two Yorkshire Townships *c.*1660–1800' and J.D. Marshall, 'Proving Ground or the Creation of Regional Identity', both in P. Swan and D. Foster, eds., *Essays in Regional and Local History* (1992), pp. 1–44.

11. Cormac Ó Grada, *Ireland: A New Economic History 1780– 1939* (1994), pp. 32–42, 60–2; L. M. Cullen, *An Economic History of Ireland Since 1660* (1972), pp. 90–1, 106–8; T. M. Devine, 'The English Connection and Irish–Scottish Development in the Eighteenth Century' in Devine, *Exploring the Scottish Past* (1995), pp. 54–73; Eric Richards, 'Margins of the Industrial Revolution' in O'Brien and Quinault, eds., *Industrial Revolution*, pp. 210–15.

12. Kenneth Morgan, *Bristol and the Atlantic Trade in the Eighteenth Century* (1993).

13. J. Butt, 'The Scottish Cotton Industry During the Industrial Revolution' and D. Dickson, 'Aspects of the Rise and Decline of the Irish Cotton Industry', both in L. M. Cullen and T. C. Smout, eds., *Scottish and Irish Economic and Social History 1600–1900* (1977), pp. 100–28; F. Geary, 'The Belfast Cotton Industry Revisited', *Irish Historical Studies*, 26 (1989), pp. 250–67.

14. Richards, 'Margins' in O'Brien and Quinault, eds., *Industrial Revolution*, pp. 204–5, 211, 214; Chris Whatley, *The Industrial Revolution in Scotland* (1997); S. J. Connolly *et al.*, eds., *Conflict, Identity and Economic Development: Ireland and Scotland, 1600– 1939* (1995).

15. John Money, *Experience and Identity* (1977), p. 277; Hudson, *Industrial Revolution*, pp. 102, 103, 105, 109.

16. T. M. Devine, *The Transformation of Rural Scotland* (1994), pp. 35–40.

17. Hudson, *Industrial Revolution*, pp. 115–31.

18. Jenkins, *Foundations of Modern Wales*, pp. 257–99, 386–426; Philip Jenkins, *A History of Moden Wales* (1992), p. 408, 'The People Above'.

19. Prys Morgan, 'From a Death to a View' in E. Hobsbawm and T. Ranger, eds., *The Invention of Tradition* (1983), pp. 43– 100; Morgan, *A New History of Wales: The Eighteenth Century Renaissance* (1981), pp. 56–62.

20. Claire O'Halloran, 'Ownership of the Past: Antiquarian Debate and Ethnic Identity in Scotland and Ireland' in Connolly *et al.*, eds., *Conflict, Identity*, pp. 135–47; Colin Kidd, 'Gaelic Antiquity and National Identity in Enlightenment Ireland and Scotland', *English Historical Review*, 109 (1994), pp. 1197–1214.

21. Hudson, *Industrial Revolution*, p. 106. Also see Money, *Experience*, p. 277.

22. Roy Porter, 'Science, Provincial Culture and Public Opinion in Enlightenment England' in Peter Borsay, ed., *The Eighteenth–Century Town* (1990), pp. 243–67.

23. E. C. Black, *The Association* (1963); Adrian Randall and Andrew Charlesworth, eds., *Markets, Market Culture and Popular Protest in Eighteenth–Century Britain and Ireland* (1996), pp. 5–6; A. Randall, 'The Industrial Moral Economy of.the Gloucestershire Weavers in the Eighteenth Century' in J. Rule, ed., *British Trade Unionism* (1988), pp. 29–51.

24. Hudson, *Industrial Revolution*, p. 111, citing Linda Colley, 'Whose Nation? Class and National Consciousness in Britain 1750–1830', *Past and Present*, 113 (1986), pp. 97– 117; and Colley, 'The Apotheosis of George III', *Past and Present*, 102 (1984), pp. 94–129.

25. Most recently Kathleen Wilson, *The Sense of the People: Politics, Culture and Imperialism in England, 1715–1785* (1995); Wilson, 'Citizenship, Empire and Modernity in the English Provinces *c.*1720–1790', *Eighteenth–Century Studies*, 29 (1995), pp. 69–96; Wilson, 'The Good, the Bad and the Impotent: Imperialism and the Politics of Identity in Georgian England' in A. Bermingham and J. Brewer, eds., *The Consumption of Culture* (1995).

26. Wilson, *Sense*, p. 432.

27. Money, *Experience*, pp. 259–61.

28. Peter Borsay, *The English Urban Renaissance* (1989), p. 286.

29. John Money, 'Freemasonry and the Fabric of Loyalism in Hanoverian England' in Eckhart Hellmuth, ed., *The Transformation of Political Culture* (1990), pp. 240–56.

30. Dror Wahrman, 'National Society, Communal Culture: An Argument About the Recent Historiography of Eighteenth–Century Britain', *Social History*, 17 (1992), pp. 48–52; Randall and Charlesworth, eds., *Markets, Market Culture*, pp. 5–6.

31. *Ibid.*, p. 45.

32. J. Habermas, *The Structural Transformation of the Public Sphere* (1962), translated by Thomas Burger, 1989; Linda Colley, *Britons: Forging the Nation 1707–1837* (1992), p. 314 n. 101;

Wahrman, 'National Society', pp. 45, 66; Wahrman, *Imagining the Middle Class* (1995), p. 193; Geoff Eley and R. Suny, eds., *Becoming National* (1996), pp. 18, 23.

33. N. T. Phillipson, 'Politics and Politeness in the Reigns of Anne and the Early Hanoverians' in J. G. A. Pocock, ed., *The Varieties of British Political Thought* (1993), pp. 211–45.

34. Borsay, *Urban Renaissance*, pp. 150–72.

35. Murray Pittock, *Inventing and Resisting Britain: Cultural Identities in Britain and Ireland, 1685–1789* (1997), pp. 98–152.

36. Wahrman, 'National Society', pp. 50–3; Bernard Bailyn, *Voyagers to the West* (1986), pp. 282–3.

37. Reed Browning, *The War of Austrian Succession* (1995).

38. Jack P. Greene, *Pursuits of Happiness: The Social Development of Early Modern British Colonies and the Formation of American Culture* (1988), pp. 101–23; 170–206; N. Landsman, 'The Provinces and the Empire' in Lawrence Stone, ed., *An Imperial State at War* (1994), pp. 258–87; Landsman, 'The Legacy of British Union for the North American Colonies' in Robertson, ed., *Union*, pp. 297–317. Also see W. J. M. Mackenzie, *Political Identity* (1978), pp. 170–2.

39. N. Landsman, 'Witherspoon and the Problem of Provincial Identity in Scottish Evangelical Culture' in Richard B. Sher and J. Smitten, eds., *Scotland and America in the Age of Enlightenment* (1990), pp. 29–45; John M. Simpson, 'James Wilson and the Making of Constitutions' in Thomas Barron *et al.*, eds., *Constitutions and National Identity* (1993), pp. 45–61; William Ferguson, *Scotland's Relations with England: A Survey to 1707* (1977), pp. 238–53.

40. Landsman, 'Witherspoon', pp. 38–42.

41. James Henretta, *Salutary Neglect: Colonial Administration Under the Duke of Newcastle* (1972), pp. viii, ix, 104, 317–18, 323–5, 344; Landsman, 'Provinces and the Empire', p. 276.

42. D. Clarke, *Arthur Dobbs* (1958); D. Helen Rankin and E. Charles Nelson, eds., *Curious in Everything: The Career of Arthur Dobbs* (1990).

43. M. Hamilton, *Sir William Johnston* (1976); Bailyn, *Voyagers*, pp. 576–85.

44. Wahrman, 'National Society', pp. 50–3; Michael Hechter, *Internal Colonialism* (1975), pp. 47–126.

45. J. McCusker and R. Menard, *The Economy of British America, 1607–1789* (1985), pp. 371, 376–7.

Notes and References

7 CULTURAL POLITICS: NATIONAL CULTURE IN A METROPOLITAN
STATE

1. Jeremy Black, 'Eighteenth-Century English Politics: Recent Work and Current Problems', *Albion*, 25 (1993), pp. 419–42; David Eastwood, 'E.P. Thompson, Britain and the French Revolution', *History Workshop Journal*, 39 (1995), pp. 79–88; Peter King, 'Edward Thompson's Contribution to Eighteenth-Century Studies', *Social History*, 21 (1996), pp. 215–28.

2. Hugh Dunthorne, *The Enlightenment* (1991); Dorinda Outram, *The Enlightenment* (1995); Roy Porter, *The Enlightenment* (1990).

3. Outram, *Enlightenment*, p. 127.

4. John Macdonald, *Memoirs of an Eighteenth-Century Footman* (first published 1790, republished 1985).

5. Peter Borsay, *The English Urban Renaissance* (1989), p. 286. The following two paragraphs are based on pp. 286–8 of Borsay's study.

6. Victor Durkacz, *The Decline of the Celtic Languages* (1983), pp. 108–22; Geraint Jenkins, *The Foundations of Modern Wales: Wales 1642–1780* (1993), pp. 386–426; Clare O'Halloran, 'Irish Recreations of the Gaelic Past', *Past and Present*, 124 (1989), pp. 69–95; Charles Withers, *Gaelic Scotland: The Transformation of a Culture Region* (1988), pp. 333–37.

7. Borsay, *Urban Renaissance*, p. 288; Philip Jenkins, *The Making of a Ruling Class: The Glamorgan Gentry 1640–1790* (1983), pp. 205–16.

8. Gavin Hamilton to Louisa Hamilton, 22 August 1755, in B. Balfour-Melvill, *The Balfours of Pilrig* (1907), pp. 131–3, as quoted in Warren McDougall, 'Gavin Hamilton, John Balfour and Patrick Neil: A Study in Publishing in Edinburgh in the Eighteenth Century' (University of Edinburgh Ph.D. thesis, 1975), p. 29.

9. Borsay, *Urban Renaissance*, p. 289; Robert Poole, '"Give us our eleven days!" Calendar Reform in Eighteenth-Century England', *Past and Present*, 149 (1995), pp. 95–139.

10. Mary Fissell, *Patients, Power and the Poor in Eighteenth-Century Bristol* (1991), p. 7.

11. Both quotations in this paragraph are from *ibid.*, pp. 14–15.

12. *Ibid.*, pp. 142, 162–3, 167–8.

13. Isobel Rae, *Knox the Anatomist* (1964); Owen Dudley Edwards, *Burke and Hare*, 2nd edn. (1993).

14. Fissell, *Patients*, pp. 149–50.

15. Alan Macfarlane, *The Origins of English Individualism* (1978), p. 165.
16. *Ibid.*, p. 199.
17. *Ibid.*, p. 202. Macfarlane has responded to criticism of his ideas in *The Culture of Capitalism* (1987), in which he remarks (p. xii) that the reviews of his book known to him consist of 160 pages of criticism of a book which was 207 pages in length!
18. Gerald Newman, *The Rise of English Nationalism* (1987), p. 127.
19. *Ibid.*, pp. 134–6.
20. *Ibid.*, pp. 95, 152–3.
21. Miles Taylor, 'John Bull and the Iconography of Public Opinion in England *c*.1712–1929', *Past and Present*, 134 (1992), p. 100.
22. Quoted in Alexander Murdoch, *The People Above: Politics and Administration in Mid-Eighteenth-Century Scotland* (1980), p. 49.
23. Joanna Innes, 'Jonathan Clark, Social History and England's Ancien Regime', *Past and Present*, 114 (1987), pp. 165–200; Jeremy Black, *Convergence or Divergence? Britain and the Continent* (1994) pp. 143–73.
24. S. J. Connolly, *Religion, Law and Power: The Making of Protestant Ireland 1660–1760* (1992), pp. 1–4; T. C. Barnard, 'Farewell to Old Ireland', *Historical Journal*, 36 (1993), pp. 909–28.
25. Eric Evans, 'National Consciousness? The Ambivalences of English Identity in the Eighteenth Century' in C. Bjorn *et al.*, eds., *Nations, Nationalism and Patriotism* (1994), pp. 145–60.
26. John Robertson, 'Franco Venturi's Enlightenment', *Past and Present*, 137 (1992), pp. 189–90, 202–3.
27. N. T. Phillipson, 'Politics, Politeness, and the Anglicisation of Early Eighteenth-Century Scottish Culture' in Roger Mason, ed., *Scotland and England 1286–1815* (1987), pp. 226–46; Phillipson, *Hume* (1989); Phillipson, 'Propriety, property and prudence: David Hume and the defence of the Revolution' in Phillipson and Quentin Skinner, eds., *Political Discourse in Early Modern Britain* (1993), pp. 303–20; Richard B. Sher, *Church and University in the Scottish Enlightenment* (1985); John Robertson, *The Scottish Enlightenment and the Militia Issue* (1985).
28. Paul Wood, *The Aberdeen Enlightenment* (1993); Andrew Hook and Richard B. Sher, eds., *The Glasgow Enlightenment* (1995); Roger Emerson, 'Did the Scottish Enlightenment Emerge in an English Cultural Province?', *Lumen: Selected Proceedings from the Canadian Society for Eighteenth-Century Studies*, 14 (1995), pp. 1–24.

29. Evidence relating to cross-cultural contact within Scottish culture generally is discussed in Alexander B. Murdoch and Richard B. Sher, 'Literary and Learned Culture' in T. M. Devine and (Rosalind M. Mitchison, eds., *People and Society in Scotland Volume I, 1760–1830* (1988), pp. 127–43.

30. Franco Venturi, *The End of the Old Regime in Europe I: The Great States of the West*, translated by R. Litchfield (1991), pp. 144–99.

31. Frances D. Dow, *Cromwellian Scotland* (1979); William Ferguson, *Scotland's Relations with England: A Survey to 1707* (1977), pp. 117–54.

32. Colin Kidd, *Subverting Scotland's Past: Scottish Whig Historians and the Creation of an Anglo-British Identity, 1689–c.1830* (1993); Kidd, 'North Britishness and the Nature of Eighteenth-Century British Patriotisms', *Historical Journal*, 39 (1996), pp. 361–82.

33. Marinell Ash, 'William Wallace and Robert the Bruce: The Life and Death of a National Myth' in Raphael Samuel and P. Thompson, eds., *The Myths We Live By* (1990), pp. 83–94; Eric Richards, 'Scotland and the Uses of Atlantic Empire' in B. Bailyn and P. Morgan, eds., *Strangers Within the Realm* (1991), pp. 67–114; Christopher A. Bayly, *Imperial Meridian: The British Empire and the World 1780–1830* (1989), pp. 81–5, 133–63.

34. Quoted in Michael Fry, *The Dundas Despotism* (1992), p. 85.

35. Murdoch, 'Lord Bute, James Stuart Mackenzie and the Government of Scotland' in K. Schweizer, ed., *Lord Bute: Essays in Reinterpretation* (1988), pp. 139–40.

36. Prys Morgan, *A New History of Wales: The Eighteenth Century Renaissance* (1981), p. 44.

37. *Ibid.*, pp. 59–62, 111–19.

38. Prys Morgan, 'From a Death to a View' in E. Hobsbawm and T. Ranger, eds., *The Invention of Tradition* (1983), p. 89.

39. Richard B. Sher, *Church and University in the Scottish Enlightenment* (1985), pp. 213–41.

40. Fry, *Dundas*, pp. 237–8, 308–9; Jack Greene, *Pursuits of Happiness: The Social Development of Early Modern British Colonies and the Formation of American Culture* (1988), pp. 101–23.

41. Roy F. Foster, *Modern Ireland 1600–1972* (1988), pp. 170–6, 180, 194; Ian McBride, 'The School of Virtue: Francis Hutcheson, Irish Presbyterians and the Scottish Enlightenment' in D. G. Boyce *et al.*, eds., *Political Thought in Ireland Since the Seventeenth Century* (1993), pp. 73–99.

42. James Conniff, 'Burke and India', *Political Research Quarterly*, 46 (1993); Conor Cruise O'Brien, *The Great Melody* (1992).
43. O'Halloran, 'Irish Recreations'; O'Halloran, 'Ownership of the Past: Antiquarian Debate and Ethnic Identity in Scotland and Ireland' in S. J. Connolly *et al.*, eds., *Conflict, Identity and Economic Development: Ireland and Scotland 1600–1939* (1995), pp. 135–47; Kidd, *Subverting*, pp. 205–15; Kidd, 'Gaelic Antiquity and National Identity in Enlightenment Ireland and Scotland', *English Historical Review*, 109 (1994).
44. O'Halloran, 'Irish Recreations', pp. 83–4.
45. *Ibid.*, p. 95.
46. *Ibid.*
47. Kidd, 'Gaelic Antiquity', p. 1210.
48. David Hempton, *Religion and Popular Culture in Britain and Ireland* (1996), pp. 93–116.

8 THE AMERICAN REVOLUTION AND THE ORIGINS OF THE SECOND BRITISH EMPIRE

1. Gordon S. Wood, *The Radicalism of the American Revolution* (1992), p. 229.
2. Simon Schama, *Citizens: A Chronicle of the French Revolution* (1989), p. 466.
3. Alexander Hamilton, 'Federalist No. 1, 27 October 1787' in James Madison Hamilton and John Jay, *The Federalist*, edited by Jacob Cooke (1961), p. 3. See John Robertson, ed., *A Union for Empire: Political Thought and the Union of 1707* (1995) pp. 36, 346.
4. Benjamin Franklin to Henry Home, Lord Kames, 11 April 1767, *The Norton Anthology of American Literature*, 3rd edn. (1989), Vol. I, pp. 394–8. Also see Franklin, *Observations Concerning the Increase of Mankind* (1751) and *The Interest of Great Britain with Regard to Her Colonies* (1760).
5. John Pocock, 'Josiah Tucker on Burke, Locke and Price; A Study in the Varieties of Eighteenth-Century Conservatism' in Pocock, *Virtue, Commerce and History* (1987), pp. 161–4.
6. Gary Nash, *The Urban Crucible: Social Change, Political Consciousness, and the Origins of the American Revolution* (1979), p. 347.
7. *Ibid.*, pp. 376–9; Joyce Appleby, 'What is Still American in the Political Philosophy of Thomas Jefferson?', *William and Mary Quarterly*, 39 (1982), pp. 287–309.

8. Colin Bonwick, *The American Revolution* (1991), pp. 81–2.
9. J. Hector St John de Crevecoeur, *Letters from an American Farmer*, ed. Albert Stone (1986 edn.), pp. 66–105; Edmund Morgan, *Inventing the People: The Rise of Popular Sovereignty in England and America* (1988), p. 290; Wood, *Radicalism of the American Revolution*, p. 192; Edward Countryman, *The American Revolution* (1985), pp. 242–5.
10. Janet Adam Smith, 'Some Eighteenth-Century Ideas of Scotland' in N. T. Phillipson and Rosalind M. Mitchison, eds., *Scotland in the Age of Improvement* (1996 edn.), pp. 107–24; Christopher A. Bayly, *Imperial Meridian: The British Empire and the World 1780–1830* (1989), pp. 81–6, 133–63.
11. Alexander Murdoch, *The People Above: Politics and Administration in Mid-Eighteenth-Century Scotland* (1980), pp. v–vi, 132–4; Richard B. Sher, *Church and University in the Scottish Enlightenment* (1985), pp. 93–147, 213–261.
12. James Bradley, *Popular Politics and the American Revolution in England* (1986), p. 59.
13. J. G. A. Pocock, '1776: The Revolution Against Parliament' in Pocock, ed., *Three British Revolutions* (1980), pp. 287–8, citing John Adams's denunciation of Bute and Mansfield as heading 'an insolent, arbitrary Scotch faction' in *The Adams Papers*, ed. L. H. Butterfield (1961), Vol. III, p. 352.
14. Dalphy Fagerstrom, 'Scottish Opinion and the American Revolution', *William and Mary Quarterly*, 3rd ser., 11 (1954), pp. 252–75; Robert Kent Donovan, 'The Popular Party of the Church of Scotland and the American Revolution' in Richard B. Sher and J. Smitten, eds., *Scotland and America in the Age of Enlightenment* (1990), pp. 81–99.
15. Alexander Murdoch, 'The Importance of Being Edinburgh: Management and Opposition in Edinburgh Politics, 1746–1784', *Scottish Historical Review*, 62 (1983), pp. 1–16, especially p. 12.
16. Gwyn A. Williams, *The Search for Beulah Land: The Welsh and the Atlantic Revolution* (1980), p. 7.
17. Colin Bonwick, *English Radicals and the American Revolution* (1977), pp. 11–12.
18. George Rudé, *Paris and London in the Eighteenth Century* (1974 edn.), p. 289.
19. E. P. Thompson, 'The Moral Economy Reviewed' in Thompson, *Customs in Common* (1991), pp. 259–351; Gary Nash, 'Artisans and Politics in Eighteenth-Century Philadelphia' in

M. Jacob and J. Jacob, eds., *The Origins of Anglo-American Radicalism* (1984), p. 178.

20. Bernard Bailyn, *Voyagers to the West* (1986), pp. 282–3; Wilson, *The Sense of the People*, pp. 206–84; H. T. Dickinson, *The Politics of the People in Eighteenth-Century Britain* (1995), pp. 221–54; Paul Langford, *Public Life and the Propertied Englishman 1689–1798* (1991), pp. 207–87, 582–6.

21. Bonwick, *Radicals*, p. 118.

22. John Derry, *English Politics and the American Revolution* (1976), p. 199; Morgan, *Inventing the People*, p. 237.

23. Colin Haydon, *Anti-Catholicism in Eighteenth-Century England* (1993), pp. 164–203; Thomas Bartlett, *The Fall and Rise of the Irish Nation* (1992), pp. 66–81; Robert Kent Donovan, *No Popery and Radicalism* (1987), pp. 50–110.

24. Philip Lawson, *Imperial Challenge: Quebec and Britain in the Age of American Revolution* (1989), p. 136; Jack Greene, *Pursuits of Happiness: The Social Development of Early Modern British Colonies and the Formation of American Culture* (1988), pp. 178–84.

25. Wilson, *The Sense of the People*, pp. 237–84; Bradley, *Popular Politics*, pp. 121–50; Bradley, *Religion, Revolution and English Radicalism* (1990), pp. 121–58.

26. R. K. Donovan, 'The Military Origins of the Roman Catholic Relief Programme of 1778', *Historical Journal*, 28 (1985), pp. 79–102.

27. Joseph W. Reed and Frederick Pottle, eds., *Boswell: Laird of Auchinleck 1778–1782* (1993 edn.), p. 48. For Robertson see Sher, *Church and University*, pp. 289–90.

28. Donovan, *No Popery*, pp. 31–2.

29. *Ibid.*, pp. 127–8.

30. *Ibid.*

31. R. B. McDowell, *Ireland in the Age of Imperialism and Revolution* (1979), p. 241.

32. Maureen Wall, *Catholic Ireland in the Eighteenth Century*, ed. Gerard O'Brien (1989), pp. 163–70.

33. Donovan, 'Military Origins', p. 93.

34. McDowell, *Ireland*, p. 241.

35. Jack Greene, 'Changing Identity in the British Caribbean' in Nicholas Canny and Anthony Pagden, eds., *Colonial Identity in the Atlantic World 1500–1800* (1987), pp. 213–66.

36. McDowell, *Ireland*, p. 245.

37. *Ibid.*, pp. 264–5.

38. *Ibid.*, p. 271.

39. *Ibid.*, p. 283.
40. Wall, *Catholic Ireland*, p. 145; McDowell, *Ireland*, p. 284.
41. Wall, *Catholic Ireland*, p. 136.
42. *Ibid.*
43. *Ibid.*, p. 137.
44. *Ibid.*, p. 145.
45. John Pocock, 'Hume and the American Revolution: Dying Thoughts of a North Briton' in Pocock, ed., *Virtue, Commerce and History* (1987), p. 128.
46. S. J. Connolly, 'Ireland, Scotland and Wales in the Hanoverian State' in Alexander Grant and Keith Stringer, eds., *Uniting the Kingdom? The Making of British History* (1995), pp. 206–7.

9 WAR AND THE NATION, 1793–1815: BRITISH IDENTITY AND THE NEW EMPIRE

1. Oliver Macdonagh, *Ireland: The Union and Its Aftermath*, 2nd edn. (1977), p. 17; Gerard O'Brien, *Anglo-Irish Politics in the Age of Grattan and Pitt* (1987), p. 163.
2. Ronald Hutton, *Charles the Second: King of England, Scotland and Ireland* (1989), p. vii.
3. Patrick K. O'Brien, 'The Political Economy of British Taxation, 1660–1815', *Economic History Review*, 41 (1988), p. 22.
4. Patrick K. O'Brien, 'Public Finance in the Wars with France 1793–1815' in H. T. Dickinson, ed., *Britain and the French Revolution, 1789–1815* (1989), p. 176.
5. *Ibid.*, p. 186.
6. Linda Colley, *Britons: Forging the Nation 1707–1837* (1992), p. 408 n. 70. Also see Michael Broers, *Europe Under Napoleon 1799–1815* (1996), pp. 261–74.
7. Michael Duffy, *Soldiers, Sugar and Seapower: The British Expeditions to the West Indies and the War Against Revolutionary France* (1987), pp. 380–4.
8. *Ibid.*, p. 386.
9. C. Bayly, 'The British Military-Fiscal State and Indigenous Resistance: India 1750–1820' in Lawrence Stone, ed., *An Imperial State at War* (1994), p. 341.
10. *Ibid.*, p. 343.
11. *Ibid.*, pp. 343–4, 348.
12. *Ibid.*, p. 349. Also see Bayly, *Indian Society and the Making of the British Empire* (1988), pp. 79–105.

13. Bayly, *Imperial Meridian: The British Empire and the World 1780–1830* (1989), pp. 166–71, 175–6, 248; Jeremy Black, *British Foreign Policy in an Age of Revolutions 1783–1793* (1994), p. 513.

14. Bayly, *Imperial Meridian*, p. 3. For more information on Colquhoun, a former Lord Provost of Glasgow, see T. M. Devine and G. Jackson, eds., *Glasgow Volume I: Beginnings to 1830* (1995), pp. 250, 293, 312; compare the perspective on Colquhoun offered in Peter Linebaugh, *The London Hanged* (1991), pp. 421–30.

15. *Ibid.*, p. 8.

16. *Ibid.*, p. 6.

17. *Ibid.*, p. 211; Michael Fry, *The Dundas Despotism* (1992), pp. 223–6; Bruce Lenman, *Integration, Enlightenment and Industrialization* (1981), pp. 80–3.

18. Bayly, *Imperial Meridian*, p. 111, quoting Wellington, also pp. 118–19; Alexander Murdoch, 'A Scottish Document Concerning Emigration to North Carolina in 1772', *North Carolina Historical Review*, 67 (1990), pp. 438–49.

19. Bayly, *Imperial Meridian*, p. 135.

20. Paul Langford, *A Polite and Commercial People* (1989), pp. 59–122, 325–9, 417–59; Langford, *Public Life and the Propertied Englishman 1689–1798* (1991), pp. 582–6.

21. Philip Jenkins, *The Making of a Ruling Class: The Glamorgan Gentry 1640–1790* (1983), pp. 193–271.

22. Lenman, *Integration*, pp. 73–128.

23. Bayly, *Imperial Meridian*, p. 127.

24. *Ibid.*, p. 196; Jacqueline Hill, 'National Festivals, the State and Protestant Ascendancy in Ireland, 1790–1820', *Irish Historical Studies*, 24 (1984), pp. 30–51; Hill, 'Popery and Protestantism, Civil and Religious Liberty', *Past and Present*, 118 (1988), pp. 105–7, 119–21, 126.

25. Nicholas Canny, 'The Marginal Kingdom: Ireland as a Problem in the First British Empire' in B. Bailyn and P. Morgan, eds., *Strangers Within the Realm* (1991), pp. 35–66.

26. Thomas Johnston, *Our Scots Noble Families*, which sold 100 000 copies when it was published as an attack on Scottish landowners in 1909, was clearly written with the Irish historical experience in mind: Graham Walker, *Thomas Johnston* (1988), pp. 9–10, 123. Also see the remarks on political attacks on Scots landowners in W. H. Fraser, *Conflict and Class: Scottish Workers 1700–1838* (1988), p. 168.

27. Thomas Bartlett, *The Fall and Rise of the Irish Nation* (1992), pp. 121–72.
28. Colley, *Britons*, pp. 237–319.
29. *Ibid.*, p. 230.
30. *Ibid.*, p. 237.
31. Alexander Murdoch, '"Beating the Lieges": The Military Riot at Ravenshaugh Toll on 5 October 1760', *Transactions of the East Lothian Antiquarian and Field Naturalists Society*, 17 (1982), pp. 39–47; Colley, *Britons*, pp. 118–19.
32. Colley, *Britons*, pp. 262–3, 277–8; John Dwyer, *Virtuous Discourse: Sensibility and Community in Late Eighteenth-Century Scotland* (1987), pp. 117–40; Clare Midgley, *Women Against Slavery: The British Campaigns 1780–1870* (1992), pp. 9–118.
33. Colley, *Britons*, p. 298.
34. Thompson, 'Which Britons' in E. P. Thompson, *Persons and Polemics* (1994), p. 320; Broers, *Europe Under Napoleon*, p. 269.
35. Thompson, 'Which Britons', p. 331.
36. Colley, *Britons*, pp. 332–4; Bartlett, *Fall and Rise*, pp. 327–47.
37. Quoted in David J. Brown, 'Henry Dundas and the Government of Scotland' (University of Edinburgh Ph.D. thesis, 1989), pp. 167–8. I am grateful to Dr Brown, now of the Scottish Record Office, for discussing this point with me.

10 EMPIRE AND ITS DISCONTENTS: ENGLISH NATIONALISM AND THE IMPERIAL STATE

1. E. P. Thompson, *The Making of the English Working Class* (1968 edn.), pp. 13–14.
2. *Ibid.*, p. 14; Linda Colley, *Britons: Forging the Nation 1707–1837* (1992), p. 298.
3. David Eastwood, 'E. P. Thompson, Britain and the French Revolution', *History Workshop Journal*, 39 (1995), p. 79.
4. E. P. Thompson, 'The Peculiarities of the English' in Thompson, *The Poverty of Theory and Other Essays* (1978), p. 58.
5. *Ibid.*, pp. 74–6.
6. Eastwood, 'E. P. Thompson', p. 82.
7. H. T. Dickinson, *The Politics of the People in Eighteenth-Century Britain* (1995), pp. 221–86; John Brims, 'The Scottish "Jacobins", Scottish Nationalism and the British Union' in Roger A. Mason, ed., *Scotland and England 1286–1815* (1987), pp. 247–65.

8. H. T. Dickinson, 'Popular Conservatism and Militant Loyalism 1789–1815' in Dickinson, ed., *Britain and the French Revolution, 1789–1815* (1989), p. 104.

9. H. T. Dickinson, ed., *Politics and Literature in the Eighteenth Century* (1974), p. 210.

10. David Eastwood, 'John Reeves and the Contested Idea of the Constitution', *British Journal for Eighteenth Century Studies*, 16 (1993), pp. 197–212; Dickinson, *Politics of the People*, pp. 280–1.

11. Dickinson, 'Popular Conservatism', p. 107.

12. *Ibid.*

13. *Ibid.*

14. B. Bailyn, *The Ideological Origins of the American Revolution* (1967), pp. 22–54; Colley, *Britons*, pp. 194–236; R. B. McDowell, *Ireland in the Age of Imperialism and Revolution* (1991), p. 283.

15. Arthur Williamson, 'Scotland, Antichrist and the Invention of Great Britain' in J. Dwyer *et al.*, eds., *New Perspectives on the Politics and Culture of Early Modern Scotland* (1982), p. 34; Colley, *Britons*, pp. 101–45; Alexander Murdoch, *The People Above: Politics and Administration in Mid-Eighteenth-Century Scotland* (1980), pp. 124–31; Murdoch, 'Lord Bute, James Stuart Mackenzie and the Government of Scotland' in K. Schweizer, ed., *Lord Bute: Essays in Reinterpretation* (1988), pp. 117–46.

16. Dickinson, 'Popular Conservatism', p. 123; Dickinson, *Politics of the People*, pp. 255–86.

17. Dickinson, *Politics of the People*, pp. 248–51; John D. Brims, 'Scottish Radicalism and the United Irishmen' in David Dickson *et al.*, eds., *The United Irishmen: Republicanism, Radicalism and Rebellion* (1993), pp. 151–66; Roger Wells, 'English Society and Revolutionary Politics in the 1790s: The Case for Insurrection' in Mark Philp, ed., *The French Revolution and British Popular Politics* (1991), pp. 188–226.

18. Thompson, *Making*, pp. 660–915.

19. David Eastwood, *Government and Community in the English Provinces, 1700–1870* (1997), p. 3.

20. Dickinson, *Politics of the People*, pp. 221–54; Thompson, *Making*, pp. 84–203.

21. Christopher A. Bayly, *Imperial Meridian: The British Empire and the World 1780–1830* (1989), pp. 151–2, 220–2; Colley, *Britons*, pp. 350–8; J. R. Oldfield, *Popular Politics and British Anti-Slavery* (1995).

22. Gwyn A. Williams, *When Was Wales?* (1985), p. 168; Prys Morgan, *A New History of Wales: The Eighteenth-Century Renaissance* (1981), pp. 111–19.
23. P. A. Brown, *The French Revolution in English History* (1918), pp. 18–19.
24. *Dictionary of National Biography*; Thompson, *Making*, pp. 19–22, 31, 132–4, 145–50.
25. 'Introduction' in H. T. Dickinson, ed., *The Political Works of Thomas Spence* (1982); Dickinson, *Politics of the People*, pp. 184–5, 188–9, 231, 241, 247, 249.
26. Colley, *Britons*, pp. 301–2.
27. Thompson, *Making*, pp. 153–4, 188–92, 521–8. Compare the treatment of the Scots and Irish in Peter Linebaugh, *The London Hanged* (1991), pp. 288–326 (Irish); pp. 47, 156, 195–6, 212, 221–2, 273, 284 (Scots).
28. Thompson, 'Peculiarities of the English', pp. 49–50; Philip Harling, 'Rethinking Old Corruption', *Past and Present*, 147 (1995), pp. 127–58.
29. John D. Brims, 'The Covenanting Tradition and Scottish Radicalism in the 1790s' in T. Brotherstone, ed., *Covenant, Charter, Party* (1989), pp. 50–62.
30. John Brims, 'The Scottish Democratic Movement in the Age of the French Revolution' (University of Edinburgh Ph.D. thesis, 1983), p. 414.
31. The text of the Claim of Right is published in W. Croft Dickinson and Gordon Donaldson, eds., *A Source Book of Scottish History*, Vol. III (1954), pp. 200–7.
32. Thomas Bartlett, *The Fall and Rise of the Irish Nation* (1992), pp. 228–342.
33. Williams, *When was Wales?* p. 170.
34. *Ibid.*, pp. 168–9.
35. Gwyn A. Williams, *The Search for Beulah Land: The Welsh and the Atlantic Revolution* (1980), p. 60.
36. Williams, *When Was Wales?* pp. 173–7; Thompson, *Making*, pp. 385–440; David Hempton, *Religion and Political Culture in Britain and Ireland* (1996), pp. 25–48, 52–3, 56–7; Callum Brown, 'Protest in the Pews. Interpreting Presbyterianism and Society in Fracture During the Scottish Economic Revolution' in T. M. Devine, ed., *Conflict and Stability in Scottish Society 1700–1850* (1990), pp. 83–105.
37. David Rollison, *The Local Origins of Modern Society: Gloucestershire 1500–1800* (1992). See David Eastwood, *Government and*

Community in the English Provinces, 1700–1870 (1997), chapter 4, 'County Communities and Patterns of Power', for a political perspective which complements Rollison's work.

38. John Lucas, *England and Englishness: Ideas of Nationhood in English Poetry 1688–1900* (1990), p. 7.
39. *Ibid.*, p. 143.
40. Ibid., p. 156.
41. *Ibid.*, p. 160. See E. P. Thompson on Clare in *Customs in Common* (1991), pp. 178–84.
42. J. M. Neeson, *Commoners: Common Right, Enclosure and Social Change in England 1700–1820* (1993), pp. 11–12.
43. *Ibid.*, p. 283.
44. *Ibid.*, p. 290.
45. Thus the contrast between Neeson, *Commoners*; Roger Wells, *Wretched Faces. Famine in Wartime England* (1988); Thompson, *Making*, pp. 515–659; and Bayly, *Imperial Meridian*; or Colley, *Britons*.
46. James Baldwin, *The Fire Next Time* (1963), p. 22.

SELECT BIBLIOGRAPHY

Anderson, Benedict, *Imagined Communities: Reflections on the Origin and Spread of Nationalism*, revised edn. (1991)

Appleby, Joyce, 'What is Still American in the Political Philosophy of Thomas Jefferson?, *William and Mary Quarterly*, 39 (1982), pp. 287–309

Appleby, Joyce, *Capitalism and a New State Order* (1984)

Armitage, David, 'Making the Empire British: Scotland in the Atlantic World 1542–1707', *Past and Present*, 155 (May 1997), pp. 34–63

Asch, R. G., ed., *Three Nations: A Common History? England, Scotland, Ireland and British History c.1600–1920* (Bochum, 1993)

Ash, Marinell, 'William Wallace and Robert the Bruce: The Life and Death of a National Myth' in Raphael Samuel and P. Thompson, eds., *The Myths We Live By* (1990), pp. 83–94

Bailyn, Bernard, *The Ideological Origins of the American Revolution* (1967)

Bailyn, Bernard, *Voyagers to the West* (1986)

Barnard, T. C., *Cromwellian Ireland* (1973)

Barnard, T. C., 'Farewell to Old Ireland', *Historical Journal*, 36 (1993), pp. 909–28

Barrow, Geoffrey, *Feudal Britain: The Completion of the Medieval Kingdoms, 1066–1314* (1956)

Bartlett, Thomas, *The Fall and Rise of the Irish Nation* (1992)

Bayly, Christopher A., *Indian Society and the Making of the British Empire* (1988)

Bayly, Christopher A., *Imperial Meridian: The British Empire and the World 1780–1830* (1989). Essential reading

Beckett, J. C., *The Making of Modern Ireland 1603–1923* (1966)

Beddard, Robert, ed., *The Revolutions of 1688* (1991)

Berg, M., *The Machinery Question* (1980)

Berg, M., *The Age of Manufactures*, 2nd edn (1993)

Berg, M., and P. Hudson, 'Rehabilitating the Industrial Revolution', *Economic History Review*, 45 (1992), pp. 24–50

Black, Jeremy, ed., *Britain in the Age of Walpole* (1984)

Black, Jeremy, 'Eighteenth-Century English Politics: Recent Work and Current Problems', *Albion*, 25 (1993), pp. 419–42

Black, Jeremy, *The Politics of Britain 1688–1800* (1993)

Black, Jeremy, *Convergence or Divergence: Britain and the Continent* (1994)

Black, Jeremy, *British Foreign Policy in an Age of Revolutions 1783–1793* (1994)

Bonwick, Colin, *English Radicals and the American Revolution* (1977)

Bonwick, Colin, *The American Revolution* (1991)

Borsay, Peter, *The English Urban Renaissance* (1989)

Bradley, James, *Popular Politics and the American Revolution in England* (1986)

Bradley, James, *Religion, Revolution and English Radicalism* (1990)

Bradshaw, Brendan, and John Morrill, eds., *The British Problem, c.1534–1707* (1996)

Brewer, John, *Party Ideology and Popular Politics at the Accession of George III* (1976)

Brewer, John, *The Sinews of Power: War, Money and the English State 1688–1783* (1989)

Brims, John D., 'The Scottish Democratic Movement in the Age of the French Revolution' (University of Edinburgh Ph.D. thesis, 1983)

Brims, John D., 'The Covenanting Tradition and Scottish Radicalism in the 1790s' in T. Brotherstone, ed., *Covenant, Charter and Party* (1989), pp. 50–62

Brims, John D., 'Scottish Radicalism and the United Irishmen' in David Dickson, D. Keogh and K. Whelan, eds., *The United Irishmen: Republicanism, Radicalism and Rebellion* (1993)

Broers, Michael, *Europe Under Napoleon 1799–1815* (1996)

Brown, David J., 'Henry Dundas and the Government of Scotland' (University of Edinburgh Ph.D. thesis, 1989)

Brown, Stewart J., ed., *William Robertson and the Expansion of Empire* (1997)

Browning, Reed, *The War of Austrian Succession* (1995)

Buckroyd, Julia, *Church and State in Scotland 1661–1681* (1980)

Burke, Peter, *Popular Culture in Early Modern Europe*, revised edn. (1994)

Cain, P. J., and A. G. Hopkins, *British Imperialism: Innovation and Expansion 1688–1914* (1993)

Calder, Angus, *Revolutionary Empire* (1981)

Canny, Nicholas, 'The Marginal Kingdom: Ireland as a Problem in the First British Empire' in B. Bailyn and P. Morgan, eds., *Strangers Within the Realm* (1991)

Canny, Nicholas, and Anthony Pagden, eds., *Colonial Identity in the Atlantic World 1500–1800* (1987)

Childs, John, *The Army, James II and the Glorious Revolution* (1980)

Clark, J. C. D., *English Society, 1688–1832: Ideology, Social Structure and Political Practice During the Ancien Regime* (1985)

Clark, J. C. D., *Revolution and Rebellion* (1986)

Clark, J. C. D., *The Language of Liberty 1660–1832* (1994)

Clarke, Tristram, 'The Scottish Episcopalians 1688–1720' (University of Edinburgh Ph.D. thesis, 1987)

Clarke, Tristram, 'The Williamite Episcopalians and the Glorious Revolution in Scotland', *Records of the Scottish Church History Society*, 24 (1992), pp. 33–52

Colley, Linda, 'The People Above in Eighteenth-Century Britain', *Historical Journal*, 24 (1981), pp. 971–9

Colley, Linda, *In Defiance of Oligarchy: The Tory Party 1714–60* (1982)

Colley, Linda, 'The Apotheosis of George III', *Past and Present*, 102 (1984), pp. 94–129

Colley, Linda, 'Whose Nation? Class and National Consciousness in Britain 1750–1830', *Past and Present*, 113 (1986), pp. 97–117

Colley, Linda, *Britons: Forging the Nation 1707–1837* (1992)

Colley, Linda, 'Britishness and Otherness: An Argument', *Journal of British Studies*, 31 (1992), pp. 309–29

Conniff, James, 'Burke and India', *Political Research Quarterly*, 46 (1993), pp. 291–309

Connolly, S. J., *Religion, Law and Power: The Making of Protestant Ireland 1660–1760* (1992)

Connolly, S. J., 'Eighteenth-Century Ireland: Colony or Ancien Regime?' in D. G. Boyce and A. O'Day, eds., *The Making of Modern Irish History* (1996), pp. 15–33

Connolly, S. J., R. Morris and R. Houston, eds., *Conflict, Identity and Economic Development: Ireland and Scotland 1600–1939* (1995)

Corfield, P. J., *Power and the Professions in Britain 1700–1850* (1995)

Countryman, Edward, *The American Revolution* (1985)

Cruickshanks, E., ed., *By Force or Default? The Revolutions of 1688–1689* (1989)

Cullen, L. M. and T. C. Smout, eds., *Scottish and Irish Economic and Social History 1600–1900* (1977)

Defoe, Daniel, *A History of the Union Between England and Scotland: With a Collection of Original Papers Relating Thereto, to which is prefixed a life of Daniel De Foe by George Chalmers* (1786)

Devine, T. M., ed., *Conflict and Stability in Scottish Society 1700–1850* (1990)

Devine, T. M., *Clanship to Crofters' War* (1994)

Devine, T. M., *The Transformation of Rural Scotland* (1994)

Devine, T. M., *Exploring the Scottish Past* (1995)

Dickinson, H. T., ed., *The Political Works of Thomas Spence* (1982)

Dickinson, H. T., 'How Revolutionary was the "Glorious Revolution" of 1688?', *British Journal for Eighteenth-Century Studies*, 11 (1988), pp. 125–42

Dickinson, H. T., ed., *Britain and the French Revolution, 1789–1815* (1989)

Dickinson, H. T., *The Politics of the People in Eighteenth-Century Britain* (1995)

Dickson, P. G. M., *The Financial Revolution in England* (1967)

Donovan, Robert K., 'The Military Origins of the Roman Catholic Relief Programme of 1778', *Historical Journal*, 28 (1985), pp. 79–102

Donovan, Robert Kent, *No Popery and Radicalism* (1987)

Dow, Frances D., *Cromwellian Scotland 1651–1660* (1979)

Duffy, Michael, *The Englishman and the Foreigner* (1986)

Duffy, Michael, *Soldiers, Sugar and Seapower: The British Expeditions to the West Indies and the War Against Revolutionary France* (1987)

Dunthorne, Hugh, *The Enlightenment* (1991)

Durkacz, Victor, *The Decline of the Celtic Languages* (1983, reissued 1995)

Dwyer, John, Roger A. Mason and Alexander Murdoch, eds., *New Perspectives on the Politics and Culture of Early Modern Scotland* (1982)

Dwyer, John, *Virtuous Discourse: Sensibility and Community in Late Eighteenth-Century Scotland* (1987)

Earle, Peter, *The Making of the English Middle Class* (1989)

Eastwood, David, 'John Reeves and the Contested Idea of the Constitution', *British Journal for Eighteenth Century Studies*, 16 (1993), pp. 197–212

Eastwood, David, 'E. P. Thompson, Britain and the French Revolution', *History Workshop Journal*, 39 (1995), pp. 79–88

Eastwood, David, *Government and Community in the English Provinces, 1700–1870* (1997)

Edwards, Owen Dudley, *Burke and Hare*, 2nd edn. (1993)

Eley, Geoff, and R. Suny, eds., *Becoming National* (1996)

Ellis, Steven G. and Sarah Barber, eds., *Conquest and Union: Fashioning a British State 1485– 1725* (1995)

Emerson, Roger, 'Did the Scottish Enlightenment Emerge in an English Cultural Province?', *Lumen: Selected Proceedings from the Canadian Society for Eighteenth-Century Studies*, 14 (1995), pp. 1–14

Evans, Eric, 'National Consciousness? The Ambivalences of English Identity in the Eighteenth Century' in C. Bjorn, A. Grant and K. Stringer, eds., *Nations, Nationalism and Patriotism* (1994), pp. 145–60

Fagerstrom, Dalphy, 'The American Revolutionary Movement in Scottish Opinion 1763–1783' (University of Edinburgh Ph.D. thesis, 1951)

Ferguson, William, *Scotland: 1689 to the Present* (1968, reissued by the Mercat Press, Edinburgh)

Ferguson, William, 'Imperial Crowns: A Neglected Facet of the Background to the Treaty of Union of 1707', *Scottish Historical Review*, 53 (1974), pp. 22–44

Ferguson, William, 'Introduction' to James Anderson, 'An Historical Essay Shewing That the Crown and Kingdom of Scotland, Is Imperial and Independent' in W. M. Gordon, ed., *The Stair Society Miscellany Three* (1992), pp. 1–27

Ferguson, William, *Scotland's Relations with England: A Survey to 1707* (1977, reissued by the Saltire Society, Edinburgh, 1994)

Fissell, Mary, *Patients, Power and the Poor in Eighteenth-Century Bristol* (1991)

Foster, Roy F., *Modern Ireland 1600–1972* (1988)

Fraser, W. H., *Conflict and Class: Scottish Workers 1700–1838* (1988)

Fry, Michael, *The Dundas Despotism* (1992)

Grant, Alexander, and Keith Stringer, eds., *Uniting the Kingdom? The Making of British History* (1995)

Greene, Jack P., *Pursuits of Happiness: The Social Development of Early Modern British Colonies and the Formation of American Culture* (1988)

Habermas, J., *The Structural Transformation of the Public Sphere*, translated by Thomas Bürger (1989 first published in German, 1962)

Habermas, J., 'Citizenship and National Identity', *Praxis International*, 12 (1992), pp. 1–19

Hancock, David, *Citizens of the World: London Merchants and the Integration of the British Atlantic Community, 1735–1785* (1995)

Harling, Philip, 'Rethinking Old Corruption', *Past and Present*, 147 (1995), pp. 127–58

Harris, Tim, *Politics Under the Later Stuarts* (1993)

Haydon, Colin, *Anti-Catholicism in Eighteenth-Century England* (1993)

Hayton, David, 'The "Country" Interest and the Party System, 1689–*c*.1720' in Clyve Jones, ed., *Party and Management in Parliament, 1660–1784* (1984), pp. 37–86

Hechter, Michael, *Internal Colonialism* (1975)

Hellmuth, Eckhart, ed., *The Transformation of Political Culture* (1990)

Hempton, David, *Religion and Popular Culture in Britain and Ireland* (1996)

Henretta, James, *Salutary Neglect: Colonial Administration Under the Duke of Newcastle* (1972)

Hill, Jacqueline, 'National Festivals, the State and Protestant Ascendancy in Ireland, 1790– 1820', *Irish Historical Studies*, 24 (1984), pp. 30–51

Hill, Jacqueline, 'Popery and Protestantism, Civil and Religious Liberty: The Disputed Lessons of Irish History 1690–1812', *Past and Present*, 118 (1988), pp. 96–129

Holmes, Geoffrey, *British Politics in the Age of Anne*, revised edn. (1987)

Holmes, Geoffrey, *The Making of a Great Power: Late Stuart and Early Georgian Britain 1660–1722* (1993)

Hook, Andrew, and Richard B. Sher, eds., *The Glasgow Enlightenment* (1995)

Hopkins, Paul, *Glencoe and the End of the Highland War* (1986)

Houston, R. A., *Scottish Literacy and the Scottish Identity* (1985)

Houston, R. A., *Social Change in the Age of Enlightenment. Edinburgh 1660–1760* (1994)

Howell, David W., *Patriarchs and Parasites: The Gentry of South-West Wales in the Eighteenth Century* (1986)

Hudson, P., *The Genesis of Industrial Capital* (1986)

Hudson, P., *The Industrial Revolution* (1992)

Hutton, Ronald, *Charles the Second: King of England, Scotland and Ireland* (1989)

Innes, Joanna, 'Jonathan Clark, Social History and England's Ancien Regime', *Past and Present*, 114 (1987), pp. 165–200

Israel, Jonathan, ed., *The Anglo-Dutch Moment* (1991)

Jacob, M., and J. Jacob, eds., *The Origins of Anglo-American Radicalism* (1984)

Jenkins, Geraint, *Literature, Religion and Society in Wales, 1660–1730* (1978)

Jenkins, Geraint, *The Foundations of Modern Wales: Wales 1642–1780* (1987, reissued 1993)

Jenkins, Philip, *The Making of a Ruling Class: The Glamorgan Gentry 1640–1790* (1983)

Jenkins, Philip, *A History of Modern Wales* (1992)

Johnston, Thomas, *Our Scots Noble Families* (1909)

Jones, J. R., ed., *Liberty Secured? Britain Before and After 1688* (1992)

Kearney, Hugh, *The British Isles: A History of Four Nations* (1989)

Kelly, James, *Prelude to Union: Anglo-Irish Politics in the 1780s* (1992)

Kidd, Colin, *Subverting Scotland's Past: Scottish Whig Historians and the Creation of an Anglo-British Identity, 1689–c.1830* (1993)

Kidd, Colin, 'Gaelic Antiquity and National Identity in Enlightenment Ireland and Scotland', *English Historical Review*, 109 (1994), pp. 1197–1214

Kidd, Colin, 'North Britishness and the Nature of Eighteenth-Century British Patriotisms', *Historical Journal*, 39 (1996), pp. 361–82

Kidd, Colin, 'Sentiment, Race and Revival: Scottish Identities in the Aftermath of Enlightenment' in Lawrence Brockliss and David Eastwood, eds., *A Union of Multiple Identities* (1997), pp. 110–26

King, Peter, 'Gleaners, Farmers and the Failure of Legal Sanctions in England 1750–1850', *Past and Present*, 125 (1989), pp. 116–50

King, Peter, 'Customary Rights and Women's Earnings: the Importance of Gleaning to the Rural Labouring Poor, 1750–1850', *Economic History Review*, 44 (1991), pp. 461–76

King, Peter, 'Edward Thompson's Contribution to Eighteenth-Century Studies', *Social History*, 21 (1996), pp. 215–28

Knox, Thomas, 'Popular Politics and Provincial Radicalism: Newcastle-upon-Tyne, 1769–85', *Albion*, 11 (1979), pp. 224–41

Langford, Paul, *A Polite and Commercial People* (1989)

Langford, Paul, *Public Life and the Propertied Englishman 1689–1798* (1991)

Lawson, Philip, *Imperial Challenge: Quebec and Britain in the Age of American Revolution* (1989)

Lenman, Bruce, *The Jacobite Risings in Britain 1689–1746* (1980, reissued by the Scottish Cultural Press, 1995)

Lenman, Bruce, *Integration, Enlightenment and Industrialization* (1981, reissued as *Integration and Enlightenment* by Edinburgh University Press, 1992)

Lenman, Bruce, *The Jacobite Clans of the Great Glen 1650–1784* (1984, reissued by the Scottish Cultural Press, 1995)

Levack, Brian, *The Formation of the British State: England, Scotland and the Union 1603–1707* (1987)

Linebaugh, Peter, *The London Hanged* (1991)

Lloyd, T. O., *The British Empire, 1558–1995*, 2nd edn. (1996)

Lucas, John, *England and Englishness: Ideas of Nationhood in English Poetry 1688–1900* (1990)

Lynch, Michael, *Scotland: A New History* (1991, paperback edn. 1992)

Macdonagh, Oliver, *Ireland: The Union and Its Aftermath*, 2nd edn. (1977)

Macfarlane, Alan, *The Origins of English Individualism* (1975)

Macfarlane, Alan, *The Culture of Capitalism* (1987)

Macinnes, Allan, *Clanship, Commerce and the House of Stuart, 1603–1788* (1996)

Mackenzie, W. J. M., *Political Identity* (1978). A sharp and succinct little book

Mason, Roger A., ed., *Scotland and England 1286–1815* (1987)

Mason, Roger A., ed., *Scots and Britons: Scottish Political Thought and the Union of 1603* (1994)

McBride, Ian, 'The School of Virtue: Francis Hutcheson, Irish Presbyterians and the Scottish Enlightenment' in D. G. Boyce, R. Eccleshall and V. Geoghegan, eds., *Political Thought in Ireland Since the Seventeenth Century* (1993), pp. 73–99

McCusker, J., and R. Menard, *The Economy of British America, 1607–1789* (1985)

McDowell, R. B., *Ireland in the Age of Imperialism and Revolution* (1979, reissued 1991)

McFarland, E. W., *Ireland and Scotland in the Age of Revolution* (1994)

Midgley, Clare, *Women Against Slavery: The British Campaigns 1780–1870* (1992)

Miller, John, 'The Earl of Tyrconnel and James II's Irish Policy 1685–1688', *Historical Journal*, 20 (1977), pp. 803–23

Mitchison, Rosalind, *Lordship to Patronage* (1983, reissued by Edinburgh University Press, 1990)

Mitchison, Rosalind, and Leah Leneman, *Sexuality and Social Control: Scotland 1660–1780* (1989)

Money, John, *Experience and Identity* (1977)

Morgan, Edmund, *Inventing the People: The Rise of Popular Sovereignty in England and America* (1988)

Morgan, Prys, *A New History of Wales: The Eighteenth Century Renaissance* (1981)

Morgan, Prys, 'From a Death to a View' in E. Hobsbawm and T. Ranger, eds., *The Invention of Tradition* (1983, reissued 1991)

Mowat, Ian, *Easter Ross: The Double Frontier, 1750–1850* (1981)

Murdoch, Alexander, *The People Above: Politics and Administration in Mid-Eighteenth-Century Scotland* (1980)

Murdoch, Alexander, 'The Advocates, the Law and the Nation in Early Modern Scotland' in W. Prest, ed., *Lawyers in Early Modern Europe and America* (1981)

Murdoch, Alexander, '"Beating the Lieges": The Military Riot at Ravenshaugh Toll on 5 October 1760', *Transactions of the East Lothian Antiquarian and Field Naturalists Society*, 17 (1982), pp. 39–47

Murdoch, Alexander, 'The Importance of Being Edinburgh: Management and Opposition in Edinburgh Politics 1746–1784', *Scottish Historical Review*, 62 (1983), pp. 1–16

Murdoch, Alexander, 'Lord Bute, James Stuart Mackenzie and the Government of Scotland' in K. Schweizer, ed., *Lord Bute: Essays in Reinterpretation* (1988), pp. 117–46

Murdoch, Alexander, 'A Scottish Document Concerning Emigration to North Carolina in 1772', *North Carolina Historical Review*, 67 (1990), pp. 438–49

Murdoch, Alexander J., 'Politics and the People in the Burgh of Dumfries, 1758–1760', *Scottish Historical Review*, 70 (1991), pp. 151–71

Murdoch, Alexander, and Richard B. Sher, 'Literary and Learned Culture' in T. M. Devine and Rosalind Mitchison, eds., *People and Society in Scotland Volume I, 1760–1830* (1988), pp. 127–43

Namier, Sir Lewis, *The Structure of Politics at the Accession of George III*, 2nd edn. (1957)

Nash, Gary, *The Urban Crucible: Social Change, Political Consciousness, and the Origins of the American Revolution* (1979)

Neeson, J. M., *Commoners: Common Right, Enclosure and Social Change in England 1700– 1820* (1993)

Newman, Gerald, *The Rise of English Nationalism* (1987)

O'Brien, Conor Cruise, *The Great Melody* (1992)

O'Brien, Gerard, *Anglo-Irish Politics in the Age of Grattan and Pitt* (1987)

O'Brien, Patrick K., 'The Political Economy of British Taxation, 1660–1815', *Economic History Review*, 41 (1988), pp. 1–32

O'Brien, Patrick K., 'Political Preconditions for Industrial Revolution' in P. K. O'Brien and R. Quinault, eds., *The Industrial Revolution and British Society* (1993), pp. 124–55

O'Brien, Patrick K., and P. A. Hunt, 'The Rise of a Fiscal State in England, 1485–1815', *Historical Research*, 66 (1993), pp. 129–76

Ó Grada, Cormac, *Ireland: A New Economic History 1780–1939* (1994)

O'Halloran, Clare, 'Irish Recreations of the Gaelic Past', *Past and Present*, 124 (1989), pp. 69–95

Ohlmeyer, Jane, ed., *From Independence to Occupation* (1995)

Oldfield, J. R., *Popular Politics and British Anti-Slavery* (1995)

Outram, Dorinda, *The Enlightenment* (1995)

Phillipson, N. T., *Hume* (1989)

Phillipson, N. T. and Rosalind M. Mitchison, eds., *Scotland in the Age of Improvement* (1970, reissued 1996)

Phillipson, N. T. and Quentin Skinner, eds., *Political Discourse in Early Modern Britain* (1993)

Philp, Mark, ed., *The French Revolution and British Popular Politics* (1991)

Phythian-Adams, Charles, ed., *Societies, Cultures and Kinship 1580–1850: Cultural Provinces and English Local History* (1993)

Pittock, Murray, *Inventing and Resisting Britain: Cultural Identities in Britain and Ireland, 1685–1789* (1997)

Pocock, J. G. A., 'British History: A Plea for a New Subject', *Journal of Modern History*, 47 (1975), pp. 601–28

Pocock, J. G. A., *The Machiavellian Moment* (1975)

Pocock, J. G. A., ed., *Three British Revolutions* (1980)

Pocock, J. G. A., 'The Limits and Divisions of British History', *American Historical Review*, 87 (1982), pp. 311–36

Pocock, J. G. A., *Virtue, Commerce and History* (1987)

Pocock, J. G. A., 'History and Sovereignty: The Historiographical Response to Europeanization in Two British Cultures', *Journal of British Studies*, 31 (1992), pp. 358–89

Pocock, J. G. A., ed., *The Varieties of British Political Thought* (1993)

Porter, Roy, 'Science, Provincial Culture and Public Opinion in Enlightenment England' in Peter Borsay, ed., *The Eighteenth-Century Town* (1990), pp. 243–67

Porter, Roy, *The Enlightenment* (1990)

Porter, Roy, 'Georgian Britain: An Ancien Regime?' *British Journal for Eighteenth Century Studies*, 15 (1992), pp. 141–4

Porter, R., and M. Teich, eds., *The Enlightenment in National Context* (1981)

Randall, Adrian, and Andrew Charlesworth, eds., *Markets, Market Culture and Popular Protest in Eighteenth-Century Britain and Ireland* (1996)

Richards, Eric, 'Scotland and the Uses of Atlantic Empire' in B. Bailyn and P. Morgan, eds., *Strangers Within the Realm* (1991), pp. 67–114

Richards, Eric, 'Margins of the Industrial Revolution' in P. K. O'Brien and R. Quinault, eds., *The Industrial Revolution and British Society* (1993), pp. 203–28

Riley, P. W. J., *The Union of England and Scotland* (1978)

Riley, P. W. J., *King William and the Scottish Politicians* (1979)

Robbins, Keith, *Nineteenth-Century Britain: Integration and Diversity* (1988)

Robertson, John, *The Scottish Enlightenment and the Militia Issue* (1985)

Robertson, John, 'Franco Venturi's Enlightenment', *Past and Present*, 137 (1992), pp. 183–206

Robertson, John, ed., A. *Union for Empire: Political Thought and the Union of 1707* (1995)

Rollison, David, *The Local Origins of Modern Society: Gloucestershire 1500–1800* (1992)

Russell, Conrad, 'The British Problem and the English Civil War,' *History*, 72 (1987), pp. 395–415

Russell, Conrad, *The Fall and Rise of the British Monarchies* (1991)

Samuel, Raphael, 'British Dimensions: Four Nations History', *History Workshop Journal*, 40 (1995), pp. iii–xxii

Schwoerer, Lois, ed., *The Revolution of 1688–1689* (1992)

Sher, Richard B., *Church and University in the Scottish Enlightenment* (1985)

Sher, Richard B., '1688 and 1788: William Robertson on Revolution in Britain and France' in Paul Dukes and John Dunkley, eds., *Culture and Revolution* (1990), pp. 98–109

Sher, Richard B., and J. Smitten, eds., *Scotland and America in the Age of Enlightenment* (1990)

Simms, J. G., *The Williamite Confiscation in Ireland 1690–1703* (1956)

Simms, J. G., *Jacobite Ireland 1685–91* (1969)

Simms, J. G., *William Molyneux of Dublin 1656–1698*, ed. P. H. Kelly (1982)

Simms, J. G., *War and Politics in Ireland, 1649–1730*, ed. David Hayton and Gerard O'Brien (1985)

Simpson, John M., 'James Wilson and the Making of Constitutions' in Thomas Barron, Owen Dudley Edwards and Patricia Storey, eds., *Constitutions and National Identity* (1993), pp. 45–61

Smout, T. C., *A History of the Scottish People, 1560–1830* (1969, paperback edn. 1972)

Smout, T. C., 'Scotland and England: Is Dependency a Symptom or a Cause of Underdevelopment?', *Review* (published by the Fernand Braudel Center for the Study of Economics, Historical

Systems and Civilisations at the State University of New York, Binghamton), 3 (1980), pp. 601–31

Smout, T. C., 'Problems of Nationalism, Identity and Improvement in Later Eighteenth Century Scotland' in T. M. Devine, ed., *Improvement and Enlightenment* (1989), pp. 1–22

Stone, Lawrence, ed., *An Imperial State at War* (1994)

Swan, P., and D. Foster, eds., *Essays in Regional and Local History* (1992)

Szechi, Daniel, 'The Hanoverians and Scotland' in M. Greengrass, ed., *Conquest and Coalescence: The Shaping of the State in Early Modern Europe* (1991)

Szechi, Daniel, *The Jacobites: Britain and Europe 1688–1788* (1994)

Szechi, Daniel, and David Hayton, 'John Bull's Other Kingdoms: Scotland and Ireland' in C. Jones, ed., *Britain in the First Age of Party 1680–1750* (1987)

Taylor, Miles, 'John Bull and the Iconography of Public Opinion in England *c*.1712–1929', *Past and Present*, 134 (1992), pp. 93–128

Thompson, E. P., *The Making of the English Working Class* (1963, paperback edn. 1968)

Thompson, E. P., 'The Peculiarities of the English' in Thompson, *The Poverty of Theory and Other Essays* (1965, reissued 1978)

Thompson, E. P., *Whigs and Hunters* (1975, paperback edn. 1977)

Thompson, E. P., *Customs in Common* (1991)

Thompson, E. P., 'Which Britons?' in Thompson, *Persons and Polemics* (1994), pp. 321–31

Thompson, M., 'Ideas of Europe During the French Revolution and Napoleonic Wars', *Journal of the History of Ideas*, 55 (1994), pp. 37–58

Tompson, Richard, *The Atlantic Archipelago: A Political History of the British Isles* (1986)

Venturi, Franco, *The End of the Old Regime in Europe I: The Great States of the West*, translated by R. Litchfield (1991)

Wahrman, Dror, 'National Society, Communal Culture: An Argument About the Recent Historiography of Eighteenth-Century Britain', *Social History*, 17 (1992), pp. 43–72

Wahrman, Dror, *Imagining the Middle Class* (1995)

Wall, Maureen, *Catholic Ireland in the Eighteenth Century*, ed. Gerard O'Brien (1989)

Weatherill, Lorna, *Consumer Behaviour and Material Culture in Britain 1660–1760* (1988)

Wells, Roger, *Wretched Faces. Famine in Wartime England* (1988)

Whatley, Chris, 'Royal Day, People's Day: The Monarch's Birthday in Scotland, c.1660– 1860' in R. A. Mason and N. Macdougall, eds., *People and Power in Scotland* (1992)

Whatley, Chris, *'Bought and Sold for English Gold'? Explaining the Union of 1707* (1994)

Whatley, Chris, *The Industrial Revolution in Scotland* (1997)

Williams, Gwyn A., *The Search for Beulah Land: The Welsh and the Atlantic Revolution* (1980)

Williams, Gwyn A., *When Was Wales?* (1985)

Williamson, Arthur H., *Scottish National Consciousness in the Age of James VI* (1979). Seminal

Williamson, Arthur H., 'George Buchanan, Civic Virtue and Commerce: European Imperialism and its Sixteenth-Century Critics', *Scottish Historical Review*, 75 (1996), pp. 20–37

Wilson, Kathleen, *The Sense of the People: Politics, Culture and Imperialism in England, 1715–1785* (1995)

Wilson, Kathleen, 'Citizenship, Empire and Modernity in the English Provinces c.1720–1790', *Eighteenth-Century Studies*, 29 (1995), pp. 69–96

Wilson, Kathleen, 'The Good, the Bad and the Impotent: Imperialism and the Politics of Identity in Georgian England' in A. Bermingham and J. Brewer, eds., *The Consumption of Culture* (1995), pp. 237–62

Withers, Charles, *Gaelic Scotland: The Transformation of a Culture Region* (1988)

Wood, Gordon S., *The Radicalism of the American Revolution* (1992)

Wormald, Jenny, ed., *Scotland Revisited* (1991)

INDEX

absolutism 23, 33, 39, 104
Africa 70
agrarian reform 9, 63
Aix-la-Chapelle, Treaty of (1748) *see*
Treaty of Aix-la-Chapelle
American empire and
settlement 68
American Revolution 12, 38, 60,
84, 106–7, 111, 112
ancien régime 97, 133
Anderson, Perry 140
Anglicisation 104
anglophone 1, 62, 132, 144, 151
Argyll *see* Campbell
Atwood, William 58

Baldwin, James, American
writer 152
Bank of Scotland 65
Barrow, Geoffrey x, 2–3, 10
Bayly, Christopher A. 11, 127, 129,
133
Beckett, J.C. ix, 3, 10
Bedingfield, James 94
Belfast; and 'regium donum' 25;
and William of Orange 48; and
Walpole's regime 60; and
economic development 76, 77;
and Enlightenment 102, 104
Belhaven, Lord speech to Scottish
Parliament (1707) 54
Benburb, Battle of (1646) 23
Berg, Maxine 75
Bewick, Thomas 150
Bill of Rights (1688) 40
Binns, John 145
Birmingham; and blue
cockades 42; and economic

development 76; Lunar Society
of 79; and popular protest 81;
and James Watt 96
Black, Jeremy ix, 59
'blue ribbon' 42
Borsay, Peter, on urban culture in
provincial England 90–2, 98
Boswell, James 116
Bourbon monarchy, of France 4,
39, 48, 107
Boyne, Battle of the (1689) 46, 53
Brewer, John 11, 65, 125
Brims, John 146
Bristol; and Atlantic trade 76; and
its medical infirmary 93–4
Britannia 87, 96
British empire; and locality 7, 67,
71; and population 130
'British' history ix, 1, 4, 10, 74–5, 87
'British liberties' 12, 72, 87, 109,
114
British patriotism 4, 134, 142; and
gender 134–5
British West Indies 69, 84, 126–7
'broad bottom' politics and 'fat ass'
opposition 42
Bryant, Arthur 124
Buccleuch, third duke of 137
Burke, Edmund 102, 141
Burke, William, murderer in
1828 94
Burnet, Gilbert 37, 40
Burney, Fanny 95
Burns, Robert 55, 148
Bute, third Earl of 110

calendar, changed in 1752 92–3
Calvinism 43; *see also* predestination

Index

Venturi, Franco 97–9

Wales; union with England 16, 32;
and Civil War 17; *Wales under the
Penal Code* 27; and commercial
development at the end of the
18th century 61, 76, 77; and
J. G. A. Pocock 74; language and
identity 78, 100; and the gentry
132; politics in 1789 144
Walker, Joseph 103
Wall, Maureen 120
Walpole, Horace 99
Walpole, Sir Robert 42, 60
War of Austrian Succession 89
'War of the Three Kingdoms'
(1638–52) 3, 10, 16, 19
Watt, James 95, 110
Wedgwood, Josiah 95
Wellesley, Richard 127
Wells, Roger 150
Whig; radicalism 42, 81, 113; Whig
party in England 55; 'Whig'
state 59; 'Whig' teleology in
history 24, 44

Wilkes, John, and the 'Wilkites' 86,
99, 112, 141
William of Orange, later King of
England, Scotland and Ireland 5,
11, 36, 37, 48; and Louis XIV of
France 39; and Scotland in
1689 43–4; and massacre of
Glencoe 1692; and Ireland 47;
and Scottish Parliament 54; and
the British state 64, 69
Williams, Edward *see* Morganwg,
Iolo
Williams, Gwyn A. 111, 147
Wilson, James 84, 110
Witherspoon, John 84, 85, 110
Wodrow, Robert 44
Wolfe, James 7, 13
Wood, Gordon (quoted) 106–7
working class 79–80, 82, 139
Wright, Joseph, of Derby, 89

Yorkshire 135–6, 139

32 607695